Illustrated Microsoft Word 5.0

John Mueller
and
Wally Wang

Wordware Publishing, Inc.

Library of Congress Cataloging-in-Publication Data

Mueller, John (John P.)
Illustrated Microsoft Word 5.0 / by John Mueller and Wally Wang.
p. cm.
Includes index.
ISBN 1-55622-021-9
1. Microsoft Word (Computer program) 2. Word processing.
I. Wang, Wally. II. Title.
Z52.5.M52M84 1989
652.557'36— dc20 89-5807
CIP

1506 Capital Avenue
Plano, Texas 75074

Printed in the United States of America

ISBN 1-55622-021-9
10 9 8 7 6 5 4 3 2 1
8909

All inquiries for volume purchases of this book should be addressed to Wordware Publishing, Inc., at the above address. Telephone inquiries may be made by calling:

(214) 423-0090

Contents

Contents (Cont.)

Recommended Learning Sequence

Recommended Learning Sequence (Cont.)

Module 1
ABOUT THIS BOOK

INTRODUCTION

This book describes how to use Microsoft Word for creative writing, business reports, form letters, and simple desktop publishing. The book explains how to use all of the Microsoft Word commands, how they work, and how to use them for writing more effectively. If you want to tap the full power of Microsoft Word, then this book can show you how.

We wrote *Illustrated Microsoft Word* for a broad range of users. For beginners, this book can explain how to create, save, and print documents with Microsoft Word. For intermediate and advanced users, this book provides explanations and working examples for using stylesheets, columns, and graphics. In addition, this book describes how to use macros, how to draw lines within a document, and how to transfer Microsoft Word documents to other word processor formats such as WordPerfect, WordStar, and even to Macintosh programs such as Microsoft Word and Microsoft Works.

Classroom instructors can use *Illustrated Microsoft Word* for teaching students the benefits of using word processing. Some of the advanced writing features that Microsoft Word offers include automatic indexing, cross-referencing text, and bookmarks. Whether you need to use Microsoft Word for writing letters and reports or for screenplays, newsletters, or technical manuals, *Illustrated Microsoft Word* can help you master the intricacies of Microsoft Word.

For a quick demonstration of Microsoft Word's many features, go through the sample session in Module 3. There you will get a chance to create and edit a document as well as experiment with outlining, spell checking, and previewing your pages before printing. As you will see, Microsoft Word can turn your computer into a word processor designed for capturing and printing your ideas quickly and easily.

ORGANIZATION

This book is arranged into small, easy-to-read modules. Each module describes a specific command, possible applications for using the command, and examples for learning how each command works.

Module 2 introduces the common commands for using Microsoft Word. Module 3 introduces you to Microsoft Word. This module guides you through a sample use for Microsoft Word so you can try the program yourself. If you want a quick overview of the common commands, then Module 3 will satisfy your curiosity for using Microsoft Word.

Modules 4 through 47 contain detailed descriptions of each Microsoft Word command. The modules appear in alphabetical order for quick reference. If you want guided instruction for learning Microsoft Word, follow the Recommended Learning Sequence at the front of this book.

Appendixes A through K contain reference information for using Microsoft Word. These appendixes explain basic desktop publishing principles you can use with Microsoft Word, how to use Microsoft Word with a mouse such as the Microsoft or Logitech Mouse, customizing Microsoft Word for different printers, creating form letters and mailing labels, converting Microsoft Word documents for other word processors, and how to use Microsoft Word's special utility programs for writing more effectively.

Appendix L contains Microsoft Word exercises for both classroom and self-teaching situations. If you use *Illustrated Microsoft Word* in a classroom, you may wish to include these exercises for student assignments. If you are learning Microsoft Word by yourself, use these exercises to check your understanding on what each module has taught you. When you can answer these questions, you are ready to move on to the next module in the learning sequence.

HARDWARE REQUIREMENTS

Microsoft Word works with versions 2.0 or greater of the PC-DOS and MS-DOS operating systems. The program will also work with the OS/2 operating system as well.

You can run the program on an IBM PC, XT, AT, PS/2, or compatible with a minimum of 384K RAM. Your computer should have a minimum of two floppy disk drives (either 5.25"or 3.5") or one floppy disk drive and one hard disk.

Microsoft Word will work with a variety of monitors and video adapters such as Monochrome, Hercules, Color Graphics Adapter (CGA), Enhanced Graphics Adapter (EGA), Virtual Graphics Array (VGA), IBM 8514/A Graphics Adapter, HP Vectra, AT&T high-resolution graphics, and the Genius Adapter with a full page monitor.

Although you can use Microsoft Word with the keyboard alone, you can also use the program with a Microsoft, IBM PS/2, Logitech mouse, or any Microsoft compatible mouse.

For printing your documents, Microsoft Word can work with a variety of name brand dot matrix, daisywheel, inkjet, and laser printers. If you use a printer that Microsoft Word doesn't support, Microsoft Word lets you create custom print drivers. Customized print drivers let you use Microsoft Word with any printer.

WHAT YOU SHOULD KNOW

The descriptions and examples in this book assume that you know how to use PC/MS-DOS with your IBM or compatible computer. You should also know how to format a floppy disk and copy, rename, and delete files. If you can do these, you are ready to use this book with Microsoft Word. If you are not familiar with these common PC/MS-DOS commands, you may wish to buy the *Illustrated MS/PC-DOS* book from Wordware Publishing, Inc.

Module 2
MICROSOFT WORD OVERVIEW

INTRODUCTION

Most word processors do little more than turn your $2,000 computer into a faster electronic typewriter. With Microsoft Word, word processing becomes more than just creating, editing, and printing text. Unlike other word processors, Microsoft Word provides a complete environment for writing from start to finish.

WRITING WITH MICROSOFT WORD

Before you start writing, you have to know what you want to say. To help you clarify your thoughts, Microsoft Word provides an outliner. The outliner lets you rapidly collect, organize, and sort ideas. Once you have organized your thoughts, you can expand on them in more detail.

This is the first step with writing: before you start writing, you have to know what you want to say. With Microsoft Word's outliner, you will know exactly what you want to say before you start writing. Writer's block is nothing more than trying to do two tasks at once: editing and creating. By outlining your thoughts first, Microsoft Word lets you create ideas. Once you have captured your thoughts in words, you can worry about editing later.

EDITING WITH MICROSOFT WORD

Microsoft Word provides standard word processing features to help you expand on your ideas. Some of these include automatic document saving to prevent accidental file loss, glossaries for inserting commonly used text, redlining for keeping track of editing changes between different versions of a document, and a dictionary and thesaurus to help you find the exact word you want to use.

Once you have written and edited a document with Microsoft Word, the next step is enhancing your writing with graphics, tables, columns, and spreadsheet data. Microsoft Word can capture and paste screen images directly into a document, format text in tables or columns, and link data from other Word documents and spreadsheets such as Microsoft Multiplan, Lotus 1-2-3, Microsoft Excel, and Microsoft Works for the PC.

If you have linked Word documents together, changes made in one document will automatically appear in any linked documents. If you have linked a spreadsheet into a document, any changes you make to the spreadsheet will automatically appear in the Word document.

In addition to linking documents to other documents or spreadsheet files, Microsoft Word also lets you cross-reference page numbers, tables, chapter headings, and footnotes. When you make changes to a document, Word will automatically keep all cross-referenced data up to date as well.

If you write long manuscripts, Microsoft Word can create an index and table of contents automatically. If you need to work on several documents at once, or if you need to see separate parts of the same document, Microsoft Word can display up to eight different windows on the screen. For nearly any type of writing, you will find that Microsoft Word has all the features you need.

PRINTING WITH MICROSOFT WORD

After organizing your thoughts in an outline, expanding on your ideas using the thesaurus and spell checker, and enhancing the appearance of your document with lines, graphics, columns, and tables, the final step involves printing. To help you see how your document will look on paper, Microsoft Word provides a print preview feature.

The print preview lets you see how your document will appear on paper before you print it. By using this feature, you can save time by not having to print a document, make changes, and then print it again.

To show you exactly how your words appear, Microsoft Word provides a text and graphics mode. In text mode, Microsoft Word shows any special formatting in different colors or highlighting. In graphics mode, Microsoft Word will show italics, bold, underlining, superscripts, and strikethrough text. By using the graphics mode, you can see exactly how your words will appear in print.

SHARING DOCUMENTS WITH MICROSOFT WORD

Microsoft Word can help you create documents from start to finish, but there may be times when you need to transfer a document from Microsoft Word to another program, such as a desktop publishing program like Ventura Publisher or PageMaker. In these cases, you can store a Microsoft Word document as an ASCII file, DCA file, or in the Microsoft Rich Text Format (RTF).

ASCII files contain text but no special formats such as underlining, bold, or strikethroughs. Since any program and computer can use an ASCII file, you can transfer Microsoft Word documents to another word processor, a desktop publishing program, or even to another computer like the Apple Macintosh.

DCA files preserve special formats such as underlining in a document. Unfortunately, not all word processors can use DCA files. For that reason, Microsoft Word can also store files in a special format developed by Microsoft called Rich Text Format or RTF.

RTF files preserve special formats such as DCA files, but unlike DCA files, RTF files can be used by any Microsoft program including the Macintosh version of Microsoft Word. Before you can save a document in DCA format, you must first save it in RTF format.

USING A MOUSE

Although you can use Microsoft Word with a keyboard, you will find the program much easier to use if you use a mouse. Microsoft Word supports any mouse that's compatible with the Microsoft mouse, such as the Logitech mouse. By using the mouse, you can choose commands directly from the menu without having to press the Esc key each time.

There are four basic actions you can do with the mouse:

Point	Move the mouse so that the pointer rests on the menu command or word you wish to select.
Click	Press the mouse button to choose whatever the pointer rests on.
Click and Hold	Press and hold down the mouse button.
Drag	Move the mouse after clicking and holding down the mouse button.

USING MICROSOFT WORD WITH WINDOWS

Microsoft Word can work with Microsoft Windows 2.0 or later, Windows/286, or Windows/386. By using Microsoft Word with Windows, you can run several programs simultaneously, cut and paste data between different programs, and take advantage of the desk accessories provided by Windows such as a clock, calculator, and notepad.

SUMMARY

Unlike other word processors, Microsoft Word provides numerous features designed specifically for writing, not just typing. Microsoft Word lets you create documents quickly and easily and share files between other programs. You can use Microsoft Word as a word processor, as a simple desktop publishing program, and as an outlining tool for organizing your thoughts. No matter how you use Microsoft Word, you will find its many features powerful and easy to use.

Module 3
A SAMPLE SESSION WITH MICROSOFT WORD

INTRODUCTION

This module gives you a chance to experiment with Microsoft Word's outlining, spell checking, and print preview capabilities. You learn to create, edit, and save a file. Later modules in this book explain these features in more detail. For now, just get acquainted with Microsoft Word.

GETTING STARTED WITH MICROSOFT WORD

Microsoft Word comes on thirteen floppy disks. Before using these disks, copy each one using the DISKCOPY command. Before copying these master disks, place a write-protect tab on each one. This insures that you cannot erase a master disk by mistake. You should always use the copies of the Microsoft Word master disks and store the original master disks in a safe place.

INSTALLING MICROSOFT WORD

You install Microsoft Word by running the Setup program provided on the Utilities 1 disk. The Setup program automatically installs Microsoft Word on your hard disk or a combination of floppy disks.

RUNNING A SAMPLE SESSION WITH MICROSOFT WORD

The following sample session shows the power of Microsoft Word as a writing tool. Before starting, make sure you are not using the Microsoft Word master disks. Begin at the DOS prompt.

1. Type **WORD** and press **Return**. Microsoft Word displays an empty, unnamed document window on the screen.

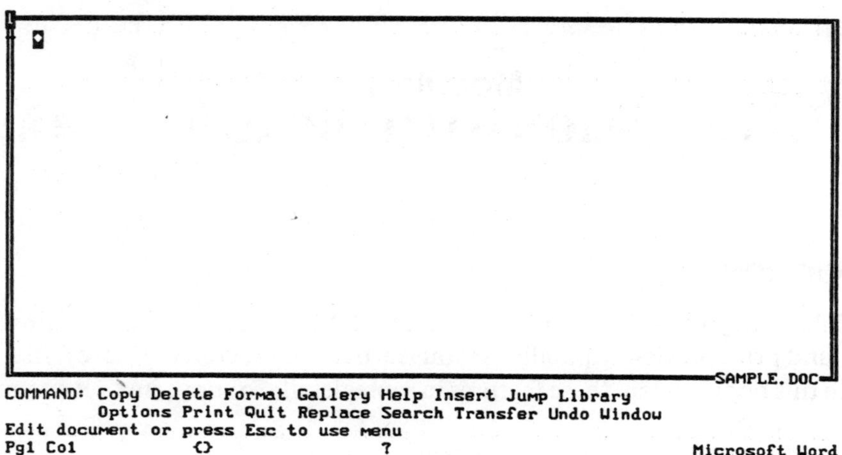

2. Press **Esc**, type **T** to choose the Transfer command, and type **S** to choose the Save command. Word asks for the document name you wish to save.
3. Type **Sample** and press **Return**. Word displays the summary information for the document. This summary information lists the creation date, the last revision date, the document title, and the author of the document.

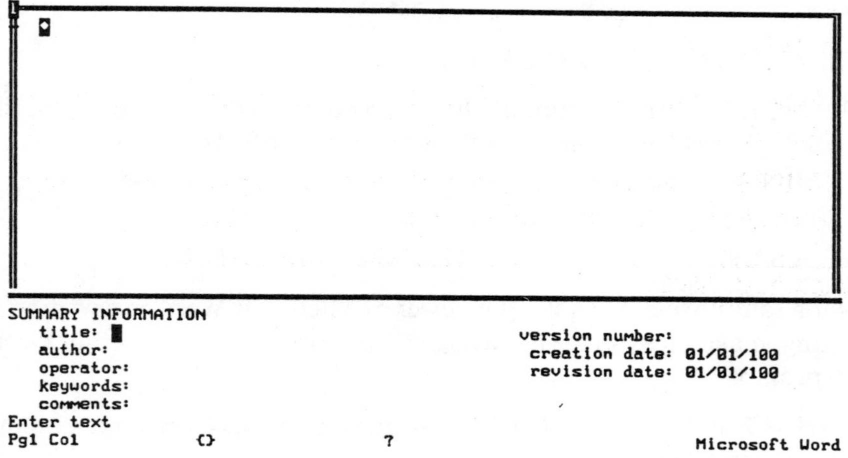

4. Press **Esc**. Notice that Word now displays the filename SAMPLE.DOC in the lower right corner of the window. If you do not specify a file extension, Word automatically adds the .DOC file extension.
5. Type **Welcome to Microsoft Word.**
6. Press **Home** to move the cursor to the beginning of the line.

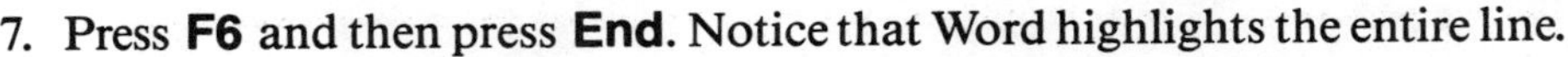

7. Press **F6** and then press **End**. Notice that Word highlights the entire line.

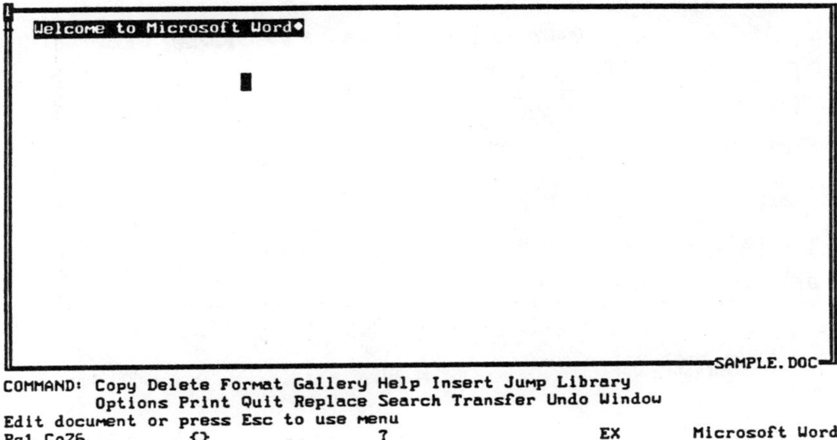

NOTE

The following steps assume you installed Word to work in the text (fast) mode and that you have a graphics monitor. If you installed word in the graphics mode, steps 8, 9, and 10 appear reversed. If you have a non-graphics display adapter, Word will not display the text in italics.

8. Press **Alt-I** for italics. Notice that Word highlights the entire sentence to show that the words appear in italics.
9. Press **Alt-F9** to switch Word from text mode to graphics mode. Notice that now Word displays the sentence in italics.

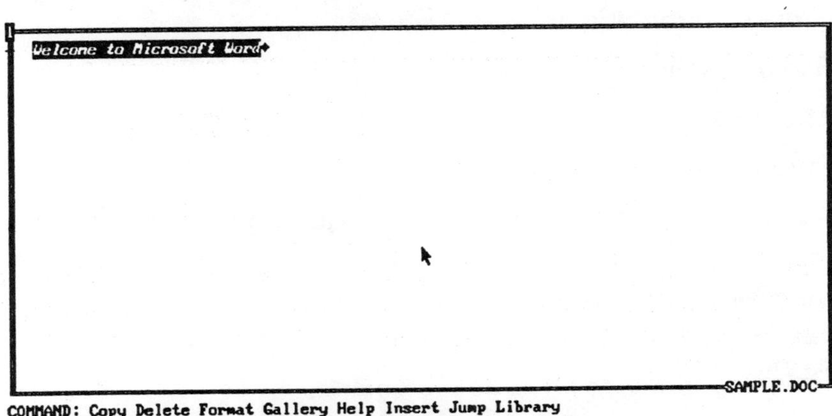

10. Press **Alt-F9** to switch Word back from graphics mode to text mode. Notice that now Word highlights the sentence but does not display the words in italics.
11. Press **Shift-F2** to switch from the document view to Microsoft Word's outlining view. Notice that Word displays the words "Level 1" at the bottom left corner of the screen. This tells you that the outline view is on the screen.
12. Press **End** and press **Return.**
13. Type **Features of Microsoft Word** and press **Return.**
14. Type **Outlining** and press **Alt-0**. Notice that Word indents this heading beneath the Features of Microsoft Word heading.

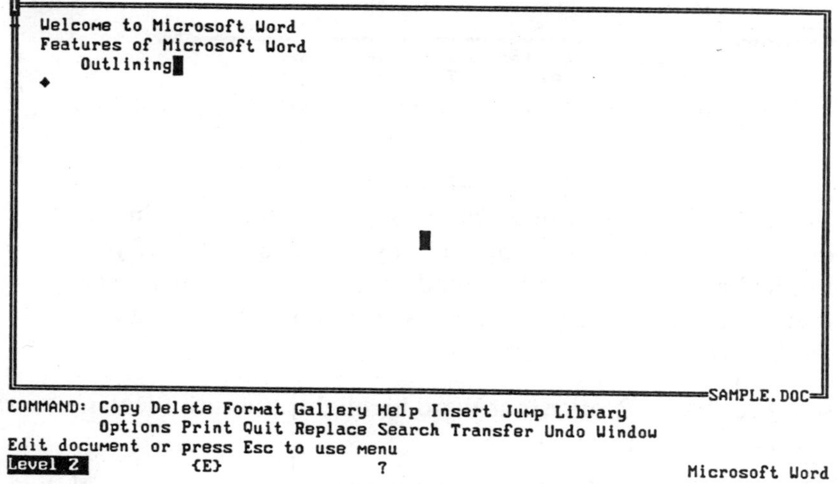

15. Press **Return.** Type **Thesaurus** and press **Return.**
16. Type **Cross-referencing** and press **Return.**
17. Type **Redlining** and press **Return.**
18. Type **Spell checking** and press **Return.**
19. Type **Print preview** and press **Return.**
20. Press **Up Arrow** seven times so the cursor appears on the Features of Microsoft Word heading.
21. Press the **gray minus** (-) key on the numeric keypad. Word collapses the outline headings. Notice that a + sign appears to show that this heading has subheadings hidden from view.

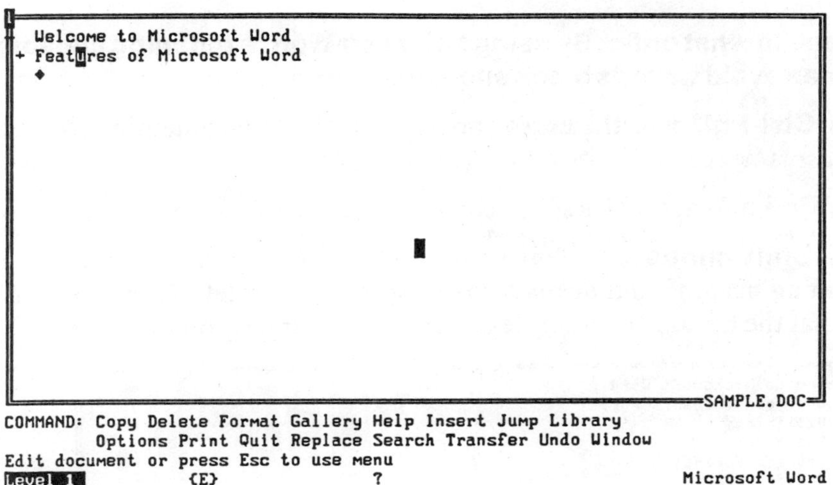

22. Press the **gray plus** (+) key on the numeric keypad. Notice that Word expands the outline heading.

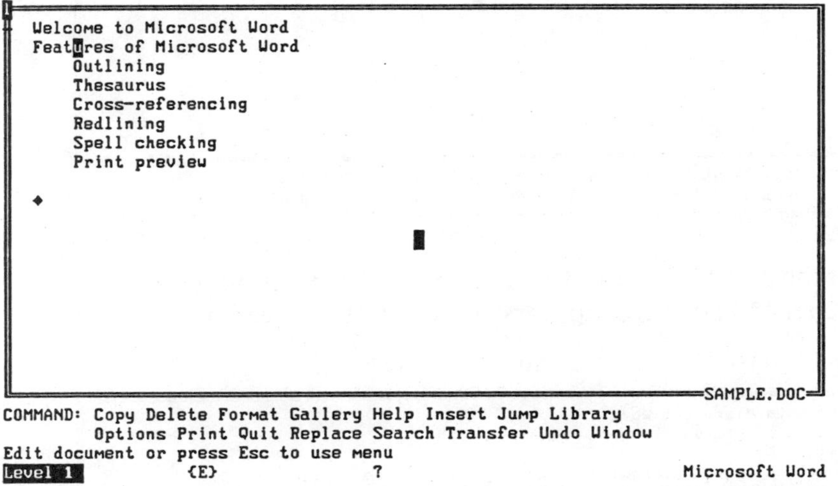

23. Press **Down Arrow** so the cursor appears on the Outlining heading. Press **End** and then press **Return**.

24. Press **Alt-P**. Notice that Word displays the message "Text" in the lower left corner of the screen.

25. Type **An outline lets you organize your thoughts before beginning to write. Most word processors help you write faster, but if you don't know what to say, then even the best word processor won't help you say it any faster. With Microsoft Word, you can organize your thoughts before writing. Then when you're ready, you'll know exactly what you want to**

say and in what order. By using Microsoft Word's outlining capabilities, you can avoid writer's block altogether.

26. Press **Ctrl-PgUp** so the cursor appears on the line containing Welcome to Microsoft Word.
27. Press **Down Arrow** twice so the cursor is on the Outlining heading.
28. Press **Shift-minus** (-). Notice that Word collapses the text beneath the Outlining heading and displays the letter "t" to the left. This letter "t" tells you that the heading contains text that does not appear on the screen.

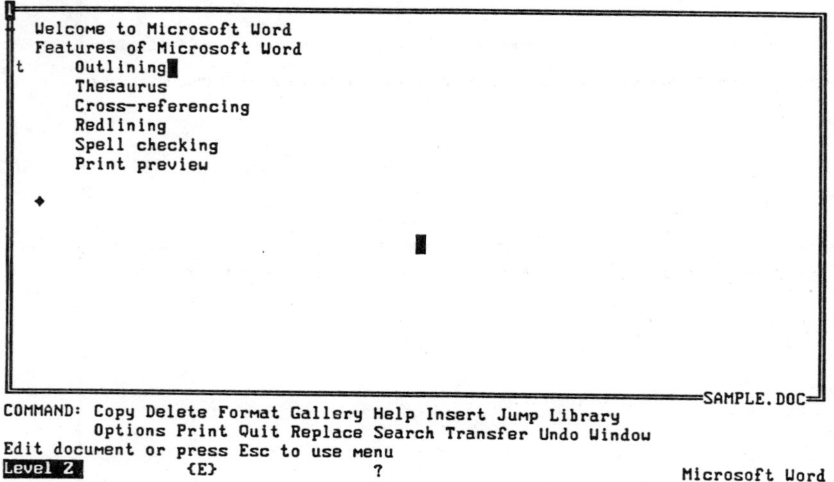

29. Press the **Shift-plus** (+) key. The text now appears on the screen. Notice that the letter "t" no longer appears at the left of the heading.
30. Press **Shift-F2** to return to document view.

```
Welcome to Microsoft Word
Features of Microsoft Word
Outlining
An outline lets you organize your thoughts before beginning
to write. Most word processors help you write faster, but if
you don't know what to say, then even the best word
processor won't help you say it any faster. With Microsoft
Word, you can organize your thoughts before writing. Then
when you're ready, you'll know exactly what you want to say
and in what order. By using Microsoft Word's outlining
capabilities, you can avoid writer's block altogether.
Thesaurus
Cross-referencing
Redlining
Spell checking
Print preview

◆
                                                    SAMPLE.DOC
COMMAND: Copy Delete Format Gallery Help Insert Jump Library
         Options Print Quit Replace Search Transfer Undo Window
Edit document or press Esc to use menu
Pg1 Co10        {E}         ?                     Microsoft Word
```

31. Press **Esc** and type **L** to choose the Library command from the Main menu. The Library menu appears at the bottom of the screen.
32. Type **S** to choose the Spell command. Word begins checking the spelling in the entire document. Word highlights any words that may be misspelled. When Word finds a misspelled word, it displays a menu at the bottom of the screen.

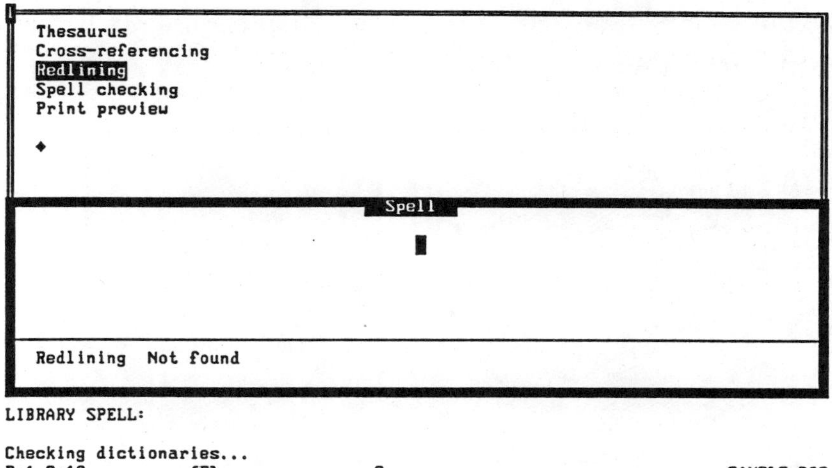

33. Press **Esc** and type **E** to exit from spell checking.
34. Press **Ctrl-F9** to choose the Print Preview command. Word displays your document on the screen.

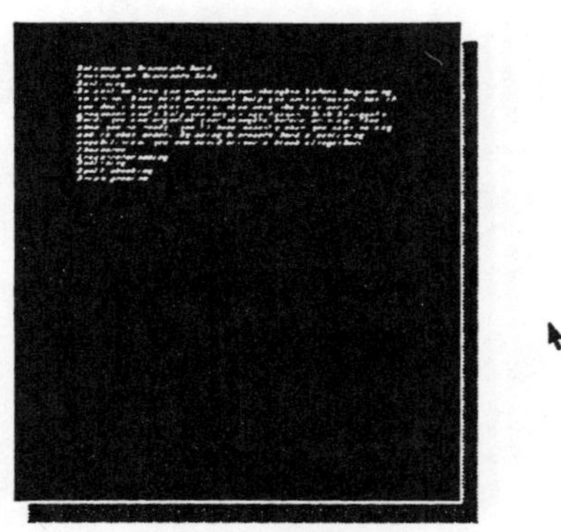

PRINT PREVIEW: Exit Jump Options Print

Use PgUp and PgDn to scroll through document
Pg1 ? SAMPLE.DOC

35. Press **Esc** and type **E** to exit from page preview.
36. Press **Esc** and type **T** to choose the Transfer command. Word displays the Transfer menu options.
37. Type **S** to choose the Save command. Press **Return**.
38. Press **Esc** and type **Q** to choose the Quit command. Word returns you to the DOS prompt.
39. Turn to Module 42 to continue the learning sequence.

Module 4
COPY

DESCRIPTION

The Copy command on the Main menu places a copy of the highlighted text in the glossary or scrap. The glossary is an area of multiple text string storage Word provides for each document. You can save the glossary to disk for future use. You can obtain a listing of current glossary entries by pressing F1 while in the Copy form. Word displays a glossary empty message when the glossary contains no entries.

```
COMMAND: Copy Delete Format Gallery Help Insert Jump Library
         Options Print Quit Replace Search Transfer Undo Window
Copies selected text to scrap or to a named glossary entry
Pg1 Li1 Co1      {}             ?                           Microsoft Word
```

The scrap contains a single text string displayed on the bottom line of the display between two curly brackets ({}). When the scrap is empty Word displays the curly brackets only. If the text length exceeds the available display area, Word displays the first seven letters, then three dots, then the last six letters. This acts as a reminder of the scrap contents.

Word provides many shortcuts for mouse users. There are no mouse commands associated specifically with this command. Generic mouse movements and commands appear in Appendix E.

APPLICATIONS

Use the Copy command to store standard text for later use in the glossary or immediate use in the scrap. The Copy command places a copy of the highlighted text in the designated area without disturbing the original copy. You can copy the highlighted text to the scrap by pressing Alt-F3.

TYPICAL OPERATION

In this example you use the Copy command to place a copy of the highlighted text in both the glossary and scrap. Begin this example at the Main menu.

1. Select the F of Forescore using the arrow keys. Press **F6**. Highlight the entire paragraph using the arrow keys. Press **Esc**. Type **C**. The Copy form appears.

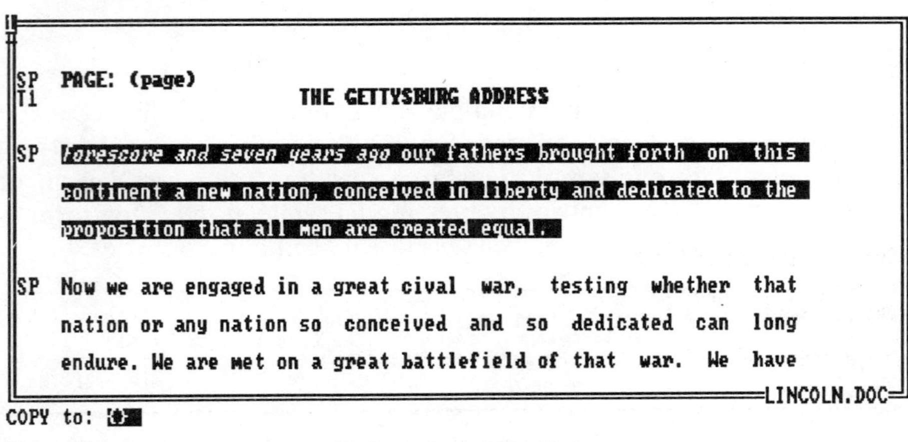

2. Press **F1**. Word displays a "List is empty" error message.
3. Type **TEMPORARY_TEXT** and press **Enter**. Word stores the text string in the glossary. Notice Word does not remove the paragraph from the edit area.

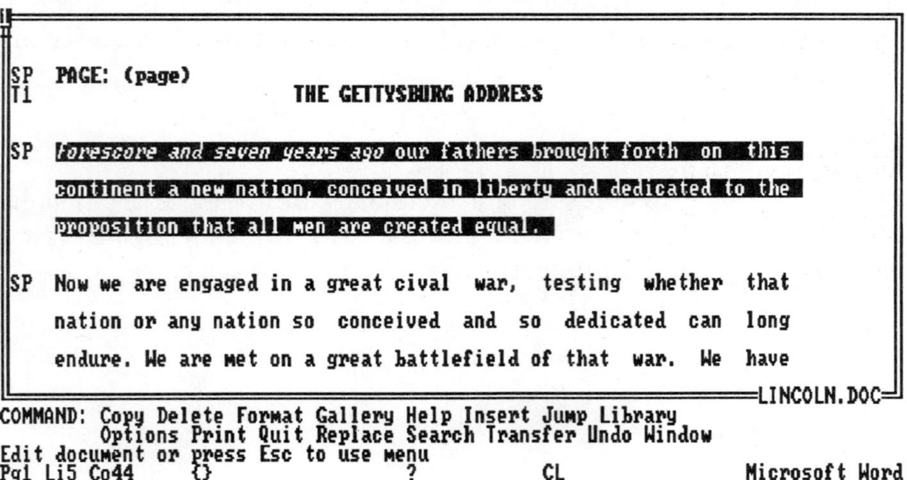

4. Press **Esc**. Type **C**, then press **F1**. Word displays a listing of glossary entries.

```
TEMPORARY_TEXT

COPY to: TEMPORARY_TEXT
Enter glossary name or press F1 to select from list
Pg1 Li5 Co44     {}              ?                          Microsoft Word
```

5. Press **Esc** twice. Type **C**, then press **Enter**. Word copies the text to the scrap.

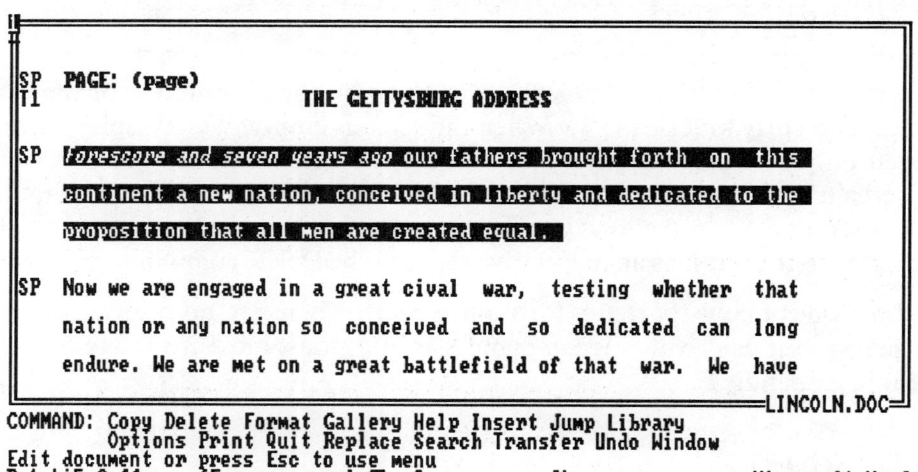

6. Turn to Module 44 to continue the learning sequence.

Module 5
DELETE

DESCRIPTION

The Delete command on the Main menu removes highlighted text from the edit area and places it in the glossary or scrap. The glossary is an area of multiple text string storage Word provides for each document. You can save the glossary to disk for future use. You can obtain a listing of current glossary entries by pressing F1 while in the Delete form. Word displays a glossary empty message when the glossary contains no entries.

```
COMMAND: Copy Delete Format Gallery Help Insert Jump Library
         Options Print Quit Replace Search Transfer Undo Window
Deletes selected text to scrap or to a named glossary entry
Pg1 Li1 Co1      {}                ?                          Microsoft Word
```

The scrap contains a single text string displayed on the bottom line of the display between two curly brackets ({ }). When the scrap is empty, Word displays the curly brackets only. If the text length exceeds the available display area, Word displays the first seven letters, then three dots, then the last six letters. This acts as a reminder of the scrap contents. Word allows you to use the Del key to move highlighted text from the display to the scrap as an alternative to using the Delete command.

Word provides many shortcuts for mouse users. There are no mouse commands associated specifically with this command. Generic mouse movements and commands appear in Appendix E.

APPLICATIONS

Use the Delete command to remove text from the edit area. It allows you to remove text more quickly than using the Backspace key. Use the glossary to save text you might use later. By saving the glossary on disk, you could use the text in standard documents. Use the scrap to save text that you want to eradicate. You cannot save the scrap to disk. Word overwrites the old scrap contents each time you place new text in the scrap.

TYPICAL OPERATION

In this example you use the Delete command to place text in both the glossary and scrap. Begin this example at the Main menu with LINCOLN.DOC loaded in the current window.

1. Press **Ctrl-PgDn**. Type **THIS IS SAMPLE TEXT TO DELETE**. Press **Home,** then **F6**, then **End**. Press **Esc**. Type **D**. The Delete form appears.

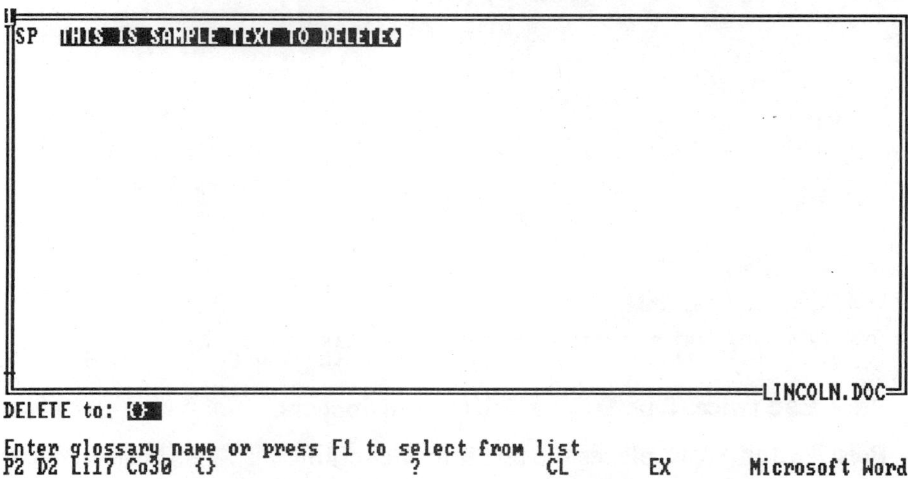

2. Press **F1**. Word displays a "List is empty" error message.

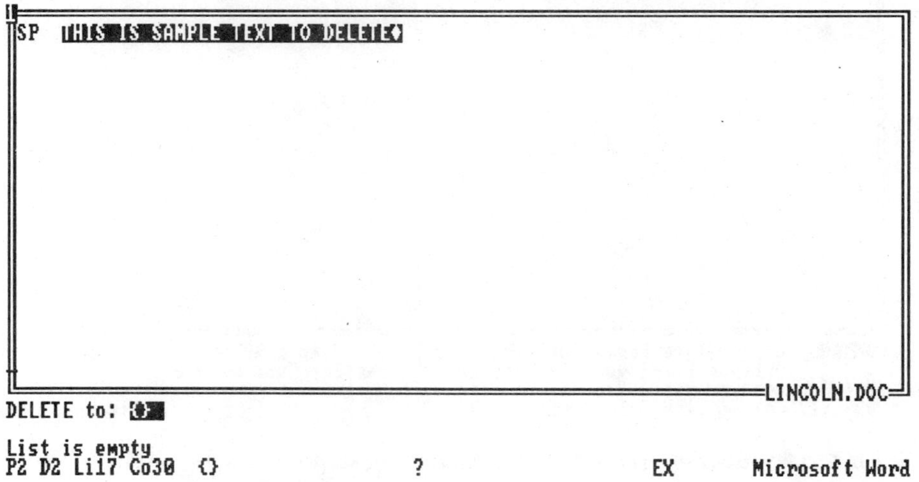

3. Type **TEMPORARY_TEXT** and press **Enter**. Word removes the text from the edit area.

4. Type **THIS IS SOME MORE SAMPLE TEXT TO DELETE.** Press **Home,** then **F6,** then **End.** Press **Esc.** Type **D.** The Delete form appears.
5. Press **F1**. Word presents a list of glossary entries.

```
TEMPORARY_TEXT






DELETE to: TEMPORARY_TEXT

Enter glossary name or press F1 to select from list
P2 D2 Li17 Co40  {}                  ?          CL       EX       Microsoft Word
```

6. Press **Esc** twice. Type **D.** The Delete form appears.
7. Press **Enter.** Word places the text into the scrap.

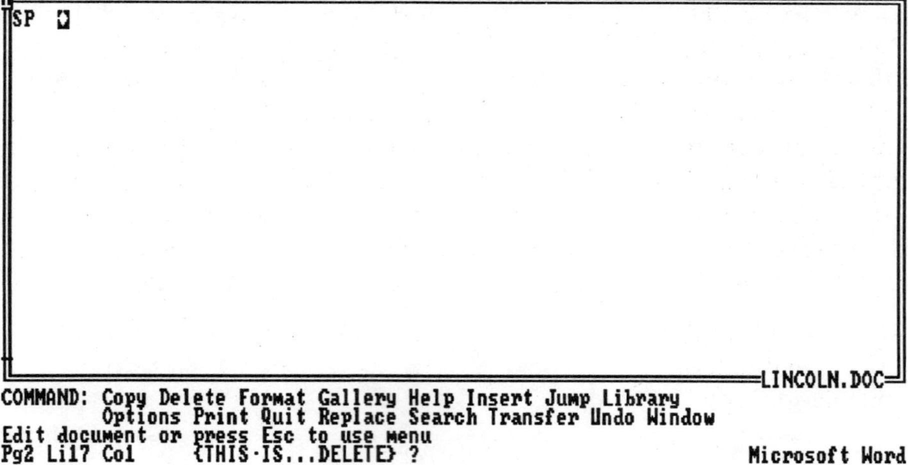

8. Turn to Module 46 to continue the learning sequence.

Module 6
FORMAT BORDER

DESCRIPTION

The Format Border command places a border around the select paragraph. Word allows you to place a complete rectangle, or any line: top, bottom, right, or left, around the paragraph. The Format Border form contains provisions for changing which lines Word prints, line thickness and style, and border color (shading). You access the Format Border command by pressing Esc and typing F, then B.

```
FORMAT: Character Paragraph Tab Border Footnote Division Running-head Stylesheet
        sEarch repLace revision-Marks pOsition Annotation bookmarK
Draws lines and boxes around selected paragraph(s)
P1 D1 C1          {that·portion}    ?          CL                 Microsoft Word
```

The Format Border form contains nine fields. The Type field tells Word what type of border to use. Selecting None means that Word does not draw a border. When you select Box, Word ignores the Left, Right, Above, and Below fields. When you select Lines, Word uses the Left, Right, Above, and Below fields to determine which lines to draw. The Line Style field controls the thickness of the border. The Color field controls the line color when using a color printer. If you use a standard printer, this field always contains black. The Background Shading field controls the level of shading within the border. You express this level as the percentage of black to white. For example, if you type 90 in this field, Word prints the background with 90% black (or selected shading color) and 10% white. If your printer does not support the extended ASCII character set, Word does not enable this feature. The Shading Color field controls the color Word uses to print the background if your printer supports color.

Word provides many shortcuts for mouse users. The mouse commands associated specifically with this command appear in Table 6-1. Generic mouse movements and commands appear in Appendix E.

TABLE 6-1. MOUSE COMMANDS

Action	*Pointing To*	*Result*
Push Left Button	Field	Word selects the field for change.
Push Left Button	Form Name	Word makes the requested changes and returns to the document.

Action	*Pointing To*	*Result*
Push Right Button	Multiple Choice Field	Word makes the requested changes and returns to the document.
Push Right Button	Fill in the Blank Field	Word displays a list of acceptable choices.
Push Right and Left Buttons	Anywhere Except the Form or Window	Word cancels the current operation and returns to Main menu.

APPLICATIONS

Use the Format Border command to enhance the appearance of your text. By placing boxes around titles and sidebars, you can make a document more readable and inviting. The use of shading to highlight a section of the document also affects the reader's desire to read.

TYPICAL OPERATION

In this example you add a border to the sample document title and headings. Begin this example at the Main menu with LINCOLN.DOC loaded in the current window.

1. Press **Ctrl-PgUp**. Press **Down Arrow** to select the title line. Press **Esc**. Type **F**, then **B**. The Format Border form appears.

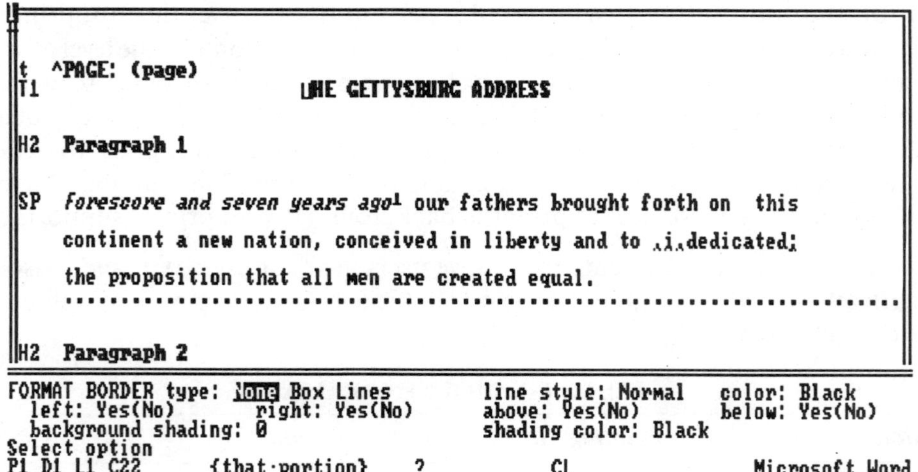

2. Press **Spacebar** twice to select Lines. Press **Tab**. Press **F1**. Word presents a listing of acceptable line styles.

```
Normal                  Bold








FORMAT BORDER type: None Box(Lines)       line style: Normal   color: Black
  left: Yes(No)       right: Yes(No)      above: Yes(No)       below: Yes(No)
  background shading: 0                   shading color: Black
Enter border line style or press F1 to select from list
P1 D1 L1 C22      {available·}     ?                           Microsoft Word
```

3. Press **Right Arrow** to select Bold. Press **Tab** to select the Above field. Press **Spacebar** to select yes. Press **Tab** to select the Below field. Press **Spacebar** to select yes. Press **Enter**. Word creates lines above and below the title.

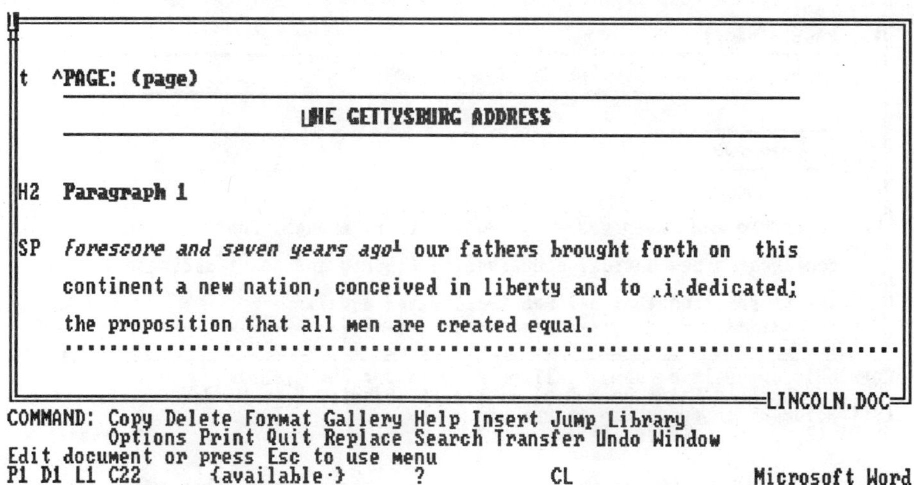

4. Press **Down Arrow** to select the first paragraph heading. Press **Esc**. Type **F**, then **B**. Select Box by pressing **Spacebar**. Press **Enter**. Word places a box around the first paragraph heading. Notice the box fills the entire width of the document.

```
t  ^PAGE: (page)
                    THE GETTYSBURG ADDRESS

  Paragraph 1

SP  Forescore and seven years ago¹ our fathers brought forth on  this
    continent a new nation, conceived in liberty and to .i.dedicated;
    the proposition that all men are created equal.
                                                          LINCOLN.DOC
COMMAND: Copy Delete Format Gallery Help Insert Jump Library
         Options Print Quit Replace Search Transfer Undo Window
Edit document or press Esc to use menu
P1 D1 L2 C13      {available·}      ?                   Microsoft Word
```

5. Press **Esc**. Type **F**, then **P**. The Format Paragraph form appears.
6. Select the Right Indent field using the arrow keys. Type **5.1**. Press **Tab**. Type **1** to change the line spacing to single spaced. Press **Enter**. Press **Home**, then **Spacebar**. The title appears centered in the border.

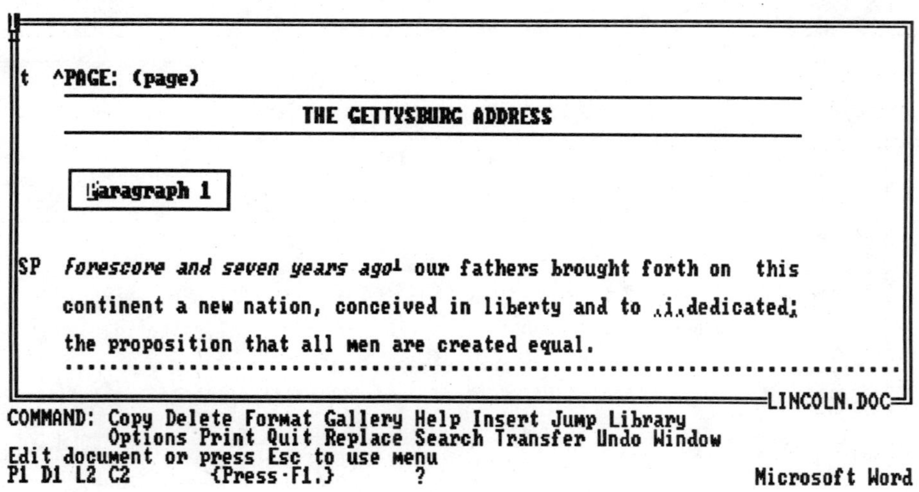

7. Press **Alt-H2** to return the heading format to normal. Press **Esc**. Type **T**, then **S**. Press **Enter**. Word saves the document.
8. Turn to Module 14 to continue the learning sequence.

Module 7
FORMAT CHARACTER

DESCRIPTION

The Format Character command on the Format menu changes the appearance of the characters used within a document. Word provides methods to change both single and groups of characters you select. You select a group of characters by placing the text cursor on the first letter of the group, pressing F6, and highlighting the group using the arrow keys. The field descriptions below assume the screen is in the graphics mode. Text mode screens use different colors or highlighting to differentiate between character formats.

```
FORMAT: Character Paragraph Tab Border Footnote Division Running-head Stylesheet
        sEarch repLace revision-Marks
Sets character format (bold, italic, hidden, etc.) and fonts
Pg1 Li1 Co1      {}               ?                         Microsoft Word
```

Word provides many shortcuts for mouse users. The mouse commands associated specifically with this form appear in Table 7-1. Generic mouse movements and commands appear in Appendix E.

TABLE 7-1. MOUSE COMMANDS

Action	*Pointing To*	*Result*
Push Left Button	Menu Selection	Word presents the requested form or submenu or executes the requested command.
Push Left Button	Field	Word selects the field for change.
Push Left Button	Form Name	Word makes the requested changes and returns to the document.
Push Right Button	Multiple Choice Field	Word makes the requested changes and returns to the document.
Push Right Button	Fill in the Blank Field	Word displays a list of available fonts for the Font Name field or available font sizes for the Font Size field.

Action	*Pointing To*	*Result*
Push Right and Left Buttons	Anywhere Except the Form or Window	Word cancels the current operation and returns to Main menu.

The Bold field changes character thickness. When selected, Word highlights the corresponding characters. Word places dot matrix printers in the emphasized mode to print bold characters. When using a laser printer, Word selects a bold resident font if available.

The Italic field slants characters to the right. When selected, Word displays the corresponding characters slanted to the right (italics). Word uses the italic character set or selects an italic resident font to print italic characters.

The Underline field places a line underneath the selected characters. Word displays the characters underlined on screen and selects the underline mode for printing (if available).

The Strikethrough field places a line in the middle of the selected characters. Word displays the characters with a horizontal line through the middle on screen. Word uses a backspace and dashed line combination for printing in most cases.

The Uppercase field changes lowercase letters to uppercase. Word uses uppercase characters for both display and printing. It does not physically change the character ASCII codes.

The Small Caps field displays uppercase characters normal size, and lowercase half size in uppercase when you select Yes. Word uses characters half the point size of uppercase characters for printing lowercase characters if available.

The Double Underline field places two lines underneath the selected characters. Word displays the characters underlined with a double thickness line on screen. It selects the underline or double underline mode for printing (if available).

The Position field changes the size and position Word prints a character with respect to the surrounding characters. For example, the Superscript selection prints characters a half line above and half the size of the surrounding characters. The Subscript selection prints characters a half line below and half the size of the surrounding characters. The Normal selection prints characters the normal size and position.

The Font Name and Font Size fields change the default character font and size. By pressing F1, you can display the font names available for the printer selected using the Print Commands form. After you select a font, you can display the available font sizes for that font. You cannot select laser printer fonts that do not exist as soft fonts on disk or as resident fonts within the printer, even if they appear as selections.

The Hidden field hides the selected text from the display and printer during normal operation. Word displays a hidden text marker on the display in place of the text. See Module 40 for a description of the hidden text marker.

APPLICATIONS

Use the Format Character form to format characters in the desired manner. The various commands offer a large variety in the way you can present the text to a reader. Appendix D tells how to use fonts and font enhancements in text.

Of all the text modifiers Word provides, the hidden text modifier provides the least esthetic and most utilitarian value. By creating an outline using hidden text, you can use the outline during writing, then hide it during printing. Hidden text also provides the means for adding non-printing notes to a document.

The strikethrough modifier is at least partially utilitarian in nature. Using strikethrough to show removed text in contracts and other documents provides an easy method of reversing the editing process.

TYPICAL OPERATION

In this example you change various character attributes on the sample document. Begin this example at the DOS prompt.

> **NOTE**
>
> The screen shots provided in this book use a Color Graphics Adapter (CGA) display to illustrate the effect of the character attribute changes. Your screen appearance will differ if you use text mode or a different display adapter type.

1. Type **WORD** and press **Enter** to start Word. Press **Esc**. Type **T**, then **L** to select the Transfer Load command. Press **F1**. Select LINCOLN.DOC using arrow keys. Press **Enter**. The Gettysburg Address appears.
2. Press **F6** then **End**. Word highlights the title and places an EX (extended selection marker) on the status line.
3. Press **Esc**. Type **F**, then **C**. The Format Character form appears.

```
[·········1·········2·········3·········4·········5·········6·········]···
                         The Gettysburg Address

Forescore and seven years  ago  our  fathers  brought  forth  on  this
continent a new nation, conceived in  liberty  and  dedicated  to  the
proposition that all men are created equal.

Now we are engaged in a great cival war, testing whether  that  nation
or any nation so conceived and so dedicated can long  endure.  We  are
met on a great battlefield of that war. We have  come  to  dedicate  a
portion of that field as a final resting place for those who here gave
their lives that that nation might live. It is altogether fitting  and
proper that we should do this.

::::::::::::::::::::::::::::::::::::::::::::::::::::::::::::::::::::::::

*  ♦

FORMAT CHARACTER bold: Yes No       italic: Yes(No)        underline: Yes(No)
        strikethrough: Yes(No)      uppercase: Yes(No)     small caps: Yes(No)
        double underline: Yes(No)   position:(Normal)Superscript Subscript
        font name: Pica             font size: 12          hidden: Yes(No)
Select option
Pg1 Li1 Co47      {}                ?          CL        EX       Microsoft Word
```

4. Press **Spacebar** to select yes. Select the Small Caps field using **Tab**. Press **Spacebar** to select yes, then **Enter**. Word bolds the title and displays lowercase letters as small capital letters.

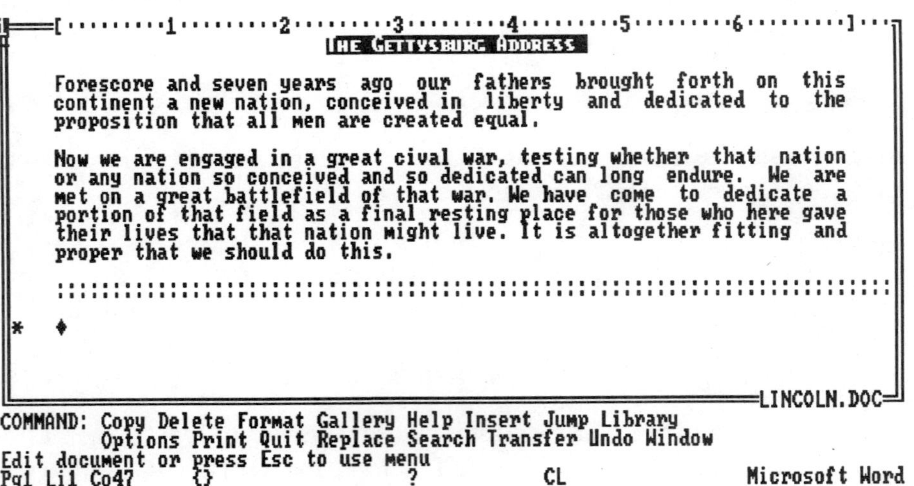

```
[·········1·········2·········3·········4·········5·········6·········]···
                         THE GETTYSBURG ADDRESS

Forescore and seven years  ago  our  fathers  brought  forth  on  this
continent a new nation, conceived in  liberty  and  dedicated  to  the
proposition that all men are created equal.

Now we are engaged in a great cival war, testing whether  that  nation
or any nation so conceived and so dedicated can long  endure.  We  are
met on a great battlefield of that war. We have  come  to  dedicate  a
portion of that field as a final resting place for those who here gave
their lives that that nation might live. It is altogether fitting  and
proper that we should do this.

::::::::::::::::::::::::::::::::::::::::::::::::::::::::::::::::::::::::

*  ♦

                                                           LINCOLN.DOC
COMMAND: Copy Delete Format Gallery Help Insert Jump Library
         Options Print Quit Replace Search Transfer Undo Window
Edit document or press Esc to use menu
Pg1 Li1 Co47      {}                ?          CL                 Microsoft Word
```

5. Press **Esc**. Type **F**, then **C**. The Format Character form appears.

6. Select the Font Name field using **Tab**. Press **F1**. Word displays the available font types for your printer installation.

```
Pica (modern a)                                   PicaD (modern b)
Elite (modern c)                                  EliteD (modern d)









FORMAT CHARACTER bold:(Yes)No       italic: Yes(No)        underline: Yes(No)
        strikethrough: Yes(No)      uppercase: Yes(No)     small caps:(Yes)No
        double underline: Yes(No)   position:(Normal)Superscript Subscript
        font name: Pica             font size: 12          hidden: Yes(No)
Enter font name or press F1 to select from list
Pg1 Li1 Co47      {}                ?          CL                Microsoft Word
```

7. Select PICAD (or a similar font on your list) using the arrow keys. Press **Tab,** then **F1**. Word displays the available font sizes for the font selected.

```
8                   12                  14                  16









FORMAT CHARACTER bold:(Yes)No       italic: Yes(No)        underline: Yes(No)
        strikethrough: Yes(No)      uppercase: Yes(No)     small caps:(Yes)No
        double underline: Yes(No)   position:(Normal)Superscript Subscript
        font name: PicaD            font size: 8           hidden: Yes(No)
Enter font size in points or press F1 to select from list
Pg1 Li1 Co47      {}                ?          CL                Microsoft Word
```

8. Select 16 point using **Right Arrow** then press **Enter**. The Main menu reappears.
9. Place the cursor on the F of Forescore using the arrow keys. Press **F6**. Highlight Forescore and seven years ago using **Right Arrow**. Press **Esc**. Type **F**, then **C**. The Format Character form appears.

10. Select Italic using **Tab**. Press **Spacebar** to select yes. Select Uppercase using **Tab**. Press **Spacebar** to select yes, then **Enter**. The highlighted text appears in all uppercase and italics.

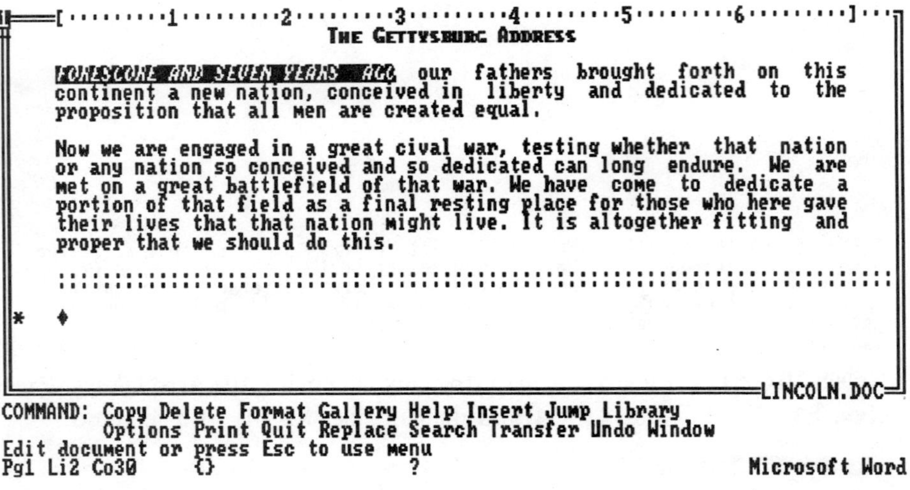

```
[········1·········2·········3·········4·········5·········6·········]···
                          THE GETTYSBURG ADDRESS

    FOURSCORE AND SEVEN YEARS AGO our fathers brought forth on this
    continent a new nation, conceived in liberty and dedicated to the
    proposition that all men are created equal.

    Now we are engaged in a great cival war, testing whether that nation
    or any nation so conceived and so dedicated can long endure. We are
    met on a great battlefield of that war. We have come to dedicate a
    portion of that field as a final resting place for those who here gave
    their lives that that nation might live. It is altogether fitting and
    proper that we should do this.

*   ♦
                                                            LINCOLN.DOC
COMMAND: Copy Delete Format Gallery Help Insert Jump Library
         Options Print Quit Replace Search Transfer Undo Window
Edit document or press Esc to use menu
Pg1 Li2 Co30     {}          ?                              Microsoft Word
```

11. Press **Esc**. Type **T**, then **S**. The Transfer Save form appears.

12. Press **Enter** to save the document. Press **Esc**. Type **Q.** The DOS prompt appears.

13. Turn to Module 16 to continue the learning sequence.

Module 8
FORMAT DIVISION

DESCRIPTION

The Format Division menu provides a list of options used to change the characteristics of a page, column, or continuous section of text. Word divides these characteristics into four groups: margins, page numbering, layout, and line numbering. You select the Format Division command by pressing Esc and typing F, then D.

```
FORMAT: Character Paragraph Tab Border Footnote Division Running-head Stylesheet
        sEarch repLace revision-Marks
Sets margins, columns, page numbers and line numbers
Pg1 Li1 Co1        {}                  ?            CL                Microsoft Word
```

Word provides many shortcuts for mouse users. The mouse commands associated specifically with this command and associated fields appear in Table 8-1. Generic mouse movements and commands appear in Appendix E.

TABLE 8-1. MOUSE COMMANDS

Action	*Pointing To*	*Result*
Push Left Button	Menu Selection	Word presents the requested form or submenu or executes the requested command.
Push Left Button	Field	Word selects the field for change.
Push Left Button	Form Name	Word makes the requested changes and returns to the document.
Push Right Button	Field	Word makes the requested changes and returns to the document.
Push Right and Left Buttons	Anywhere Except the Form or Window	Word cancels the current operation and returns to Main menu.

MARGIN The Format Division Margin command changes the distances between the edge of the page and the top, bottom, right, and left sides of the text. It also changes the gutter margin. The gutter margin adds extra space to the inside edge of a page for binding (see figure below). Finally, the Margin command contains fields for page length, page width, running head position, and footer position. The Page Length and Page Width fields tell Word the size paper. The Running Head Position From Top field tells Word where to place running heads appearing at the top of the page (headers). The From Bottom field tells Word where to place running heads appearing at the bottom of the page (footers). The Mirror Margins field assists you in creating two-sided documents. You set the margins for a left page; Word automatically reverses these margins for a right page when you select Yes. The Use As Default field allows you to select the current margins as the default margins for all documents not using stylesheets.

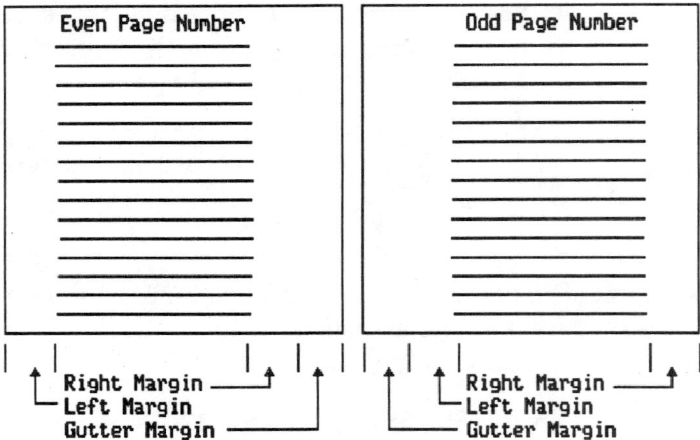

PAGE-NUMBERS The Format Division Page-Numbers command changes the position and numbering sequence for the page numbers. The first field allows you to turn page numbering off or on. When you select Yes, the From Left and From Top fields tell Word where to place the page number. Word uses two different methods to number pages. By selecting continuous, you tell Word to start at page 1 and number through to the end of the document. The other field allows you to start/stop numbering at the specified page. Word provides five different numbering schemes: Arabic, upper or lowercase Roman, and upper or lowercase alphabetic.

LAYOUT The Format Division Layout command changes the method Word uses to print a page. You can change where Word prints the footnotes, the number of columns, and the width between columns. In addition, this command also defines the scope of the division definition. Table 8-2 lists the division scope types and their definitions.

TABLE 8-2. FORMAT DIVISION SCOPE TYPES

Type	*Definition*
Page	Word creates a page break at the new division definition. The new parameters take effect on the text immediately after the division break.
Continuous	Word uses text from the text appearing after the division definition to fill up the current page (if necessary). It then begins the new definition with text appearing on the next page.
Column	Word creates a column break at the new division definition. The new text appears in the next column of the same page (if possible). The new parameters take effect on the text immediately below the division break.
Even	Word creates a page break at the new division definition. The new parameters take effect on the text immediately after the division break. If the text begins on an odd page number, Word inserts an additional page break to force the text to begin on an even page.
Odd	Word creates a page break at the new division definition. The new parameters take effect on the text immediately after the division break. If the text begins on an even page number, Word inserts an additional page break to force the text to begin on an odd page.

LINE-NUMBERS The Format Division Line-Numbers command changes the numbering sequence, position, and increment for line numbers added to documents. The first field controls whether Word places line numbers in your document. If you select Yes, Word places line numbers in your document. Word provides three methods of restarting the line numbers. The Page field restarts the line numbers at the beginning of each page. The division field restarts the line numbers at the beginning of each division break. Finally, the continuous field prevents Word from restarting the line numbering throughout the document.

APPLICATIONS

Use the Format Division menu and associated fields to change the characteristics of a column, page, or entire document. When creating legal documents, use the line numbering field to automatically number contract lines. Use the page numbering field to change the page number appearance between the front matter and text of a document. By changing the division definition at the column level, you can define multiple columns of variable widths.

TYPICAL OPERATION

In this example you change various aspects of the page layout for your sample document. Begin this example at the DOS prompt.

1. Type **WORD** and press **Enter** to start Word. Press **Esc**. Type **T**, then **L** to select the Transfer Load command. Press **F1**. Select LINCOLN.DOC using arrow keys. Press **Enter**. The Gettysburg Address appears.
2. Press **Ctrl-PgDn**. Word goes to the end of the document.
3. Type the following text. **Forescore and seven years ago our fathers brought forth on this continent a new nation, conceived in liberty and dedicated to the proposition that all men are created equal.**
4. Press **Ctrl-PgUp**. Word goes to the beginning of the document.
5. Press **Esc**. Type **F**, then **D**. The Format Division menu appears.

```
FORMAT DIVISION: Margins Page-numbers Layout line-Numbers

Sets margins, page length, and running head position for current division
Pg1 Li4 Co61      {}                  ?                              Microsoft Word
```

6. Press **Enter**. The Format Division Margins form appears.

```
FORMAT DIVISION MARGINS
       top: 1"                     bottom: 1"
       left: 1.25"                  right: 1.25"
       page length: 11"             width: 8.5"        gutter margin: 0"
       running-head position from top: 0.5"           from bottom: 0.5"
       mirror margins: Yes(No)                         use as default: Yes(No)
Enter measurement
Pg1 Li4 Co60      {}                  ?                              Microsoft Word
```

7. Type **.75** and press **Tab**. Type **.75** and press **Tab**. Type **.75** and press **Tab**. Type **.75** and press **Enter**. Notice a double row of dots appears at the bottom of the document. Word changes the document margins.

```
*   The Gettysburg Address
*   Forescore and seven years ago our fathers brought forth on this
    continent a new nation, conceived in liberty and dedicated to the
    proposition that all men are created equal.
    ::::::::::::::::::::::::::::::::::::::::::::::::::::::::::::::::::::::
*   ♦

                                                              LINCOLN.DOC
```

8. Press **Esc**. Type **F**, then **D**, then **P**. The Format Division Page-Numbers form appears.

```
FORMAT DIVISION PAGE-NUMBERS: Yes No      from top: 0.5"     from left: 7.25"
       numbering:(Continuous)Start        at:                number format:(1)I i A a
Select option
Pg1 Li1 Co1       {}                ?            CL                 Microsoft Word
```

9. Press **Spacebar** to select yes, then **Tab**. Type **10.5** then press **Tab**. Type **4.25** then press **Enter**. Word changes the position of the page number. (The change does not appear on screen, only when printed.)
10. Press **Esc**. Type **F**, then **D**, then **L**. The Format Division Layout form appears.

```
FORMAT DIVISION LAYOUT footnotes: Same-page End
       number of columns: 1        space between columns: 0.5"
          division break:(Page)Continuous Column Even Odd
Select option
Pg1 Li1 Co1       {}                ?                               Microsoft Word
```

11. Press **Enter**. The Main menu reappears.
12. Press **Esc**. Type **F**, then **D**, then **N**. The Format Division Line-Numbers form appears.

```
FORMAT DIVISION LINE-NUMBERS: Yes No                    from text: 0.4"
       restart at:(Page)Division Continuous             increments: 1
Select option
Pg1 Li1 Co1       {}                ?                               Microsoft Word
```

13. Press **Spacebar** to select yes, then **Enter**. Word adds line numbers to the document. (The change does not appear on screen, only when printed.)
14. Press **Esc**. Type **T**, then **S**. The Transfer Save form appears.
15. Press **Enter**. Word displays a file save message. The Main menu appears.
16. Press **Esc**. Type **Q**. The DOS prompt appears.
17. Turn to Module 10 to continue the learning sequence.

Module 9
FORMAT FOOTNOTE

DESCRIPTION

The Format Footnote command places footnotes in your document. Word places a group of characters or an automatic reference number next to the referenced text. It places the footnote at the end of the document. The Format Division Layout command changes the position where Word prints the footnote. Word allows you to choose between same page and end of document. You access this command by pressing Esc and typing F, then F again.

```
FORMAT: Character Paragraph Tab Border Footnote Division Running-head Stylesheet
        sEarch repLace revision-Marks pOsition Annotation bookmarK
Inserts reference mark. Jumps to document end where you type footnote
P1 D1 C1          {-}              ?          CL                  Microsoft Word
```

The Format Footnote form contains a single field. If you don't enter a number in the field, Word automatically uses the next number in sequence. You can also use any sequence of characters as the footnote reference. Word uses only the first character.

Word provides many shortcuts for mouse users. There are no mouse commands associated specifically with this command. Generic mouse movements and commands appear in Appendix E.

APPLICATIONS

Use the Format Footnote command to add footnotes to your document. Footnotes are especially useful for identifying copyrighted or quoted material. You can also use footnotes to further explain the nature of a phrase or other ambiguous text.

TYPICAL OPERATION

In this example you add a footnote to the example document. Begin this example at the Main menu with LINCOLN.DOC loaded in the current window.

1. Place the text cursor between the words ago and our in the first paragraph using the arrow keys. Press **Esc**. Type **F**, then **C**. Select the Position field by pressing

Tab. Press **Spacebar** to change the character format to superscript. Press **Esc** twice. Type **F**, then **F** again. The Format Footnote form appears.

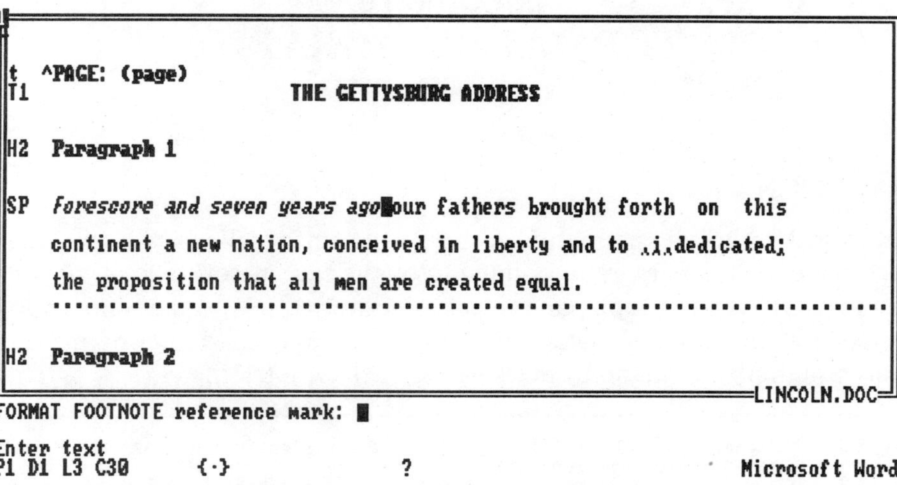

2. Press **Enter**. Word places a 1 between ago and our. It provides an area to type the footnote text at the end of the document.

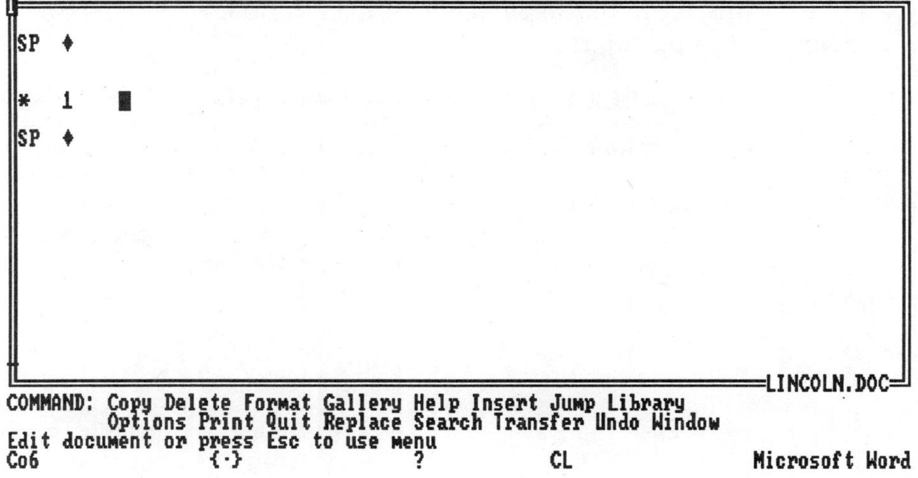

3. Press **Tab**. Type **87 years ago**. Press **Ctrl-PgUp**. Press **Esc**. Type **P**, then **V**. The Print Preview display appears. Notice the footnote appears at the bottom of the first page.
4. Exit Preview. Press **Esc**. Type **T**, then **S**. Press **Enter**. Word saves the document.
5. Turn to Module 6 to continue the learning sequence.

Module 10
FORMAT PARAGRAPH

DESCRIPTION

The Format Paragraph command on the Format menu allows you to change the characteristics of the paragraph pointed to by the text cursor. It consists of a form containing various paragraph parameters. In some cases, Word does not change the displayed appearance of the paragraph, only the manner used to print it. Access the Format Paragraph command by pressing Esc then typing F then P.

```
FORMAT: Character Paragraph Tab Border Footnote Division Running-head Stylesheet
        sEarch repLace revision-Marks
Sets paragraph alignment, indent, line spacing; adds side-by-side format
Pg1 Li1 Co1      {}              ?                              Microsoft Word
```

Word provides many shortcuts for mouse users. The mouse commands associated specifically with this form appear in Table 10-1. Generic mouse movements and commands appear in Appendix E.

TABLE 10-1. MOUSE COMMANDS

Action	*Pointing To*	*Result*
Push Left Button	Menu Selection	Word presents the requested form or submenu or executes the requested command.
Push Left Button	Field	Word selects the entry for change.
Push Left Button	Form Name	Word makes the requested changes and returns to the document.
Push Right Button	Field	Word makes the requested changes and returns to the document.
Push Right Button	[on Ruler and Drag	Word changes the Left Indent value.
Push Right Button	] on Ruler and Drag	Word changes the Right Indent value.
Push Right Button	¦ on Ruler and Drag	Word changes the First Line value.
Push Right and Left Buttons	Anywhere Except the Form or Window	Word cancels the current operation and returns to Main menu.

The Alignment field changes paragraph alignment. The Left selection provides an even left margin and ragged right margin. The Centered selection provides ragged left and right margins with the text centered between the margins. The Right selection provides an even right margin and ragged left margin. The Justified selection provides even right and left margins. When using the Justified selection, Word inserts extra spaces between each word until the right edge of the text aligns with the right margin.

The Left Indent, First Line, and Right Indent fields add extra space between the margins and the edge of the text. The Left Indent field changes the space between the left margin and all lines of text in a paragraph. The First Line field changes the space between the left margin and the first line of text. The Right indent field changes the space between the right margin and all lines of text in a paragraph. By combining one or more fields you can create various effects. For example, if you wanted to create an outdented paragraph (a paragraph where the first line extends further to the left than the rest of the lines) you would type a positive number in the Left Indent field and a negative number in the First Line field.

The Line Spacing, Space Before, and Space After fields affect the number of spaces between paragraphs and lines of text. The Line Spacing field tells Word how many spaces to add between lines of text. For example, if you wanted to use double spacing, you would type a 2 in the Line Spacing field. You can use fractional spacing (for instance .75) to get more lines to the inch. The Space Before field changes the number of blank lines Word adds before the paragraph text begins. The Space After field changes the number of blank lines Word adds after the paragraph text ends.

The Keep Together field prevents Word from splitting a paragraph at a page break when you select Yes. Instead, Word places the entire paragraph on the next page.

The Keep Follow field prevents Word from splitting two paragraphs at a page or column break. Use this field to keep titles with their associated paragraphs automatically.

The Side by Side field changes the way Word prints paragraphs. By formatting the paragraphs correctly, you can place two paragraphs beside each other. This particular feature works best using stylesheets. See Module 20 for a complete description.

APPLICATIONS

Use the Format Paragraph command to change the characteristics of the paragraph pointed to by the text cursor. Each field changes the printed appearance of the paragraph as described above. By combining various fields, you can create any special effect you want.

TYPICAL OPERATION

In this example you change the format of the sample document using the Format Paragraph form. Begin this example at the DOS prompt.

1. Type **WORD** and press **Enter** to start Word. Press **Esc**. Type **T**, then **L** to select the Transfer Load command. Press **F1**. Select LINCOLN.DOC using the arrow keys. Press **Enter**. The Gettysburg Address appears.

2. With the cursor on the title, press **Esc**. Type **F**, then **P**. The Format Paragraph form appears.

```
FORMAT PARAGRAPH alignment: Left Centered Right Justified
     left indent: 0"          first line: 0"          right indent: 0"
     line spacing: 1 li       space before: 0 li      space after: 0 li
     keep together: Yes(No)   keep follow: Yes(No)    side by side: Yes(No)
Select option
Pg1 Li1 Co1      {}                  ?                                 Microsoft Word
```

3. Select Centered by pressing **Spacebar**. Select Space After by pressing **Tab** six times. Type **1** and press **Enter**. Word centers the title, then adds a space between the title and the paragraph below.

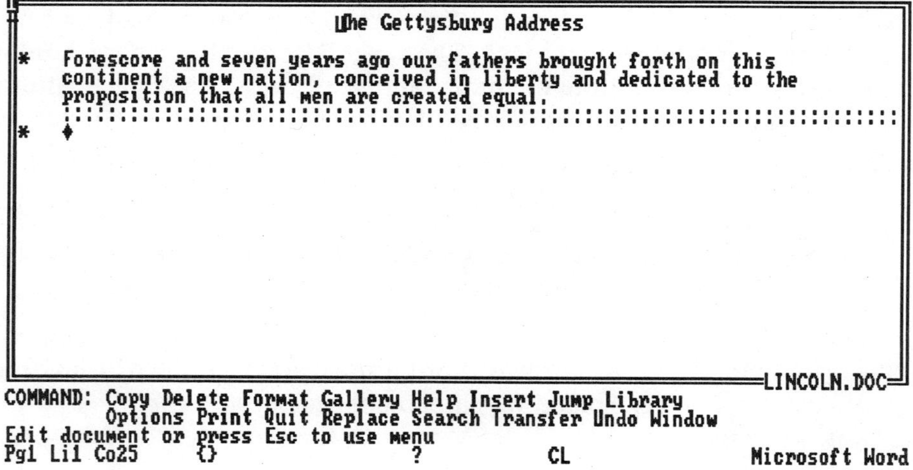

4. Press **Down Arrow**. Press **Esc**. Type **F**, then **P**. The Format Paragraph form appears.

5. Select Justified by pressing **Spacebar**. Select Space After by pressing **Tab** six times. Type **1** and press **Enter**. Word justifies the text, then adds a space between the title and the end pointer. Notice Word justifies the last line of text.

```
                    The Gettysburg Address

Forescore and seven years  ago  our  fathers  brought  forth  on  this
continent a new nation, conceived in  liberty  and  dedicated  to  the
proposition     that     all      men      are      created      equal.
```

6. Select the end of the paragraph using the arrow keys. Press **Enter**. Type the following text.

   Now we are engaged in a great civil war, testing whether that nation or any nation so conceived and so dedicated can long endure. We are met on a great battlefield of that war. We have come to dedicate a portion of that field as a final resting place for those who here gave their lives that that nation might live. It is altogether fitting and proper that we should do this.

7. Press **Enter**. Notice Word does not justify the last lines of either text paragraph and the second paragraph used the format of the first paragraph.

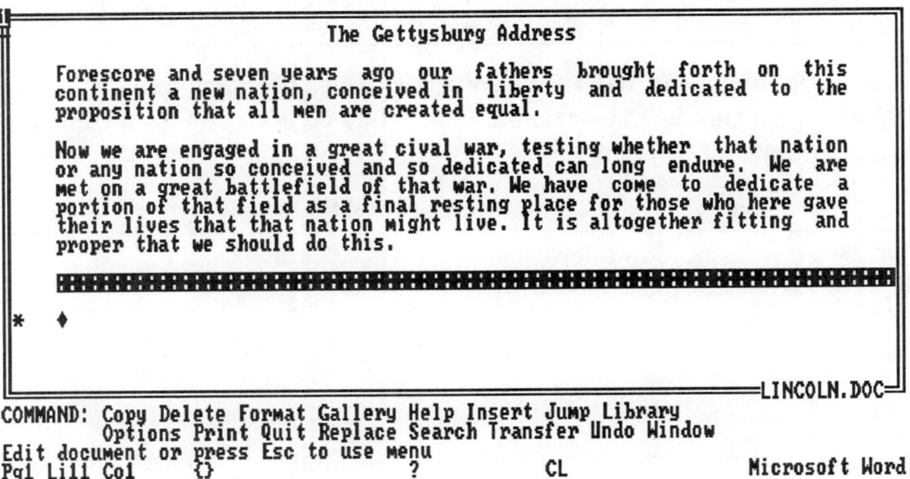

8. Press **Esc**. Type **T**, then **S**. The Transfer Save form appears.
9. Press **Enter**. Word displays a file save message. The Main menu appears.
10. Press **Esc**. Type **Q**. The DOS prompt appears.
11. Turn to Module 7 to continue the learning sequence.

Module 11
FORMAT REPLACE

DESCRIPTION

The Format Replace command allows you to search for a particular style and replace it with another. As with the Format Search command, Word allows you to search for the style key code or fill out the character or paragraph form fields. After you tell Word what search parameters to use, Word asks for the replace criteria. In essence, this command performs for paragraph formatting what the Replace command performs for text. You access this command by pressing Esc and typing F, then L.

```
FORMAT: Character Paragraph Tab Border Footnote Division Running-head Stylesheet
        sEarch replace revision-Marks pOsition Annotation bookmarK
Searches for and replaces formats or applied styles
P1 D1 C1           {Search·}          ?          CL                Microsoft Word
```

Word provides many shortcuts for mouse users. The mouse commands associated specifically with this form appear in Table 11-1. Generic mouse movements and commands appear in Appendix E.

TABLE 11-1. MOUSE COMMANDS

Action	*Pointing To*	*Result*
Push Left Button	Menu Selection	Word presents the requested form or submenu or executes the requested command.
Push Left Button	Field	Word selects the field for change.
Push Left Button	Form Name	Word makes the requested changes and returns to the document.
Push Right Button	Multiple Choice Field	Word makes the requested changes and returns to the document.
Push Right Button	Fill in the Blank Field	Word displays a list of acceptable choices.
Push Right and Left Buttons	Anywhere Except the Form or Window	Word cancels the current operation and returns to Main menu.

CHARACTER The Format Replace Character command allows you to search for a character based on a description you provide. Word presents a form containing the same elements as the Format Character form. Module 7 contains a complete description of the fields in this form. The Confirm field determines if Word asks to replace the format for each occurrence it finds. After you fill out the form describing what to look for, Word presents another copy of the form containing what to replace it with. This command does not apply to formats created using stylesheets.

PARAGRAPH The Format Replace Paragraph command allows you to search for a paragraph based on a description you provide. Word presents a form containing the same elements as the Format Paragraph form. Module 10 contains a complete description of the fields in this form. The Confirm field determines if Word asks to replace the format for each occurrence it finds. After you fill out the form describing what to look for, Word presents another copy of the form containing what to replace it with. This command does not apply to formats created using stylesheets.

STYLE The Format Replace Style command allows you to find a character, paragraph, or division using the two-character key code. The Key Code field contains the one- or two-character key code of the desired style. The With field contains the replacement two-character key code. The Confirm field selects whether Word asks for confirmation before each replacement.

APPLICATIONS

Use the Format Replace command to find a particular division, paragraph, or character based on its style and replace it with another style. This command allows you to find unusual or incorrect styles quickly. It also allows you to quickly change the format of some paragraphs using a specific style, without affecting all the paragraphs using that style.

TYPICAL OPERATION

In this example you search for and replace styles in the sample document. Begin this example at the Main menu with LINCOLN.DOC loaded in the current window.

1. Press **Ctrl-PgUp**. Press **Esc**. Type **F**, then **L**. The Format Replace menu appears.

```
FORMAT REPLACE: Character Paragraph Style

Searches for and replaces character formats
P1 D1 C1          {Search·}          ?                    Microsoft Word
```

2. Select Style by pressing **Right Arrow**. Press **Enter**. The Format Replace Style form appears.

```
FORMAT REPLACE STYLE key code: █           with:
                     confirm:(Yes)No
Enter one or two letter key code for style
P1 D1 C1          { }            ?          CL                  Microsoft Word
```

3. Type **H2**. Press **Tab**. Type **SP**. Press **Tab**, then **Spacebar** for yes, then **Enter**. Word finds the first occurrence of the H2 style and asks if you want to replace it.

```
t  ^PAGE: (page)
                      THE GETTYSBURG ADDRESS

H2  Paragraph 1

SP  Forescore and seven years ago¹ our fathers brought forth on  this
    continent a new nation, conceived in liberty and to .i.dedicated;
    the proposition that all men are created equal.
    ..................................................................
                                                        LINCOLN.DOC
FORMAT REPLACE STYLE key code: H2          with: SP
                     confirm:(Yes)No
Enter Y to replace, N to skip and continue, or Esc to cancel █
P1 D1 L2 C13      { }            ?          CL                  Microsoft Word
```

4. Type **Y**, then **N**, then **N**. Word replaces the first occurrence of H2 but not the rest. Word indicates the number of replacements on the message line.

```
t  ^PAGE: (page)
                      THE GETTYSBURG ADDRESS

SP   Paragraph 1

SP  Forescore and seven years ago¹ our fathers brought forth on  this
    continent a new nation, conceived in liberty and to .i.dedicated;
    the proposition that all men are created equal.
    ..................................................................
                                                        LINCOLN.DOC
COMMAND: Copy Delete Format Gallery Help Insert Jump Library
         Options Print Quit Replace Search Transfer Undo Window
1 replacement made
P1 D1 C1          { }            ?          CL                  Microsoft Word
```

5. Press **Esc**. Type **F**, then **L,** then **C**. The Format Replace Character form appears.

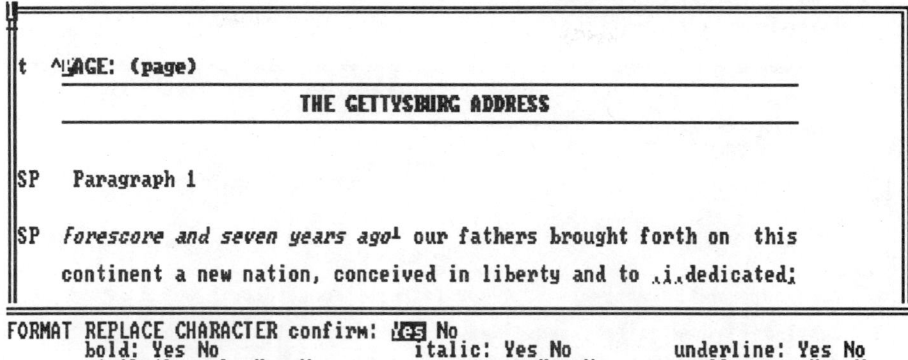

6. Select the Hidden field by pressing **Tab**. Press **Spacebar** to select yes. Press **Enter**. The Replace With Character Format form appears.

7. Select the Bold field by pressing **Tab**. Press **Spacebar** for yes. Press **Enter**. Word finds the first occurrence of hidden text and asks if you want to replace it with the new style.

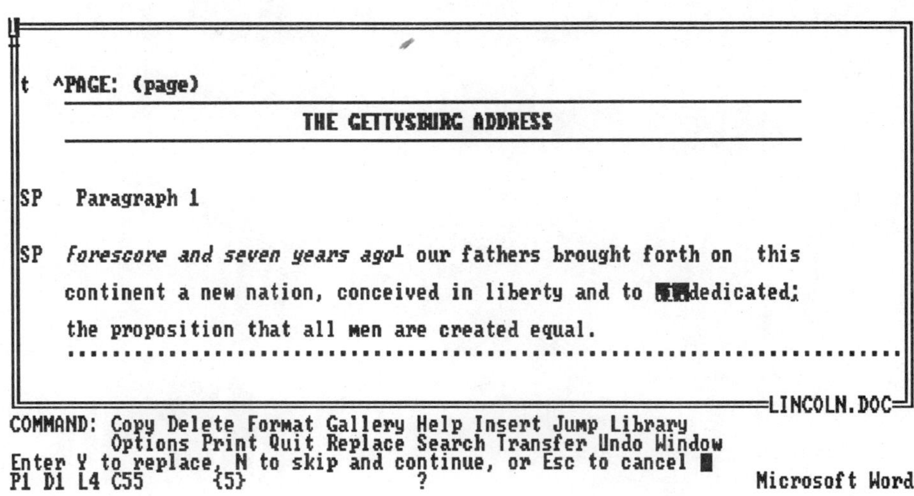

8. Type **Y** for the first two occurrences of hidden text. Type **N** for all succeeding occurrences. Word replaces only the first two occurrences and displays the number of replacements on the message line.

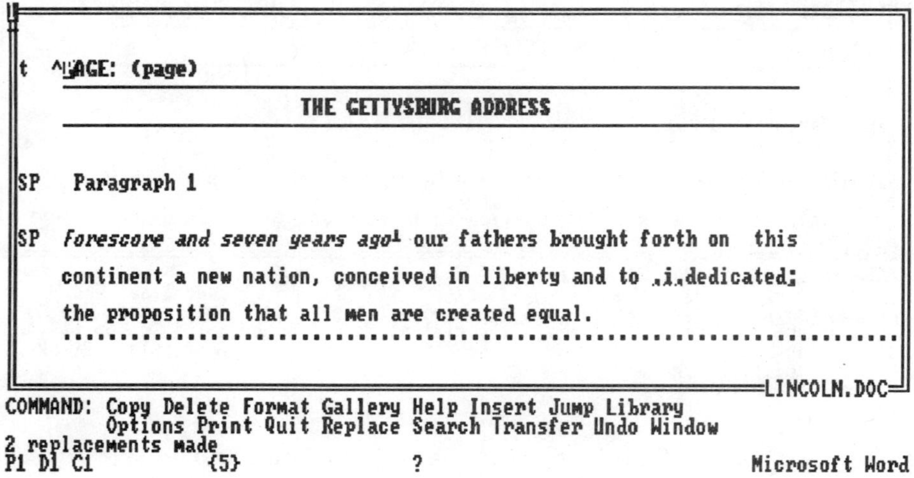
t ^PAGE: (page)

THE GETTYSBURG ADDRESS

SP Paragraph 1

SP *Forescore and seven years ago*[1] our fathers brought forth on this continent a new nation, conceived in liberty and to .i.dedicated; the proposition that all men are created equal.

LINCOLN.DOC

COMMAND: Copy Delete Format Gallery Help Insert Jump Library
Options Print Quit Replace Search Transfer Undo Window
2 replacements made
P1 D1 C1 {5} ? Microsoft Word

9. Turn to Module 12 to continue the learning sequence.

Module 12
FORMAT REVISION-MARKS, FORMAT ANNOTATION, FORMAT BOOKMARK

DESCRIPTION

These three commands work together to provide standard document editing features. The Format Revision-Marks command defines the way Word displays document revisions. It also provides the means of accepting new revisions and undoing old revisions. You select the revision marks feature by pressing Esc, typing F, then M, then O, and selecting Yes in the Add Revision-Marks field. The Format Annotation command adds comments to your document. In many respects, the Format Annotation command works the same as the Format Footnote command. However, unlike footnotes, annotations usually reflect review comments or comments printed on the outside margin of a document. To access the Format Annotation command press Esc and type F, then A. The Format Bookmark command places a marker in your text. When you need to find that position in your document, the Format Bookmark command assists you in finding it. You access the Format Bookmark command by pressing Esc and typing F, then K.

```
FORMAT: Character Paragraph Tab Border Footnote Division Running-head Stylesheet
        sEarch repLace revision-Marks pOsition Annotation bookmarK
Controls revision marks (redlining) in text
P1 D1 C1          {}              ?            CL                  Microsoft Word
```

REVISION-MARKS The Format Revision-Marks menu contains four commands. The Format Revision-Marks Options command controls the appearance of the revision marks and whether Word uses revision marks. The Format Revision-Marks Accept-Revisions command tells Word to add inserted text and remove deleted text. The Format Revision-Marks Undo-Revisions command allows you to remove inserted text and unmarked deleted text. The Format Revision-Marks Search command finds the next revision. It always searches from the top of the document to the bottom.

The Format Revision-Marks Options form contains three fields. The Add Revision-Marks field determines whether Word uses revision marks or performs actual insertions and deletions. By selecting Yes, you use revision marks. The Inserted Text field defines how Word presents inserted text on screen. Word always presents deleted text with a strikethrough attribute. The Revision Bar Position field determines where Word places the margin indicators showing revised text. If you select None, Word doesn't use revision bars.

ANNOTATION The Format Annotation form contains three fields. The Mark field tells Word what characters to use beside a sequential number. For example, if you placed your initials in the Mark field and inserted your first annotation, Word would use your initials followed by 1 to mark the annotation. The Insert Date field determines if Word places the date at the beginning of the annotation. The Insert Time field determines if Word places the time at the beginning of the annotation.

BOOKMARK The Format Bookmark form contains a single field. Always use a descriptive name to assist you in remembering the purpose of the bookmark. You find previously inserted bookmarks using the Jump Bookmark command described in Module 29.

APPLICATIONS

Use the Format Revision-Marks command to control the appearance and use of revision marks in your document. By using revision marks instead of actually editing your document, you can remove unneeded changes later. The Format Revision-Marks Accept-Revisions and Format Revision-Marks Undo-Revisions commands allow you to accept or reject revisions to your document. You can also use revision marks when editing contracts to show requirements added or deleted as a result of negotiations.

Use the Format Annotation command to add comments, either temporary or permanent, to your document. Temporary comments include ideas on how to improve the document or notes on how certain document features affect your business. Permanent comments include notes on technical papers. By selecting the side-by-side formatting feature for the affected paragraphs, you can place a marker in the paragraph text, and print the comment as a sidebar.

Use the Format Bookmark command to assist you in finding different areas in your document. You can also include this feature for others. By adding the appropriate annotation and bookmarks, you can show the document originator all the paragraphs affected by your comment.

TYPICAL OPERATION

In this example you use the Format Revision-Marks, Format Annotation, and Format Bookmark commands to edit the sample document. Begin this example at the Main menu with LINCOLN.DOC loaded in the current window.

1. Select the word Forescore by pressing arrow keys. Press **F8** to highlight the entire word. Press **Esc**. Type **F**, then **M**. The Format Revision-Marks menu appears.

```
FORMAT REVISION-MARKS: Options accept-Revisions Undo-revisions Search

Turns redlining on or off. Sets revision marking options
P1 D1 L3 C10      {}                  ?                            Microsoft Word
```

2. Press **Enter** to select Options. The Format Revision-Marks Options form appears.

```
FORMAT REVISION-MARK OPTIONS
        add revision marks: Yes No
        inserted text: Normal Bold(Underlined)Uppercase Double-underlined
        revision bar position:(None)Left Right Outside
Select option
P1 D1 L3 C10      {}                  ?                            Microsoft Word
```

3. Press **Spacebar** to select yes for revision marks. Press **Tab** twice to select the Revision Bar Position field. Press **Spacebar** to select left, then **Enter**. The Main menu appears. Notice the letters MR appear on the status line. This signifies Word is using revision marks instead of actually performing edits.

4. Press **Del**. Word places a line through Forescore instead of deleting it.

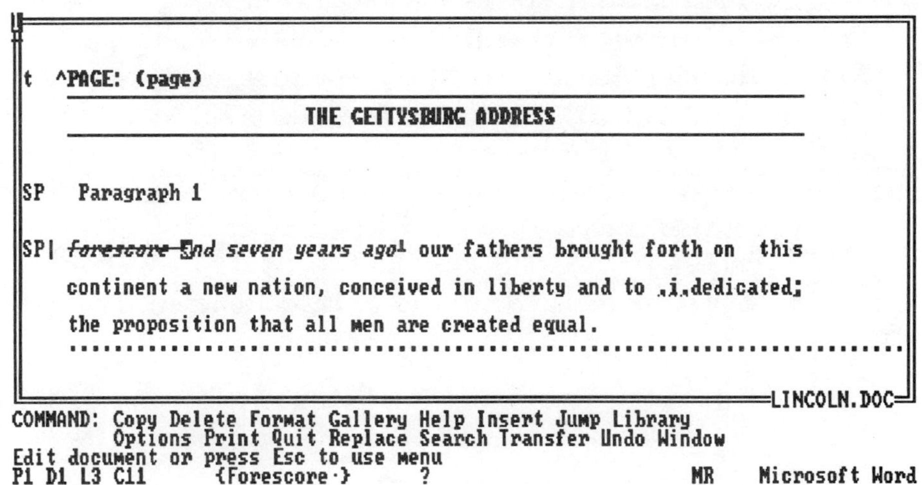

5. Type **Fourscore.** Word places a line under the new text.

```
t  ^PAGE: (page)
                         THE GETTYSBURG ADDRESS
SP   Paragraph 1
SP| forescore-fourscore and seven years ago¹ our fathers brought
    forth on this continent a new nation, conceived in liberty and to
    .i.dedicated; the proposition that all men are created equal.
    ..................................................................
                                                            LINCOLN.DOC
COMMAND: Copy Delete Format Gallery Help Insert Jump Library
         Options Print Quit Replace Search Transfer Undo Window
Edit document or press Esc to use menu
P1 D1 L3 C21      {t}              ?                   MR    Microsoft Word
```

6. Press **Ctrl-PgUp**. Press **Esc**. Type **F**, then **M**, then **S**. Word finds the first occurrence of a revision mark.

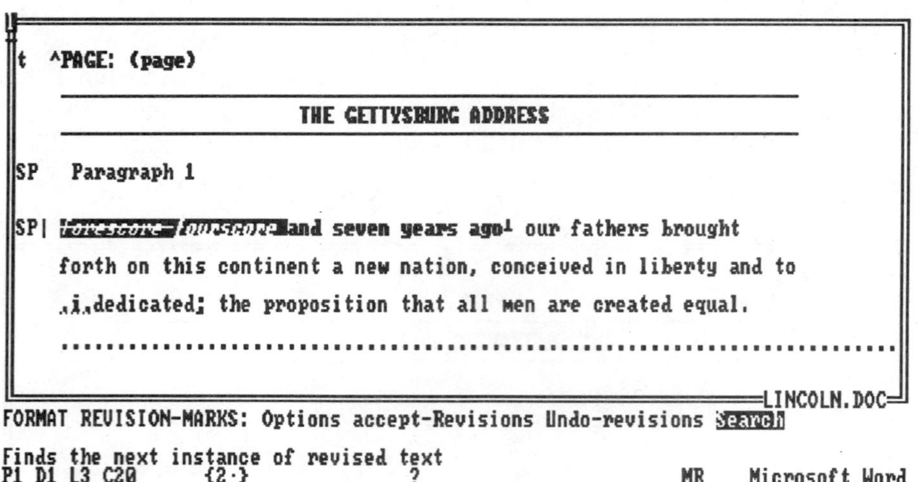

7. Press **R** to accept the revisions. Word removes the revision marks and performs the revision.

```
t  ^PAGE: (page)
          ____________________________________________________
                      THE GETTYSBURG ADDRESS
          ____________________________________________________
SP   Paragraph 1

SP  Fourscore and seven years ago¹ our fathers brought forth on this
    continent a new nation, conceived in liberty and to .i.dedicated;
    the proposition that all men are created equal.
    ..........................................................................
                                                              LINCOLN.DOC
FORMAT REVISION-MARKS: Options accept-Revisions Undo-revisions Search

Finds the next instance of revised text
P1 D1 L3 C1        {2·}           ?                     MR    Microsoft Word
```

8. Press **Esc** to return from the Format Revision-Marks menu. The Main menu appears.

9. Select the end of the Paragraph 2 line by pressing arrow keys. Press **Esc**. Type **F**, then **A**. The Format Annotation form appears.

```
FORMAT ANNOTATION mark: █
           insert date: Yes(No)                   insert time: Yes(No)
Enter text
P2 D1 L1 C12       {·}            ?                     MR    Microsoft Word
```

10. Type **INITIALS**. Press **Tab**, then **Spacebar** to select yes for date. Press **Tab** then **Spacebar** to select yes for time. Press **Enter**. Word creates an annotation entry. Notice this entry contains a 2 at the beginning. The footnote entry created in Module 9 counts as 1. Notice also, the entry shows with a changebar to the left. By adding annotation using revision marks, you can remove it easily.

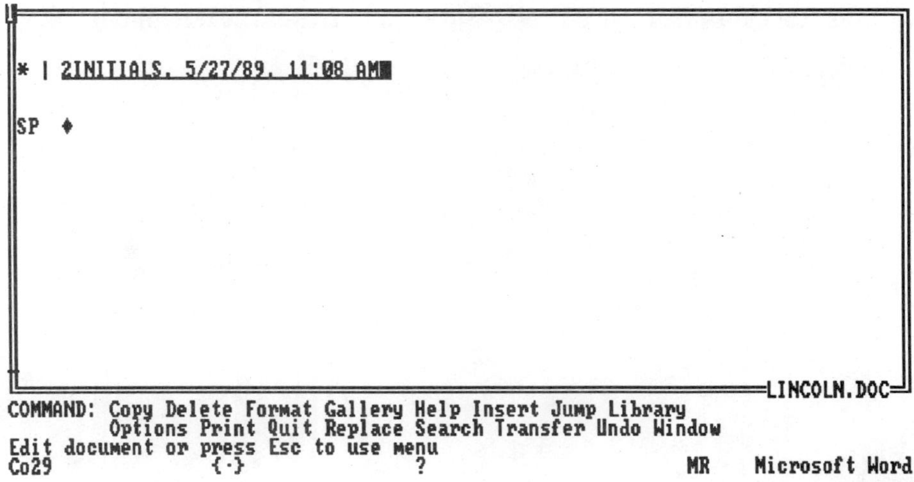

11. Press **Ctrl-PgUp**. Press **Esc**. Type **P**, then **V**. The Print Preview display appears. Notice the footnote appears on the bottom of page 1; the annotation appears on the bottom of page 2.

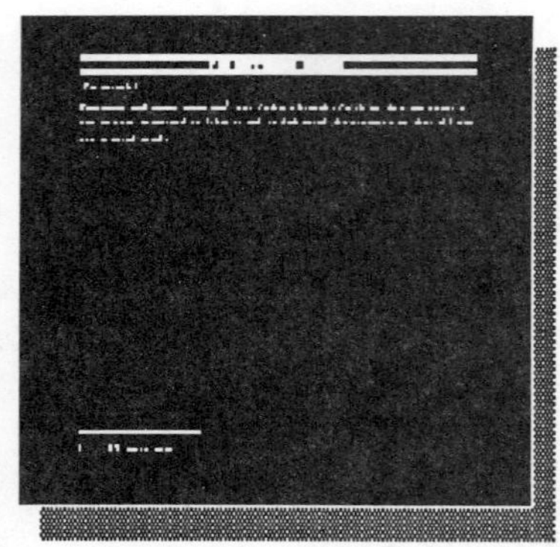
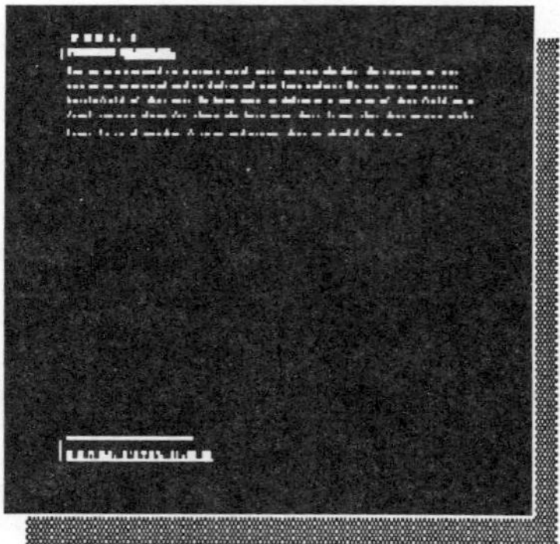

```
PRINT PREVIEW: Exit Jump Options Print

Use PgUp and PgDn to scroll through document
P1 D1      P2 D1                     ?                MR       LINCOLN.DOC
```

12. Exit Preview. Select Paragraph 1 by pressing arrow keys. Press **Esc**. Type **F**, then **K**. The Format Bookmark form appears.

```
FORMAT BOOKMARK name: █

Enter bookmark name or press F1 to select from list
P1 D1 L2 C1        {·}              ?                MR     Microsoft Word
```

13. Type **PARA1**. Press **Enter**. Select Paragraph 2 by pressing arrow keys. Press **Esc**. Type **F**, then **K**. Type **PARA2**. Press **Enter**. Select Paragraph 3 by pressing arrow keys. Press **Esc**. Type **F**, then **K**. Type **PARA3**. Press **Enter**.
14. Press **Esc**. Type **T**, then **S**. Press **Enter**. Word saves the document.
15. Turn to Module 17 to continue the learning sequence.

Module 13
FORMAT RUNNING-HEAD

DESCRIPTION

The Format Running-Head command allows you to place a heading at the top or bottom of a sequence of pages. You access the Format Running-Head command by pressing Esc and typing F, then R. If you want to use the default Running-Head settings, press Alt-F2 to place a running head at the bottom of a page, or press Ctrl-F2 to place a running head at the top of a page.

```
FORMAT: Character Paragraph Tab Border Footnote Division Running-head Stylesheet
        sEarch repLace revision-Marks pOsition Annotation bookmarK
Defines and positions the selected paragraph(s) as a running head
P1 D1 L1 C1       {entire·}        ?                        Microsoft Word
```

The Format Running-Head form contains five fields. The Position field determines if Word places the running head at the top or bottom of the page. Word uses the settings in the Format Division Margins form Running-Head Position From Top field for header page position, and From Bottom field for footers page position. The Odd Pages, Even Pages, and First Page fields work together to determine on which pages Word places the running head. The Odd Pages field affects all odd numbered pages except the first page. The Even Pages field affects all even numbered pages except the first page. The First Page field affects only the first page. The Alignment field determines if Word positions the running head starting at the normal margin or at the edge of the paper. By selecting the edge of the paper, you can place running heads in the margins of a document.

Word provides many shortcuts for mouse users. There are no mouse commands associated specifically with this command. Generic mouse movements and commands appear in Appendix E.

APPLICATIONS

Use the Format Running-Head command to place running heads at the top or bottom of your document. Word does not restrict the number of lines a running head consumes. You can also include any of the seven standard glossary entries in your running head. For example, you could place the document name and page number on even pages and the chapter name and page number on odd pages. Running heads also provide a convenient method of ensuring tables contain the appropriate information on the top of every page. By making the table title and column heading a running head, you force Word to perform this tedious task.

TYPICAL OPERATION

In this example you create several types of running heads. Begin this example at the Main menu with LINCOLN.DOC loaded in the current window.

1. Select the P of Page by pressing arrow keys. Press **Esc**. Type **F**, then **R**. The Format Running-Head form appears.

```
FORMAT RUNNING-HEAD position: Top Bottom None
       odd pages:(Yes)No  even pages:(Yes)No  first page: Yes(No)
       alignment:(Left-margin)Edge-of-paper
Select option
P1 D1 L1 C1        {entire·}         ?                           Microsoft Word
```

2. Press **Spacebar** to select Top. Press **Tab** three times to select the First Page field. Press **Spacebar** to select yes, then **Enter**. Word shows the line of text as a running head. Notice the style bar shows a lowercase t and a carat (t ∧).

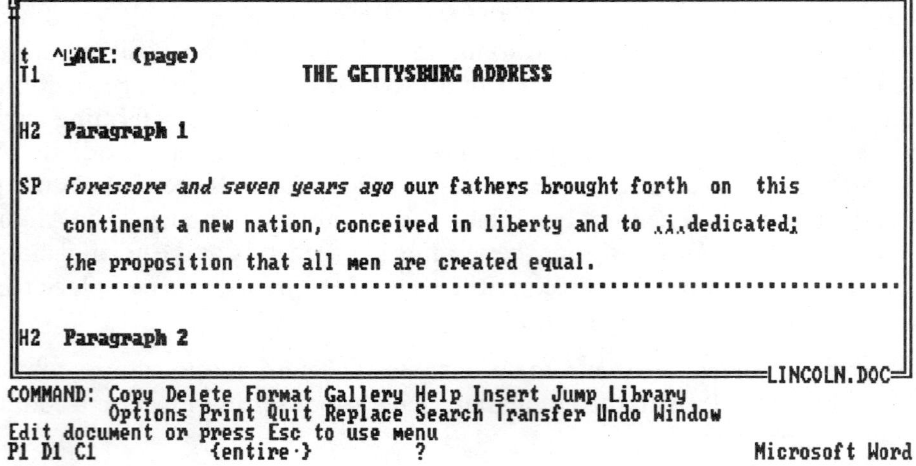

3. Press **Esc**. Type **P**, then **V**. The Print Preview display appears. Notice the header appears on both pages near the top.

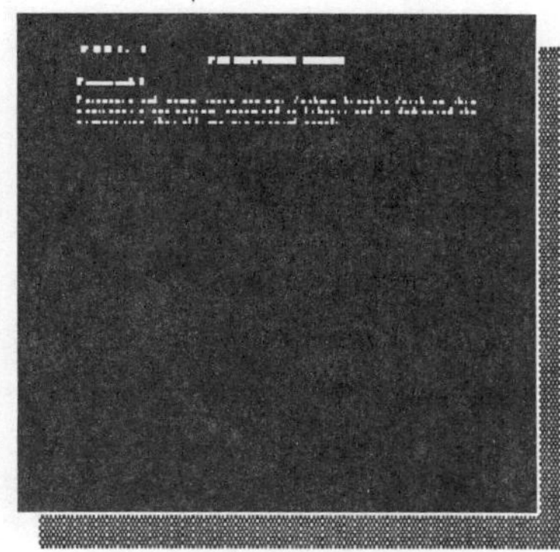

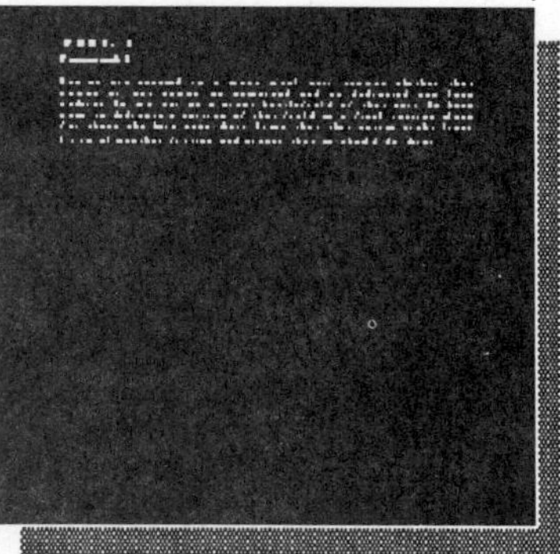

```
PRINT PREVIEW: Exit Jump Options Print

Use PgUp and PgDn to scroll through document
P1 D1     P2 D1                       ?          CL                    LINCOLN.DOC
```

4. Exit Print Preview. Press **Esc**. Type **F**, then **R**. The Format Running-Head form appears.

5. Press **Spacebar** to select Bottom. Press **Enter**. Word shows the line of text as a running head. Notice the style bar shows a lowercase b and a carat (b ∧).

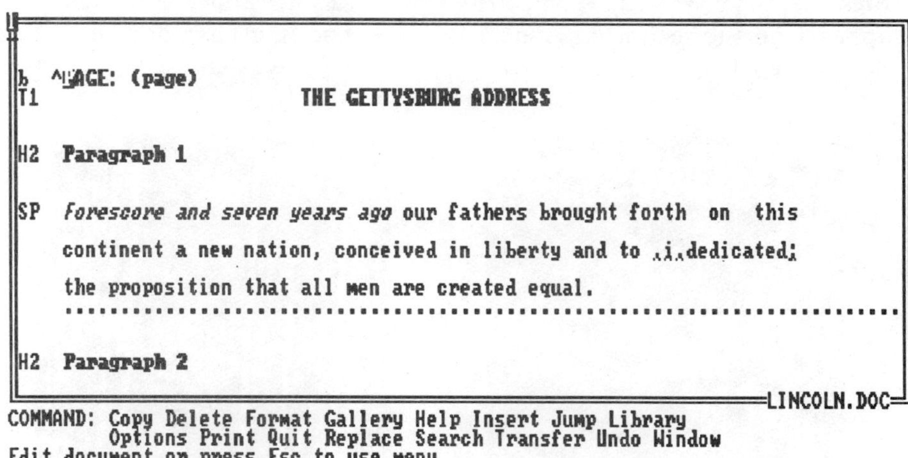

6. Press **Esc**. Type **P**, then **V**. The Print Preview display appears. Notice the header appears on both pages near the bottom.

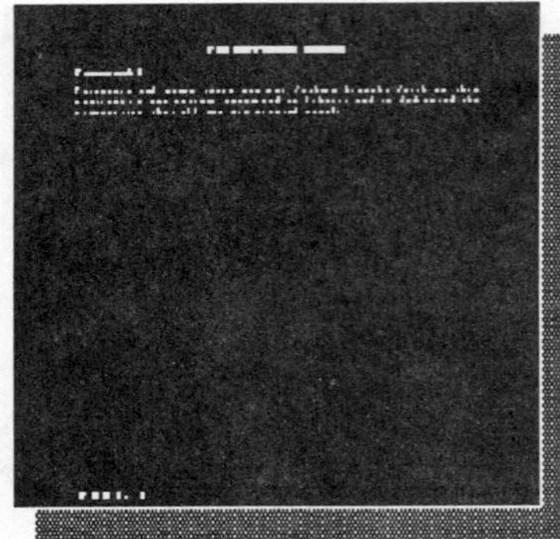

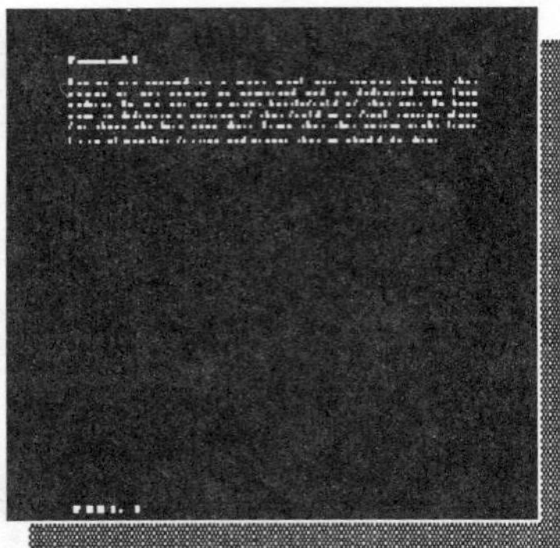

```
PRINT PREVIEW: Exit Jump Options Print

Use PgUp and PgDn to scroll through document
P1 D1     P2 D1                   ?                                LINCOLN.DOC
```

7. Repeat step 4. Press **Spacebar** to select Top. Press **Tab** three times to select the First Page field. Press **Spacebar** for no, then **Enter**. Word shows the line of text as a running head. Notice the style bar shows a lowercase t and a carat (t ∧).

8. Press **Esc**. Type **P**, then **V**. The Print Preview display appears. Notice the header appears on the second page near the top. The first page does not contain a running head.

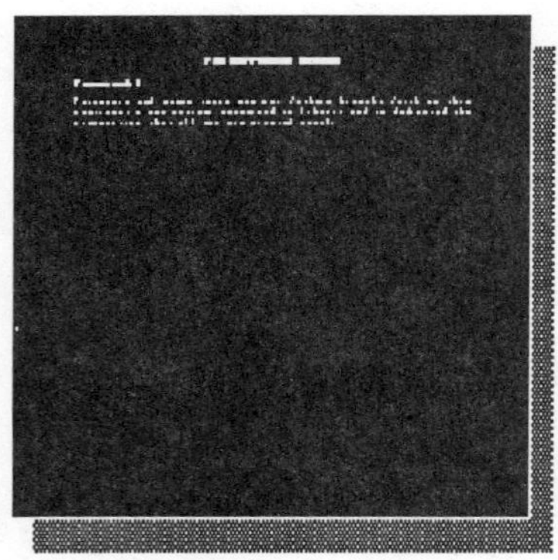

```
PRINT PREVIEW: Exit Jump Options Print

Use PgUp and PgDn to scroll through document
P1 D1     P2 D1                   ?                                LINCOLN.DOC
```

9. Exit Print Preview. Press **Esc**. Type **T**, then **S**. Press **Enter**. Word saves the document.

10. Turn to Module 9 to continue the learning sequence.

Module 14
FORMAT SEARCH

DESCRIPTION

The Format Search command allows you to find a division, paragraph, or character based on its style. When searching for a character or paragraph, Word provides a method of describing the format. This allows you to find the particular character or paragraph in documents not using a particular style. A second method of finding the style uses the two-character style code. Word finds the first occurrence of the style and highlights the paragraph. You access the Format Search command by pressing Esc and typing F, then E.

```
FORMAT: Character Paragraph Tab Border Footnote Division Running-head Stylesheet
        sEarch repLace revision-Marks pOsition Annotation bookmarK
Searches for formats or applied styles
P1 D1 C1          {Style·}        ?            CL                 Microsoft Word
```

Word provides many shortcuts for mouse users. The mouse commands associated specifically with this form appear in Table 14-1. Generic mouse movements and commands appear in Appendix E.

TABLE 14-1. MOUSE COMMANDS

Action	*Pointing To*	*Result*
Push Left Button	Menu Selection	Word presents the requested form or submenu or executes the requested command.
Push Left Button	Field	Word selects the field for change.
Push Left Button	Form Name	Word makes the requested changes and returns to the document.
Push Right Button	Multiple Choice Field	Word makes the requested changes and returns to the document.
Push Right Button	Fill in the Blank Field	Word displays a list of acceptable choices.
Push Right and Left Buttons	Anywhere Except the Form or Window	Word cancels the current operation and returns to Main menu.

CHARACTER The Format Search Character command allows you to search for a character based on a description you provide. Word presents a form containing the same elements as the Format Character form. Module 7 contains a complete description of the fields in this form. This command does not apply to formats created using stylesheets.

PARAGRAPH The Format Search Paragraph command allows you to search for a paragraph based on a description you provide. Word presents a form containing the same elements as the Format Paragraph form. Module 10 contains a complete description of the fields in this form. This command does not apply to formats created using stylesheets.

STYLE The Format Search Style command allows you to find a character, paragraph, or division using the two-character key code. The Key Code field contains the one- or two-character key code of the desired style. The direction field selects whether Word searches up or down the document from the text cursor position.

APPLICATIONS

Use the Format Search command to find a particular division, paragraph, or character based on its style. This command allows you to find unusual or incorrect styles quickly.

TYPICAL OPERATION

In this example you search for a particular paragraph using the Format Search command. Begin this example at the Main menu with LINCOLN.DOC loaded in the current window.

1. Press **Ctrl-PgUp**. Press **Esc**. Type **F**, then **E**. The Format Search menu appears.

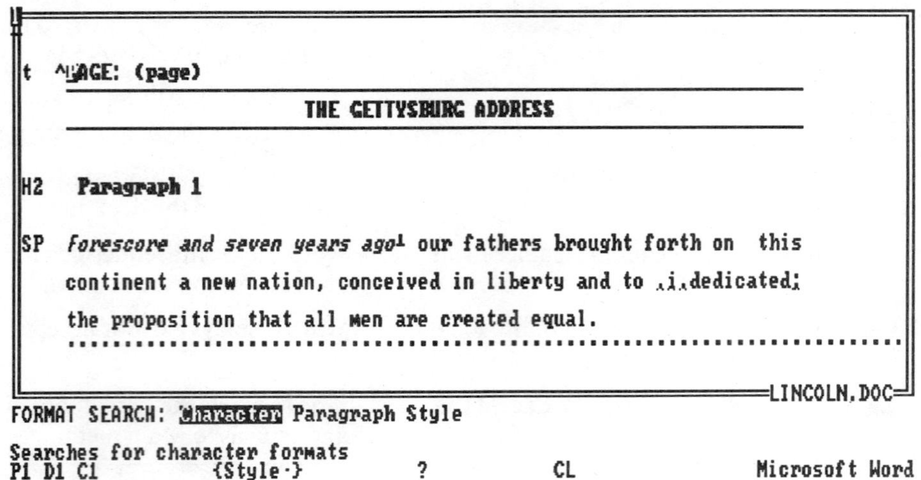

2. Select Style by pressing **Right Arrow**. Press **Enter**. The Format Search Style form appears.

```
FORMAT SEARCH STYLE key code: █          direction: Up(Down)

Enter one or two letter key code for style
P1 D1 C1            {Style·}         ?            CL              Microsoft Word
```

3. Type **H2** and press **Enter**. Word finds the first occurrence of the H2 style.

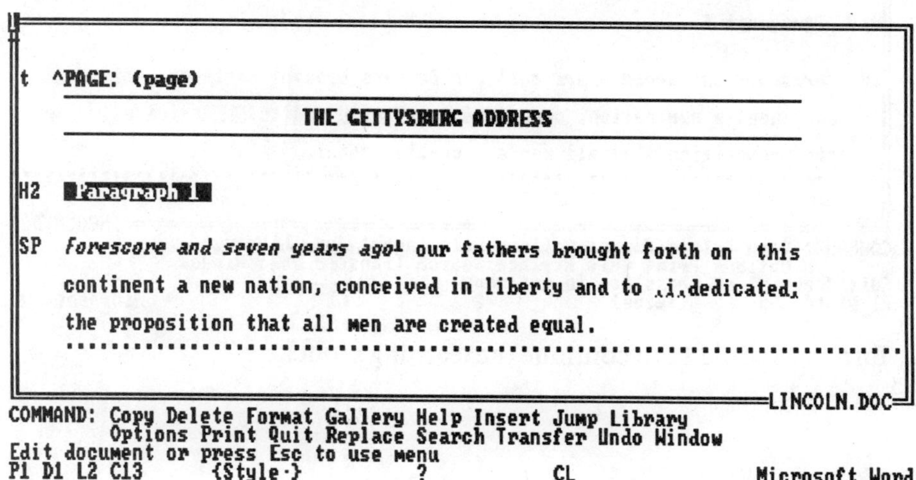

```
t  ^PAGE: (page)
                    THE GETTYSBURG ADDRESS

H2  Paragraph 1

SP  Forescore and seven years ago¹ our fathers brought forth on  this
    continent a new nation, conceived in liberty and to .i.dedicated:
    the proposition that all men are created equal.
    ..........................................................................
                                                              LINCOLN.DOC
COMMAND: Copy Delete Format Gallery Help Insert Jump Library
         Options Print Quit Replace Search Transfer Undo Window
Edit document or press Esc to use menu
P1 D1 L2 C13        {Style·}         ?            CL              Microsoft Word
```

4. Press **Esc**. Type **F**, then **E**, then **C**. The Format Search Character form appears.

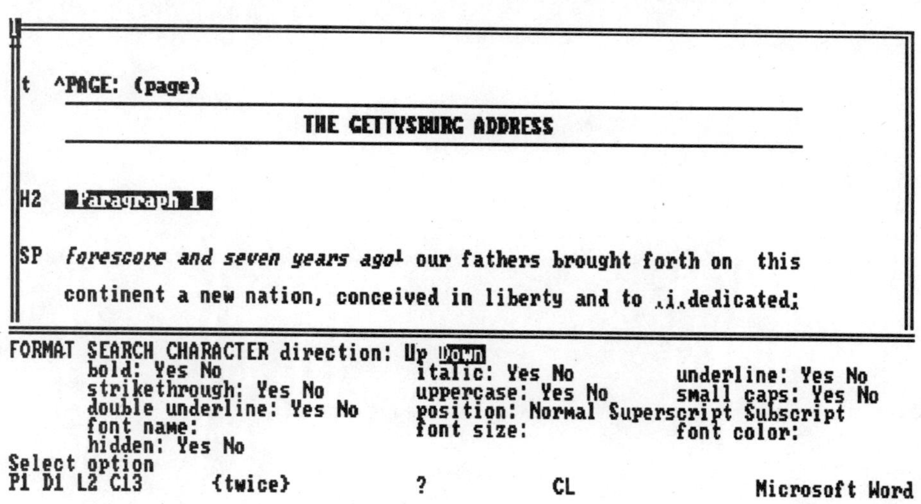

```
t  ^PAGE: (page)
                    THE GETTYSBURG ADDRESS

H2  Paragraph 1

SP  Forescore and seven years ago¹ our fathers brought forth on  this
    continent a new nation, conceived in liberty and to .i.dedicated:

FORMAT SEARCH CHARACTER direction: Up Down
       bold: Yes No                  italic: Yes No          underline: Yes No
       strikethrough: Yes No         uppercase: Yes No       small caps: Yes No
       double underline: Yes No      position: Normal Superscript Subscript
       font name:                    font size:              font color:
       hidden: Yes No
Select option
P1 D1 L2 C13        {twice}          ?            CL              Microsoft Word
```

5. Select the Hidden field by pressing **Tab**. Press **Spacebar** to select yes. Press **Enter**. Word finds the first occurrence of hidden text.

```
t  ^PAGE: (page)
                     THE GETTYSBURG ADDRESS

H2  Paragraph 1

SP  Forescore and seven years ago¹ our fathers brought forth on  this
    continent a new nation, conceived in liberty and to   dedicated;
    the proposition that all men are created equal.
    ...................................................................
                                                          LINCOLN.DOC
COMMAND: Copy Delete Format Gallery Help Insert Jump Library
         Options Print Quit Replace Search Transfer Undo Window
Edit document or press Esc to use menu
P1 D1 L4 C55      {twice}          ?          CL          Microsoft Word
```

6. Turn to Module 11 to continue the learning sequence.

Module 15
FORMAT STYLESHEET

DESCRIPTION

The Format Stylesheet menu of the Format menu contains all the commands required to manage document interaction with an attached stylesheet. It also contains the means for attaching a stylesheet to a document. While using a stylesheet with a document, Word allows access to the default Alt key formatting codes by prefixing them with an X. For example, normally you select the standard character for a highlighted group of characters by pressing Alt-Spacebar. When using a stylesheet with a document you would press Alt-X then Spacebar to achieve the same effect.

```
FORMAT: Character Paragraph Tab Border Footnote Division Running-head Stylesheet
        sEarch repLace revision-Marks
Attaches style sheet, applies styles, records new styles
Pg1 Li1 Co25     {}                  ?                CL              Microsoft Word
```

Word provides many shortcuts for mouse users. The mouse commands associated specifically with this command appear in Table 15-1. Generic mouse movements and commands appear in Appendix E.

TABLE 15-1. MOUSE COMMANDS

Action	*Pointing To*	*Result*
Push Left Button	Menu Selection	Word presents the requested form or submenu or executes the requested command.
Push Left Button	Field	Word selects the field for change.
Push Left Button	Form Name	Word makes the requested changes and returns to the document.

Action	Pointing To	Result
Push Right Button	Field	Word provides a list of acceptable choices. When requesting filename choices, Word provides the list in the current directory. To get a list of the files in another directory, change the Transfer Options entry or point to the correct drive/ directory name on the file listing. When requesting any other choices, Word uses the contents of the currently attached stylesheet and print driver for information.
Push Right Button	Field	Word makes the requested changes and returns to the document.
Push Right and Left Buttons	Anywhere Except the Form or Window	Word cancels the current operation and returns to Main menu.

ATTACH The Format Stylesheet Attach command provides the means to match a stylesheet to a document. To get a listing of stylesheets in the current directory, press F1.

CHARACTER The Format Stylesheet Character command changes the format of the highlighted characters. By pressing F1, you can obtain a listing of character styles contained in the attached stylesheet. You can also change the character format by pressing the appropriate Alt key combination (the two-letter definition you provided when creating the stylesheet).

PARAGRAPH The Format Stylesheet Paragraph command reformats the paragraph pointed to by the text cursor or any number of highlighted paragraphs. This command changes the tab settings, but does not affect the character formatting. By pressing F1, you can obtain a listing of paragraph styles contained in the attached stylesheet. You can also change the paragraph format by pressing the appropriate Alt key combination (the two-letter definition you provided when creating the stylesheet).

DIVISION The Format Stylesheet Division command creates a new division formatted as defined in the selected division definition. By pressing F1, you can obtain a listing of division styles contained in the attached stylesheet. You can also change the division definition by pressing the appropriate Alt key combination (the two-letter definition you provided when creating the stylesheet).

RECORD The Format Stylesheet Record command creates a new definition in the currently attached stylesheet. This command works exactly the same as the Gallery Insert command discussed in Module 22. Word automatically formats the new definition like the character, paragraph, or division currently pointed to by the text cursor. After leaving this command, a marked paragraph or division contains the appropriate style marker on the left edge of the display.

APPLICATIONS

Use this menu to control all aspects of the interface between a document and an attached stylesheet. Since a stylesheet reduces both the time and effort used to create a document, many of the stylesheet commands contained on the menu also appear as control key combinations. For example, to use a character, paragraph, or division definition appearing in a stylesheet, you only need to press Alt then the style marker letters. You can also record a new stylesheet definition by pressing Alt-F10 while inside a document. Word automatically creates a new definition as described above.

Because Word provides easy access to the stylesheet commands, you can include them in macros. This allows you to create standard documents quickly and efficiently. It also completely automates the process of creating standard documents, ensuring they all look uniform.

TYPICAL OPERATION

In this example you attach the previously created stylesheet to the sample document. The example then guides you through the process of reformatting the document using the stylesheet definitions. Begin this example at the Main menu with LINCOLN.DOC loaded in the current window.

1. Press **Esc**. Type **F**, then **S**. The Format Stylesheet menu appears.

```
FORMAT STYLESHEET: Attach Character Paragraph Division Record

Attaches style sheet
Pg1 Li1 Co25     {}                ?                          Microsoft Word
```

2. Press **Enter**. The Format Stylesheet Attach form appears.

```
FORMAT STYLESHEET ATTACH: C:\MW\001?\NORMAL.STY

Enter filename or press F1 to select from list
Pg1 Li1 Co25     {}                ?          CL              Microsoft Word
```

3. Press **F1**. Word displays a list of stylesheets in the current directory.

```
LINCOLN.STY          NORMAL.STY







FORMAT STYLESHEET ATTACH: LINCOLN.STY

Enter filename or press F1 to select from list (17934336 bytes free)
Pg1 Li1 Co25     {}                ?          CL                Microsoft Word
```

4. Select LINCOLN.STY by pressing arrow keys. Press **Enter**. The Main menu appears.
5. Press **Esc**. Type **F**, then **S**, then **D**. The Format Stylesheet Division form appears.

```
FORMAT STYLESHEET DIVISION: █

Enter division style or press F1 to select from list
Pg1 Li1 Co25     {}                ?          CL                Microsoft Word
```

6. Press **F1**. Word presents a list of division definitions.

```
SD Division Standard (Standard Divisio)







FORMAT STYLESHEET DIVISION: Division Standard

Enter division style or press F1 to select from list
Pg1 Li1 Co25     {}                ?          CL                Microsoft Word
```

7. Select STANDARD DIVISION by pressing arrow keys. Press **Enter**. The Main menu appears.
8. Press **PgDn**. Notice the SD (style marker) on the left side of the division marker.

```
    to add or detract. The world will little note, nor long remember,
    what we say here, but it can never forget what they did here.  It
    is for us  the  living,  rather  to  be  dedicated  here  to  the
    unfinished work which they who fought here have thus far so nobly
    advanced. It is rather, to be dedicated here to  the  great  task
    remaining before us -- that  from  these  honored  dead  we  take
    increased devotion to that cause for which  they  gave  the  last
    full measure of devotion -- that  we  here  highly  resolve  that
    these dead shall not have died in vain -- that this nation, under
    God, shall have a new birth of freedom -- and that government  of
    the people, by the people, for the people, shall not perish  from
    this earth.

SD  ::::::::::::::::::::::::::::::::::::::::::::::::::::::::::::::::::::::


SP  ♦
                                                               LINCOLN.DOC
COMMAND: Copy Delete Format Gallery Help Insert Jump Library
         Options Print Quit Replace Search Transfer Undo Window
Edit document or press Esc to use menu
Pg2 Li4 Co22      {}            ?          CL             Microsoft Word
```

9. Press **PgUp**. Select the title by pressing arrow keys. Press **Esc**. Type **F**, then **S**, then **P**. The Format Stylesheet Paragraph form appears.

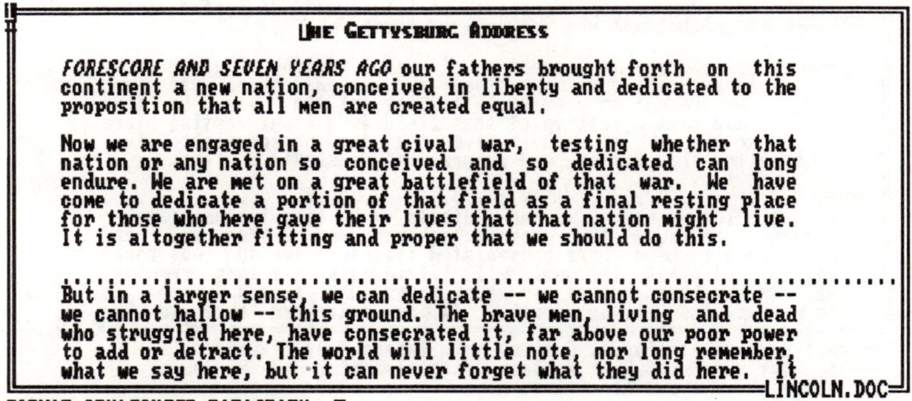

```
                         THE GETTYSBURG ADDRESS

    FORESCORE AND SEVEN YEARS AGO our fathers brought forth  on  this
    continent a new nation, conceived in liberty and dedicated to the
    proposition that all men are created equal.

    Now we are engaged in a great cival  war,  testing  whether  that
    nation or any nation so  conceived  and  so  dedicated  can  long
    endure. We are met on a great battlefield of that  war.  We  have
    come to dedicate a portion of that field as a final resting place
    for those who here gave their lives that that nation might  live.
    It is altogether fitting and proper that we should do this.

    ......................................................................
    But in a larger sense, we can dedicate -- we cannot consecrate --
    we cannot hallow -- this ground. The brave men, living  and  dead
    who struggled here, have consecrated it, far above our poor power
    to add or detract. The world will little note, nor long remember,
    what we say here, but it can never forget what they did here.  It
                                                               LINCOLN.DOC
FORMAT STYLESHEET PARAGRAPH: █

Enter paragraph style or press F1 to select from list
Pg1 Li1 Co22      {}            ?          CL             Microsoft Word
```

10. Press **F1**. Word displays a list of paragraph definitions.

```
SP Paragraph Standard (Standard Paragr) T1 Paragraph Heading level 1 (Gettysbu)









FORMAT STYLESHEET PARAGRAPH: Paragraph Standard

Enter paragraph style or press F1 to select from list
Pg1 Li1 Co22     {}                ?          CL                 Microsoft Word
```

11. Select PARAGRAPH HEADING LEVEL 1 by pressing arrow keys. Press **Enter**. The Main menu appears. Notice Word changes the paragraph style, but not the text style.

```
T1                     THE GETTYSBURG ADDRESS
     FORESCORE AND SEVEN YEARS AGO our fathers brought forth  on  this
     continent a new nation, conceived in liberty and dedicated to the
     proposition that all men are created equal.

     Now we are engaged in a great cival  war,  testing  whether  that
     nation or any nation so  conceived  and  so  dedicated  can  long
     endure. We are met on a great battlefield of that  war.  We  have
     come to dedicate a portion of that field as a final resting place
     for those who here gave their lives that that nation might  live.
     It is altogether fitting and proper that we should do this.
..........................................................................
     But in a larger sense, we can dedicate -- we cannot consecrate --
     we cannot hallow -- this ground. The brave men, living  and  dead
     who struggled here, have consecrated it, far above our poor power
     to add or detract. The world will little note, nor long remember,
     what we say here, but it can never forget what they did here.  It
     is for us  the  living,  rather  to  be  dedicated  here  to  the
                                                            LINCOLN.DOC
COMMAND: Copy Delete Format Gallery Help Insert Jump Library
         Options Print Quit Replace Search Transfer Undo Window
Edit document or press Esc to use menu
Pg1 Li1 Co22     {}                ?          CL                 Microsoft Word
```

12. Press **F6** then **End**. Press **Esc**. Type **F**, then **S**, then **C**. The Format Stylesheet Character form appears.

```
FORMAT STYLESHEET CHARACTER: █

Enter character style or press F1 to select from list
Pg1 Li1 Co44     {}                ?          CL       EX        Microsoft Word
```

13. Press **F1**. Word displays a list of character styles.

```
 Character Standard                       IT Character 1 (Italic Characters)









FORMAT STYLESHEET CHARACTER: Character Standard

Enter character style or press F1 to select from list
Pg1 Li1 Co44     {}                ?          CL        EX        Microsoft Word
```

14. Select CHARACTER STANDARD by pressing arrow keys. Press **Enter**. Word changes the title character style to the character definition for T1.

15. Select the first paragraph by pressing arrow keys. Press **F6**, then **Ctrl-PgDn**. Press **Alt-S**. Type **P**. Word changes the paragraph formatting to match the definition for a standard paragraph.

16. Press **Alt-X** then **Spacebar**. Word changes the character format of the selected paragraphs to the standard character definition.

```
T1                     THE GETTYSBURG ADDRESS

SP  Forescore and seven years ago our fathers brought forth  on  this
    continent a new nation, conceived in liberty and dedicated to the
    proposition that all men are created equal.

SP  Now we are engaged in a great cival  war,  testing  whether  that
    nation or any nation so  conceived  and  so  dedicated  can  long
    endure. We are met on a great battlefield of that  war.  We  have
    come to dedicate a portion of that field as a final resting place
    for those who here gave their lives that that nation might  live.
                                                          LINCOLN.DOC
COMMAND: Copy Delete Format Gallery Help Insert Jump Library
         Options Print Quit Replace Search Transfer Undo Window
Edit document or press Esc to use menu
Pg2 Li16 Co1     {}                ?          CL                  Microsoft Word
```

17. Select the F of Forescore by pressing arrow keys. Press **F6**. Highlight FORESCORE AND SEVEN YEARS AGO by pressing arrow keys. Press **Alt-I**. Type **T**. Word changes the character format of the selected text to italics.

```
T1                     THE GETTYSBURG ADDRESS

SP  Forescore and seven years ago our fathers brought forth  on  this
    continent a new nation, conceived in liberty and dedicated to the
    proposition that all men are created equal.

SP  Now we are engaged in a great cival  war,  testing  whether  that
    nation or any nation so  conceived  and  so  dedicated  can  long
    endure. We are met on a great battlefield of that  war.  We  have
    come to dedicate a portion of that field as a final resting place
    for those who here gave their lives that that nation might  live.
                                                           LINCOLN.DOC
COMMAND: Copy Delete Format Gallery Help Insert Jump Library
         Options Print Quit Replace Search Transfer Undo Window
Edit document or press Esc to use menu
Pg1 Li2 Co29     {}           ?          CL               Microsoft Word
```

18. Press **Esc**. Type **T**, then **S**. The Transfer Save form appears.
19. Press **Enter**. Word displays a file save message. The Main menu appears.
20. Turn to Module 24 to continue the learning sequence.

Module 16
FORMAT TAB

DESCRIPTION

The Format Tab menu contains three commands. The first command sets tabs, the second clears single tabs, the third clears all tabs. You access the Format Tab command by pressing Esc, then typing F then T.

```
FORMAT: Character Paragraph Tab Border Footnote Division Running-head Stylesheet
        sEarch repLace revision-Marks
Sets, clears, and moves tab stops
Pg1 Li1 Co1     {}            ?                               Microsoft Word
```

Word provides many shortcuts for mouse users. The mouse commands associated specifically with the Format Tab command appear in Table 16-1. Generic mouse movements and commands appear in Appendix E.

TABLE 16-1. MOUSE COMMANDS

Action	*Pointing To*	*Result*
Push Left Button	Menu Selection	Word presents the requested form or submenu or executes the requested command.
Push Left Button	Field	Word selects the field for change.
Push Left Button	Form Name	Word makes the requested changes and returns to the document.
Push Left Button	Rule	Word places the default tab type on the ruler line. Define the default tab type using the Alignment and Leader Char entries.
Push Right Button	Field	Word makes the requested changes and returns to the document.
Push Right and Left Buttons	Tab on Ruler	Word removes the tab setting.
Push Right and Left Buttons	Anywhere Except the Form or Window	Word cancels the current operation and returns to Main menu.

SET The Format Tab Set form contains three fields. The first field is the tab location in inches. Word displays a ruler to make entering tab positions easier. By pressing the F1 key, you can directly place tab settings on the ruler by pressing the Ins key. Pressing the Del key while on the ruler removes the tab setting pointed to by the ruler cursor. The second field is the alignment type. The Left selection aligns characters to the left of the tab. The Center selection centers the characters at the tab position. The Right selection aligns characters to the right of the tab. The Decimal selection aligns characters to the right of the tab until you enter a decimal point. It then aligns characters to the left of tab. The Vertical selection doesn't actually create a tab stop; instead, it places a vertical line at that position. As you add lines, it places vertical lines at the appropriate positions. The third field is the leader character. Word provides four leader characters including: blank (none), . (dot), - (dash), and _ underscore).

CLEAR The Format Tab Clear form contains only a single field, the tab location to clear in inches. By pressing the F1 key, you can obtain the exact measurement of the tab you wish to remove by highlighting it on the ruler line.

RESET-ALL The Format Tab Reset-All command does not use a form. Instead, it immediately clears all active tabs when selected.

APPLICATIONS

Use the Format Tab menu to select which subfunction you would like to perform. By using tabs in place of spaces, you can easily change the positions of table fields by simply redefining the tab stops. Using decimal tabs makes it easier to align columns of numbers or monetary figures. The vertical tab makes it exceptionally easy to place vertical lines in your tables by eliminating the need to physically place them there. Using the dot leader for a table of contents eliminates the need to physically place dots between chapter titles and associated page numbers. The underscore leader makes it easy to add underlined fields to tables or extend the ends of headings to meet the right edge of the paper.

TYPICAL OPERATION

In this example you learn how to add and delete tabs using the three menu selections on the Format Tab menu. You also see how easy it is to differentiate between tab and leader types by looking at the ruler. Begin this example at the DOS prompt.

1. Type **WORD** and press **Enter** to start Word. Press **Esc**. Type **T**, then **L** to select the Transfer Load command. Press **F1**. Select LINCOLN.DOC using the arrow keys. Press **Enter**. The Gettysburg Address appears.

2. Press **Esc**. Type **F**, then **T**. The Format Tab menu appears.

```
FORMAT TAB: Set Clear Reset-all

Sets tab position and alignment in selected paragraph(s)
Pg1 Li1 Co25     {}                ?                         Microsoft Word
```

3. Type **S**. The Format Tab Set form appears.

```
FORMAT TAB SET position: █
        alignment:(Left)Center Right Decimal Vertical   leader char:(Blank). - _
Enter measurement
Pg1 Li1 Co25     {}                ?           CL            Microsoft Word
```

4. Type **3** and press **Enter**. The Main menu reappears.
5. Press **Esc**. Type **F**, then **T**, then **S**. The Format Tab Set form appears.
6. Press **F1**. A ruler cursor appears on the ruler line. Notice an L replaced the 3 on the ruler line during the previous tab setting sequence. Word places a 0 in the Position field.

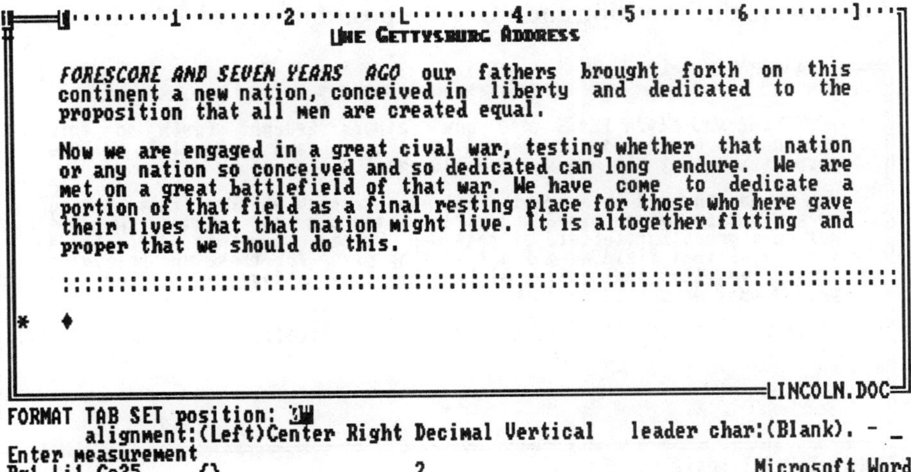

7. Position the ruler cursor halfway between 1 and 2 using **Right Arrow**. Press **Ins**. Word places an L on the position pointed to by the ruler cursor.

```
[·········1····[]····2·········L·········4·········5·········6·········]···
                         THE GETTYSBURG ADDRESS

  FORESCORE AND SEVEN YEARS AGO our fathers brought forth on this
  continent a new nation, conceived in liberty and dedicated to the
  proposition that all men are created equal.

  Now we are engaged in a great cival war, testing whether that nation
  or any nation so conceived and so dedicated can long endure. We are
  met on a great battlefield of that war. We have come to dedicate a
  portion of that field as a final resting place for those who here gave
  their lives that that nation might live. It is altogether fitting and
  proper that we should do this.

  :::::::::::::::::::::::::::::::::::::::::::::::::::::::::::::::::::::::

*  ♦

                                                            LINCOLN.DOC
FORMAT TAB SET position: █
     alignment:(Left)Center Right Decimal Vertical   leader char:(Blank). - _
Enter measurement
Pg1 Li1 Co25     {}                ?          CL               Microsoft Word
```

8. Press **Tab** then **Spacebar** to select Center in the Alignment field. Press **Tab** then **Spacebar** to select a dot leader. Press **Tab** then **F1** to access the ruler. Position the ruler cursor one mark past 2 using **Right Arrow.** Press **Ins.** Word places a dot leader in the 2 position and a C on the position pointed to by the ruler cursor.

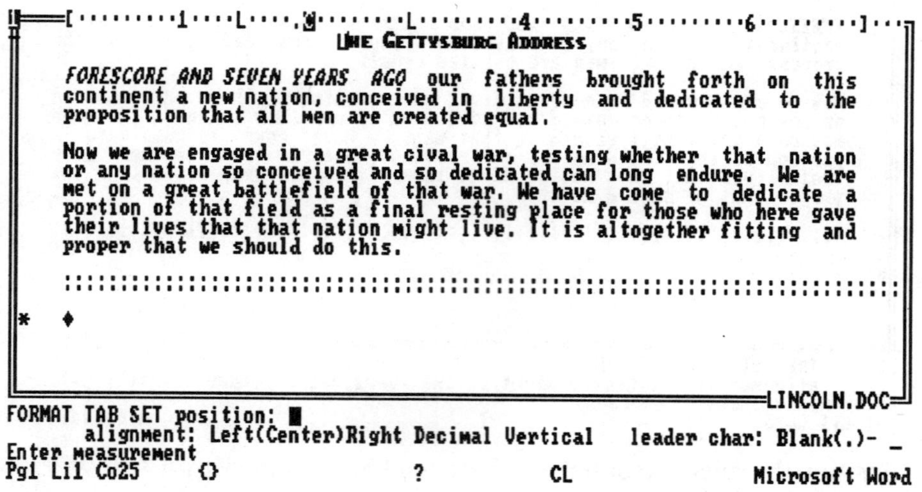

```
[·········1····L····.[]·········L·········4·········5·········6·········]···
                         THE GETTYSBURG ADDRESS

  FORESCORE AND SEVEN YEARS AGO our fathers brought forth on this
  continent a new nation, conceived in liberty and dedicated to the
  proposition that all men are created equal.

  Now we are engaged in a great cival war, testing whether that nation
  or any nation so conceived and so dedicated can long endure. We are
  met on a great battlefield of that war. We have come to dedicate a
  portion of that field as a final resting place for those who here gave
  their lives that that nation might live. It is altogether fitting and
  proper that we should do this.

  :::::::::::::::::::::::::::::::::::::::::::::::::::::::::::::::::::::::

*  ♦

                                                            LINCOLN.DOC
FORMAT TAB SET position: █
     alignment: Left(Center)Right Decimal Vertical   leader char: Blank(.)- _
Enter measurement
Pg1 Li1 Co25     {}                ?          CL               Microsoft Word
```

9. Press **Tab** then **Spacebar** to select Right in the Alignment field. Press **Tab** then **Spacebar** to select a dash leader. Press **Tab** then **F1** to access the ruler. Position the ruler cursor two marks past 2 using **Right Arrow**. Press **Ins.** Word places a dash leader next to the C and an R on the position pointed to by the ruler cursor.

```
[·········1····L····.C-[]······L·········4·········5·········6·········]···
                        THE GETTYSBURG ADDRESS

FORESCORE AND SEVEN YEARS AGO our fathers brought forth on this
continent a new nation, conceived in liberty and dedicated to the
proposition that all men are created equal.

Now we are engaged in a great cival war, testing whether that nation
or any nation so conceived and so dedicated can long endure. We are
met on a great battlefield of that war. We have come to dedicate a
portion of that field as a final resting place for those who here gave
their lives that that nation might live. It is altogether fitting and
proper that we should do this.

::::::::::::::::::::::::::::::::::::::::::::::::::::::::::::::::::::::::::

*  ♦

                                                             LINCOLN.DOC
FORMAT TAB SET position: █
      alignment: Left Center(Right)Decimal Vertical    leader char: Blank .(-)_
Enter measurement
Pg1 Li1 Co25     {}              ?                          Microsoft Word
```

10. Press **Tab** then **Spacebar** to select Decimal in the Alignment field. Press **Tab** then **Spacebar** to select an underline leader. Press **Tab** then **F1** to access the ruler. Position the ruler cursor four marks past 2 using **Right Arrow**. Press **Ins**. Word places an underline leader next to the R and a D on the position pointed to by the ruler cursor.

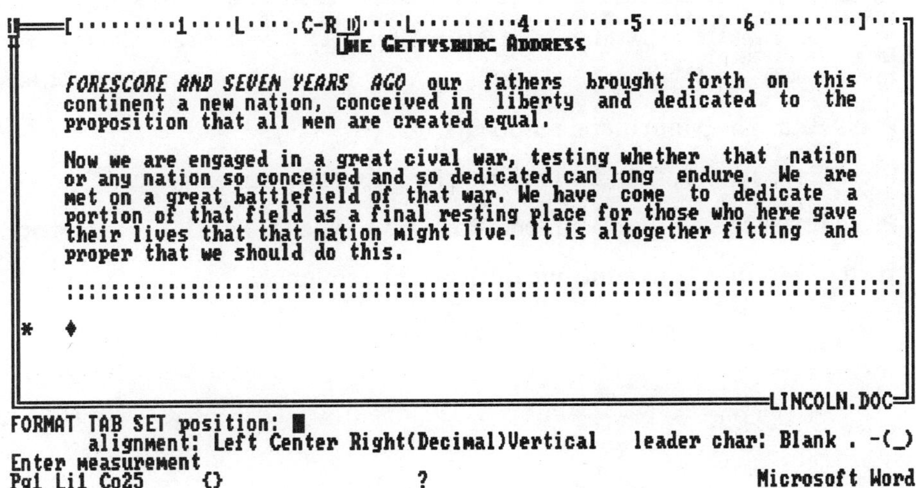

```
[·········1····L····.C-R_D···L·········4·········5·········6·········]···
                        THE GETTYSBURG ADDRESS

FORESCORE AND SEVEN YEARS AGO our fathers brought forth on this
continent a new nation, conceived in liberty and dedicated to the
proposition that all men are created equal.

Now we are engaged in a great cival war, testing whether that nation
or any nation so conceived and so dedicated can long endure. We are
met on a great battlefield of that war. We have come to dedicate a
portion of that field as a final resting place for those who here gave
their lives that that nation might live. It is altogether fitting and
proper that we should do this.

::::::::::::::::::::::::::::::::::::::::::::::::::::::::::::::::::::::::::

*  ♦

                                                             LINCOLN.DOC
FORMAT TAB SET position: █
      alignment: Left Center Right(Decimal)Vertical    leader char: Blank . -(_)
Enter measurement
Pg1 Li1 Co25     {}              ?                          Microsoft Word
```

11. Press **Enter**. The Main menu reappears.

12. Press **Esc**. Type **F**, then **T**, then **C**. The Format Tab Clear form appears.

```
FORMAT TAB CLEAR position: █

Enter list of measurements
Pg1 Li1 Co25     {}              ?          CL              Microsoft Word
```

13. Press **F1**. A ruler cursor appears in the 0 position.
14. Press **Right Arrow**. Notice Word automatically selects the first tab.
15. Press **Enter**. Word deletes the tab stop.
16. Press **Esc**. Type **F**, then **T**, then **R**. Word removes the rest of the tabs.
17. Press **Esc**. Type **F**, then **T**, then **S**. The Format Tab Set form appears. Notice that no tabs appear on the ruler.

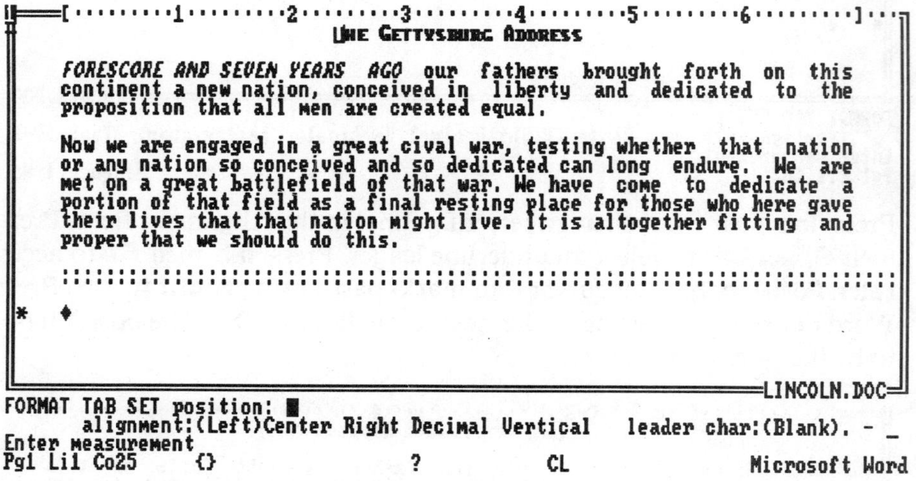

```
[·········1·········2·········3·········4·········5·········6·········]···
                           THE GETTYSBURG ADDRESS

FORESCORE AND SEVEN YEARS AGO our fathers brought forth on this
continent a new nation, conceived in liberty and dedicated to the
proposition that all men are created equal.

Now we are engaged in a great cival war, testing whether that nation
or any nation so conceived and so dedicated can long endure. We are
met on a great battlefield of that war. We have come to dedicate a
portion of that field as a final resting place for those who here gave
their lives that that nation might live. It is altogether fitting and
proper that we should do this.
::::::::::::::::::::::::::::::::::::::::::::::::::::::::::::::::::::::::::
*  ♦

                                                               LINCOLN.DOC
FORMAT TAB SET position: █
     alignment:(Left)Center Right Decimal Vertical    leader char:(Blank). - _
Enter measurement
Pg1 Li1 Co25     {}              ?          CL              Microsoft Word
```

18. Press **Esc**. The Main menu reappears.
19. Press **Esc**. Type **T**, then **S**. The Transfer Save form appears.
20. Press **Enter** to save the document. Press **Esc**. Type **Q**. The DOS prompt appears.
21. Turn to Module 41 to continue the learning sequence.

Module 17
GALLERY COPY

DESCRIPTION

The Gallery Copy command allows you to copy the formatting parameters of a style to the scrap. The gallery scrap is totally separate from the main program scrap. By pressing the Ins key, you can place the contents of the scrap in the gallery. This creates a new gallery entry. You access the Gallery Copy command from the Main menu by pressing Esc, typing G, selecting the entry you wish to copy, and typing C.

```
GALLERY: Copy Delete Exit Format Help
         Insert Name Print Transfer Undo
Copies selected style(s) to scrap
              {}          ?                     Microsoft Word
```

Word provides many shortcuts for mouse users. There are no mouse commands associated specifically with this command. Generic mouse movements and commands appear in Appendix E.

APPLICATIONS

The Gallery Copy command is especially useful when you need to create several gallery styles which differ in only one or two aspects. By creating the styles in this manner, you save the time required to duplicate all the formatting characteristics contained in each style.

TYPICAL OPERATION

In this example you create a new gallery entry using the Gallery Copy command. Begin this example at the Main menu with LINCOLN.DOC loaded in the current window.

1. Press **Esc**. Type **G**. The Gallery menu appears.
2. Select T1 by pressing arrow keys. Press **C**. The contents of the T1 style appear in the scrap.

```
1    SD Division Standard                             Standard Division
       Page break. Page length 11"; width 8.5". Page # format Arabic at
       10.5" from top, 4.25" from left. Top margin 1"; bottom 1"; left 1";
       right 1". Top running head at 0.5". Bottom running head at 0.5".
       Footnotes on same page.
2    SP Paragraph Standard                            Left, Elite
       Elite (modern c) 10/24. Flush left, space after 1 li.
3    T1 Paragraph Heading level 1                     Centered, Bold, All Caps
       Pica (modern a) 12 Bold Uppercase. Centered, space after 1 li (keep
       with following paragraph).
4    H2 Paragraph Heading level 2                     Bold, Same as SP
       EliteD (modern d) 10/12 Bold Uppercase. Flush left, space before 2
       li (keep in one column, keep with following paragraph).
5    RH Paragraph Running Head                        Left Justified
       Pica (modern a) 12. Flush left.
6    TD Paragraph 1                                   Terms & Definitions
       Elite (modern c) 10/24. Flush left, Left indent 0.5" (first line
       indent -0.5"), space after 2 li (keep in one column). Tabs at: 0.5"
       (left flush).
                                                              WORDWARE.STY
GALLERY: Copy Delete Exit Format Help
         Insert Name Print Transfer Undo
Copies selected style(s) to scrap
                 {Paragraph He...} ?                          Microsoft Word
```

3. Press **Ctrl-PgDn**. Press **Ins**. A copy of the original T1 style appears in the position pointed to by the cursor.

```
       indent -1.5"), space after 1 li. Tabs at: 1.5" (left flush), 6.5"
       (right flush).
15   T1 Paragraph Heading level 1                     Centered, Bold, All Caps
       Pica (modern a) 12 Bold Uppercase. Centered, space after 1 li (keep
       with following paragraph).

                                                              WORDWARE.STY
GALLERY: Copy Delete Exit Format Help
         Insert Name Print Transfer Undo
Copies selected style(s) to scrap
                 {Paragraph He...} ?                          Microsoft Word
```

4. Press **Esc**. Select the new copy of the T1 style by pressing **Up Arrow**. Press **Del** to remove the extra copy. Press **E** to exit Gallery. The Main menu appears.

5. Turn to Module 23 to continue the learning sequence.

Module 18
GALLERY DELETE

DESCRIPTION

The Gallery Delete command allows you to remove unneeded styles from a stylesheet. It places the deleted style in the scrap. This allows you to use the Gallery Undo command (discussed in Module 26) to retrieve it if required. Unfortunately, the scrap stores only one style. If you delete or copy another style, Word cannot recover the previous one. You access the Gallery Delete command from the Main menu by pressing Esc, typing G, selecting the desired paragraph, and typing D.

```
GALLERY: Copy Delete Exit Format Help
         Insert Name Print Transfer Undo
Deletes selected style(s) to scrap
            {}                ?           CL                  Microsoft Word
```

Word provides many shortcuts for mouse users. There are no mouse commands associated specifically with this command. Generic mouse movements and commands appear in Appendix E.

APPLICATIONS

Use the Gallery Delete command to remove any unneeded styles from your stylesheet. By removing these unneeded styles, you reduce the possibility of another person incorrectly formatting a document by using the style.

TYPICAL OPERATION

In this example you remove a style from the sample stylesheet. Begin this example at the Main menu with LINCOLN.DOC loaded in the current window.

1. Press **Esc**. Type **G**. The Gallery menu appears.
2. Press **Ctrl-PgDn**, then **Up Arrow** to select the last stylesheet entry. Type **D**. Word removes the gallery entry. Notice Word places the gallery entry in the scrap.

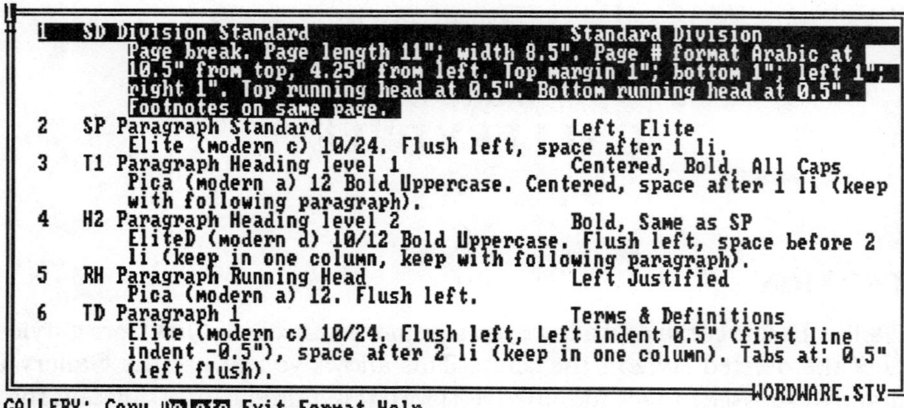


```
GALLERY: Copy Delete Exit Format Help
         Insert Name Print Transfer Undo
Deletes selected style(s) to scrap
                   {Paragraph He...} ?           CL                 Microsoft Word
```

3. Press **Esc**. Type **T**, then **S**. Press **Enter**. Word saves the stylesheet.
4. Type **E**. The Main menu appears.
5. Turn to Module 26 to continue the learning sequence.

Module 19
GALLERY EXIT

DESCRIPTION

The Gallery Exit command of the Gallery menu returns you to the Main menu. The gallery is an area used by Word to contain the stylesheet. It consists of both a menu and an editing area. The default stylesheet contained in the gallery is the one used by the current document (or NORMAL.STY if the current document does not use a specialized stylesheet). Since the gallery is completely separate from the document, you do not need to save your document before going to the gallery. Also, you do not need to save your stylesheet before seeing its effect on the document. Because of this, you can reload the old version of the stylesheet if the changes made during the last editing session in the gallery adversely affect the appearance of the document.

```
GALLERY: Copy Delete Exit Format Help
         Insert Name Print Transfer Undo
Exits gallery and returns to document window
_                  {}             ?                        Microsoft Word
```

Word provides many shortcuts for mouse users. There are no mouse commands associated specifically with this command. Generic mouse movements and commands appear in Appendix E.

APPLICATIONS

Use the Gallery Exit command whenever you need to get back to the Main menu after a stylesheet editing session. Unlike the Quit command on the Main menu, the Gallery Exit command does not automatically ask you if you want to save the stylesheet.

TYPICAL OPERATION

In this example you exit from the gallery to the Main menu. Begin this example at the DOS prompt.

1. Type **WORD** and press **Enter**. The Word introductory screen, then the Main menu appear.
2. Press **Esc**. Type **G**. The Gallery menu and edit area appear.

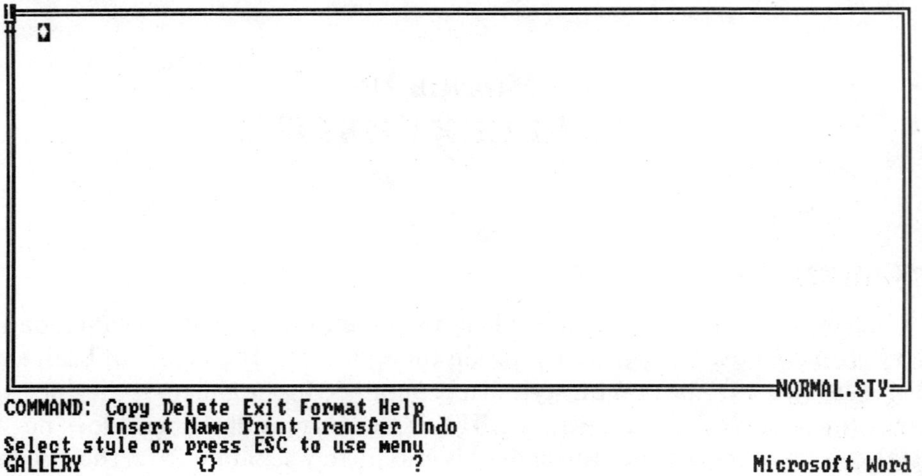

3. Type **E**. The Main menu and edit area appear. Notice the Gallery menu is always active; Word requires no Esc key sequence before executing a command.
4. Press **Esc**. Type **Q**. The DOS prompt appears.
5. Turn to Module 21 to continue the learning sequence.

Module 20
GALLERY FORMAT

DESCRIPTION

The Gallery Format command of the Gallery menu automatically selects one of three user interfaces based on whether the highlighted definition concerns a character, paragraph, or division. When modifying a division definition, Word displays a menu containing commands for margins, page numbers, layout, and line numbers. When modifying a paragraph definition, Word displays a menu containing commands to change the default character, paragraph, tab, or border definition. When modifying a character definition, Word displays the Gallery Format Character form only.

```
COMMAND: Copy Delete Exit Format Help
         Insert Name Print Transfer Undo
Sets formats for selected style(s)
GALLERY          {}              ?          CL               Microsoft Word
```

Word provides many shortcuts for mouse users. The mouse commands associated specifically with this menu and commands appear in Table 20-1. Generic mouse movements and commands appear in Appendix E.

TABLE 20-1. MOUSE COMMANDS

Action	*Pointing To*	*Result*
Push Left Button	Menu Selection	Word presents the requested form or submenu or executes the requested command.
Push Left Button	Field	Word selects the field for change.
Push Left Button	Form Name	Word makes the requested changes and returns to the document.
Push Right Button	Field	Word makes the requested changes and returns to the document.
Push Right and Left Buttons	Anywhere Except the Form or Window	Word cancels the current operation and returns to Main menu.

MARGIN The Gallery Format Division Margin form changes the distances between the edge of the page and the top, bottom, right, and left sides of the text. It also changes the gutter margin. The gutter margin adds extra space to the inside edge of a page for binding. Module 8 contains a diagram showing the margin areas. Finally, the Gallery Format Division Margin form contains fields for page length, page width, running head position, and footer position.

PAGE-NUMBERS The Gallery Format Division Page-Numbers form changes the position and numbering sequence for page numbers. The first field allows you to turn page numbering off or on. Word uses two different methods to number pages. By selecting continuous, you tell Word to start at page 1 and number through to the end of the document. The other command allows you to start/stop numbering at the specified page. Word provides five different numbering schemes: Arabic, upper or lowercase Roman, and upper or lowercase alphabetic.

LAYOUT The Gallery Format Division Layout form changes the method Word uses to print a pages. You can change where Word prints the footnotes, the number of columns, and the width between columns. In addition, this form also defines the scope of the division definition. Module 8 contains a table listing the division scope types and their definitions.

LINE-NUMBERS The Gallery Format Division Line-Numbers form changes the numbering sequence, position, and increment for line numbers added to documents. Word provides three methods of restarting the line numbers. The Page command restarts the line numbers at the beginning of each page. The division command restarts the line numbers at the beginning of each division break. Finally, the continuous command prevents Word from restarting the line numbering throughout the document.

CHARACTER The Gallery Format Character form contains the same elements as the one accessed using the Main menu. Module 7 contains a complete description of this form.

PARAGRAPH The Gallery Format Paragraph form contains the same elements as the one accessed using the Main menu. Module 10 contains a complete description of this form.

TAB The Gallery Format Tab form contains the same elements as the one accessed using the Main menu. Module 16 contains a complete description of this form.

BORDER The Gallery Format Border form allows you to place a box or lines around a paragraph. For example, if you wanted to place a border around the title of a document, you would use this command. The Type field determines what type of border you use. By selecting none, you tell Word not to place a border around the paragraph. When you select box, Word places a complete box around the paragraph. When you select lines, Word looks at the Left, Right, Above, and Below fields. Word places the lines that you selected around the paragraph. One way to use this is to place a line above and below a title. The Line Style field changes the line thickness. The normal selection uses a single-pixel line. The bold selection uses a two-pixel line. The double selection uses two single-pixel lines placed one pixel apart.

APPLICATIONS

Use the Gallery Format Division menu and associated commands to change the characteristics of a column, page, or entire document. When creating legal documents, use the line numbering command to automatically number contract lines. Use the page numbering command to change the page number appearance between the front matter and text of a document. By changing the division definition at the column level, you can define multiple columns of variable widths.

Use the Format Character form to format characters in the desired manner. The various commands offer a large variety in the way you can present the text to a reader. Appendix D tells how to use fonts and font enhancements in text. Module 7 contains a complete description of all the Gallery Format Character form functions.

Use the Gallery Format Paragraph command to change the characteristics of the paragraph definition pointed to by the cursor. Each field changes the printed appearance of the paragraph as described above. By combining various fields, you can create any special effect you want.

Use the Gallery Format Tab menu to select which subfunction you would like to perform. By using tabs in place of spaces, you can easily change the positions of table fields by simply redefining the tab stops. Using decimal tabs makes it easier to align columns of numbers or monetary figures. The vertical tab makes it exceptionally easy to place vertical lines in your tables by removing the need to place them there physically. Using the dot leader for a table of contents eliminates the need to place dots between chapter titles and associated page numbers. The underscore leader makes it easy to add underlined fields to tables or extend the ends of headings to meet the right edge of the paper.

Use the Gallery Format Border form to tell Word how to enhance the appearance of your document. Using lines to separate various sections of the document improves readability and draws the reader's attention to the new section.

TYPICAL OPERATION

In this example you format the previously created stylesheet. You also add two new definitions to the stylesheet. Begin this example at the Main menu with LINCOLN.DOC loaded in the current window.

1. Press **Esc**. Type **G**, then **F**. The Gallery Format Division menu appears.

```
FORMAT DIVISION: Margins Page-numbers Layout line-Numbers

Sets margins,page length and running head position for selected style
GALLERY          {}                ?                                Microsoft Word
```

2. Press **M**. The Gallery Format Division Margins form appears.

```
FORMAT DIVISION MARGINS top:        bottom: 1"       left: 1.25"  right: 1.25"
                  page length: 11"   width: 8.5"     gutter margin: 0"
          running-head position from top: 0.5"       from bottom: 0.5"
Enter measurement
GALLERY          {}                ?            CL                  Microsoft Word
```

3. Select the Left field by pressing **Tab**. Type **1**. Select the Right field by pressing **Tab**. Type **1** and press **Enter**. Word makes the appropriate changes to the division definition.

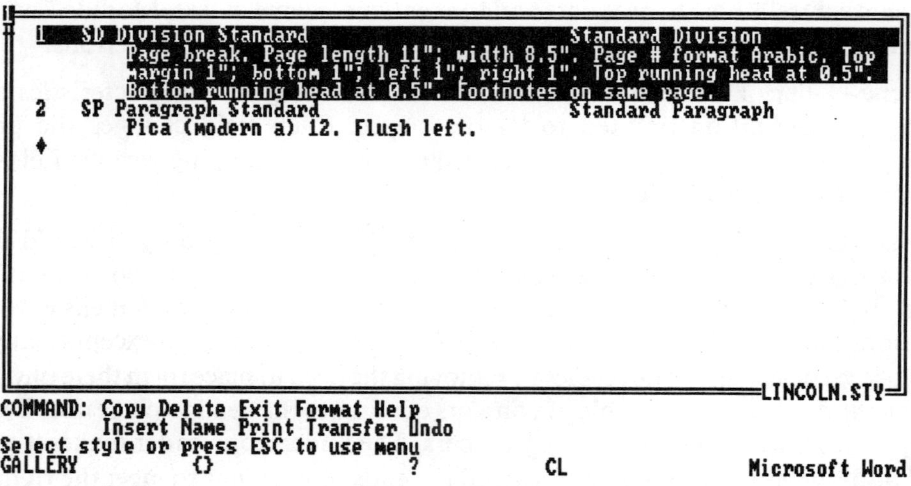

4. Select the Standard Paragraph definition by pressing **Down Arrow**. Type **F**. The Gallery Format menu appears. Notice how it differs from the Gallery Format Division menu.

```
FORMAT: Character Paragraph Tab Border

Sets character format and font for selected style(s)
GALLERY          {}                ?                                Microsoft Word
```

5. Type **P**. The Gallery Format Paragraph form appears.

```
FORMAT PARAGRAPH alignment: Left Centered Right Justified
     left indent: 0"           first line: 0"          right indent: 0"
     line spacing: 1 li        space before: 0 li      space after: 0 li
     keep together: Yes(No)    keep follow: Yes(No)    side by side: Yes(No)
Select option
GALLERY          {}                   ?                          Microsoft Word
```

6. Select JUSTIFIED by pressing **Spacebar**. Select the Line Spacing field by pressing **Tab**. Type **1.5**. Select the Space Before field by pressing **Tab**. Type **1**. Press **Enter**. Word makes the appropriate changes to the paragraph definition.

```
1   SD Division Standard                        Standard Division
       Page break. Page length 11"; width 8.5". Page # format Arabic. Top
       margin 1"; bottom 1"; left 1"; right 1". Top running head at 0.5".
       Bottom running head at 0.5". Footnotes on same page.
2   SP Paragraph Standard                       Standard Paragraph
       Pica (modern a) 12/18. Justified, space before 1 li.
♦

                                                             LINCOLN.STY
COMMAND: Copy Delete Exit Format Help
         Insert Name Print Transfer Undo
Select style or press ESC to use menu
GALLERY          {}                   ?          CL              Microsoft Word
```

7. Press **Down Arrow**. Type **I**. Type **T1**. Press **Tab**. Select PARAGRAPH by pressing **Spacebar**. Press **Tab**, then **F1**. Select HEADING LEVEL 1 by pressing arrow keys. Press **Tab**. Type **Gettysburg Heading** and press **Enter**. Word inserts a new paragraph heading into the stylesheet. Notice the new paragraph automatically assumes the formatting parameters of the standard paragraph.

8. Type **F**, then **P**. Select CENTERED by pressing **Spacebar**. Select the Keep Follow field by pressing **Tab**. Press **Spacebar** to select yes, then **Enter**. Word changes the paragraph definition.

9. Type **F**, then **C**. The Gallery Format Character form appears.

```
FORMAT CHARACTER bold: Yes No       italic: Yes(No)        underline: Yes(No)
       strikethrough: Yes(No)       uppercase: Yes(No)     small caps: Yes(No)
       double underline: Yes(No)    position:(Normal)Superscript Subscript
       font name: Pica              font size: 12          hidden: Yes(No)
Select option
GALLERY          {}                   ?          CL              Microsoft Word
```

10. Press **Spacebar** to select bold. Select the Uppercase field by pressing **Tab**. Press **Spacebar** for yes, then **Enter**. Word changes the paragraph definition.

```
COMMAND: Copy Delete Exit Format Help
         Insert Name Print Transfer Undo
Select style or press ESC to use menu
GALLERY         {}                  ?          CL                    Microsoft Word
```

11. Press **Down Arrow**. Type **I**. Type **IT**, then press **Tab** three times. Type **Italic Characters** and press **Enter**. Word inserts the new character definition. Notice the new character definition assumes the formatting parameters of the standard paragraph character definition.
12. Type **F**. The Gallery Format Character form appears.
13. Select the Italic field by pressing **Tab**. Press **Spacebar** for yes, then **Enter**. Word changes the character definition.

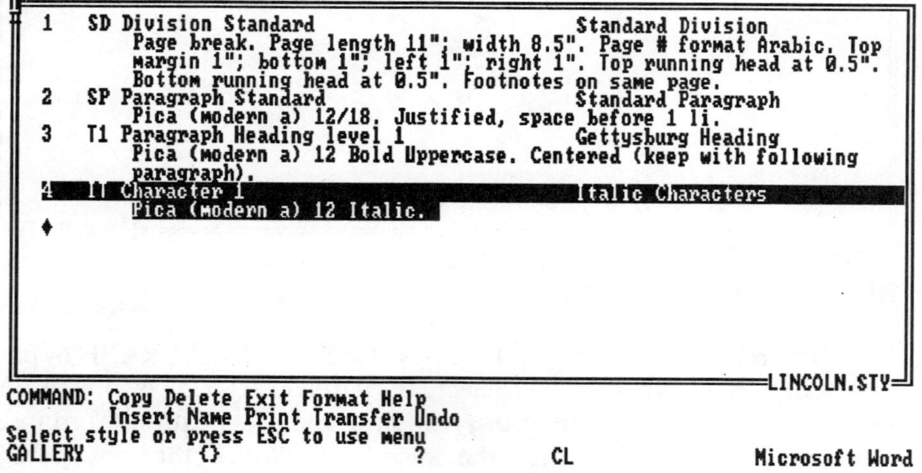

```
 1    SD Division Standard                       Standard Division
         Page break. Page length 11"; width 8.5". Page # format Arabic. Top
         margin 1"; bottom 1"; left 1"; right 1". Top running head at 0.5".
         Bottom running head at 0.5". Footnotes on same page.
 2    SP Paragraph Standard                      Standard Paragraph
         Pica (modern a) 12/18. Justified, space before 1 li.
 3    T1 Paragraph Heading level 1               Gettysburg Heading
         Pica (modern a) 12 Bold Uppercase. Centered (keep with following
         paragraph).
 4    IT Character I                             Italic Characters
         Pica (modern a) 12 Italic.
 ♦
                                                                  LINCOLN.STY
COMMAND: Copy Delete Exit Format Help
         Insert Name Print Transfer Undo
Select style or press ESC to use menu
GALLERY         {}                  ?          CL                    Microsoft Word
```

14. Type **T**, then **S**. Press **Enter**. Word saves the changes to LINCOLN.STY.
15. Press **E**, then **N**. The Main menu appears.
16. Turn to Module 15 to continue the learning sequence.

Module 21
GALLERY HELP

DESCRIPTION

The Gallery Help command on the Gallery menu works similarly to the Help command on the Main menu (see Module 27 for a comparative description of the Main menu Help command). Both commands provide context sensitive help using the same basic menu. The difference between the two commands is the way Word provides the help. The help screens provided in the Gallery menu contain specific help for stylesheets.

```
COMMAND: Copy Delete Exit Format Help
         Insert Name Print Transfer Undo
Provides quick reference information and lessons
GALLERY        {}              ?                         Microsoft Word
```

Word provides many shortcuts for mouse users. There are no mouse commands associated specifically with this command. Generic mouse movements and commands appear in Appendix E.

APPLICATIONS

Use the Gallery Help command whenever you need information about a Gallery function or menu selection. You can ask for context sensitive help at any time by pressing Alt-H. Press H alone to receive non-context sensitive help.

TYPICAL OPERATION

In this example you use the Gallery Help command. You will see differences between the Gallery Help command and the Help command on the Main menu. Begin this example at the Main menu.

1. Press **Esc**. Type **G**. The Gallery menu and edit area appear.

2. Type **H**. The Gallery Help screen appears.

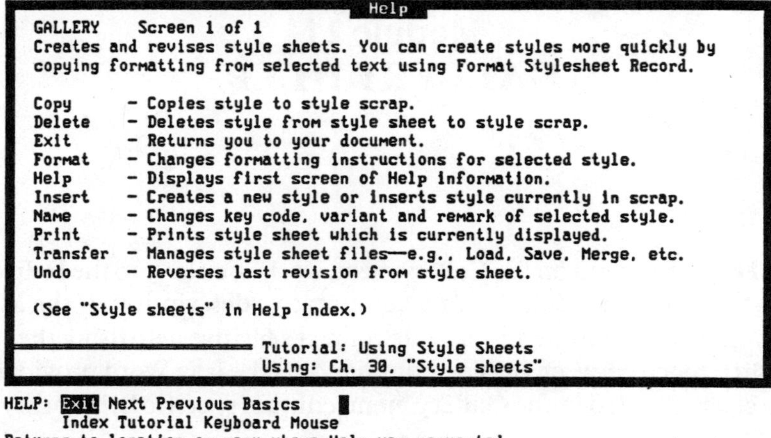

3. Type **N**. The Gallery Copy Help screen appears.

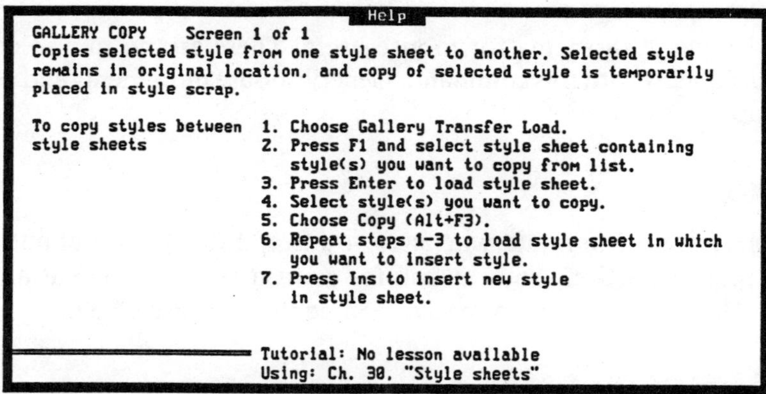

4. Type **P**. The previous Gallery Help screen appears.
5. Type **B**. The Basic Help page appears.

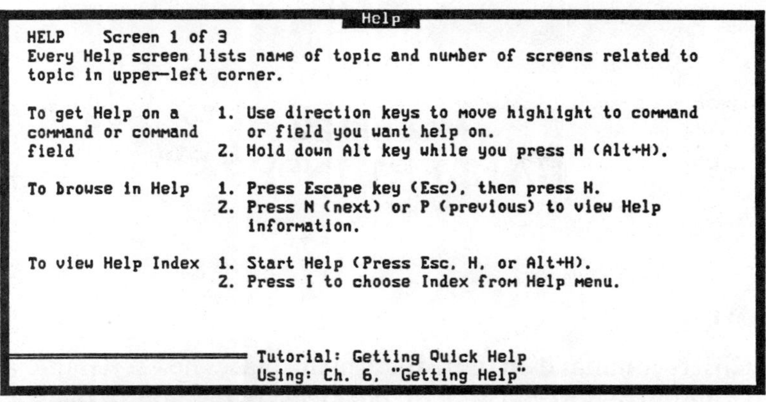


```
HELP: Exit Next Previous Basics
      Index Tutorial Keyboard Mouse
Returns to location or menu where Help was requested
                  {}             ?                           NORMAL.STY
```

6. Type **I**. The Help index appears.

```
Align Left             Glossaries             Repaginate
Align Right            Graphics               Repeat
Annotations            Headers                Replace
ASCII file             Hidden text            Revision marks
Autosave               Hyphens                Ruler
Backup                 Indent                 Running heads
Block                  Index                  Save
Bold                   Italics                Screen borders
Bookmarks              Jump                   Search
Bulleted list          Justify                Select text
Calculate              Keyboard               Show layout
Center                 Leader character       Side by side
Colors                 Line break             Small caps
Columns                Line drawing           Sort
Commands               Line spacing           Speed keys
Copy                   Load document          Spell
Cross referencing      Macros                 Spreadsheet link
Delete                 Mailing labels         Strikethrough
Division break         Margins                Style sheets

HELP INDEX: Align Left

Select Help topic: press PgDn for more topics
                  {}             ?                           NORMAL.STY
```

8. Type **T**. The Tutorial menu appears.

9. Press **Esc**. The Gallery menu appears.
10. Press **Alt-H**. The Help menu appears. Notice the Gallery Copy Help page appears rather than the general Style Sheet Help page.
11. Type **R** then type **E**. The Gallery menu appears, then the Main menu appears.
12. Turn to Module 22 to continue the learning sequence.

Module 22
GALLERY INSERT

DESCRIPTION

The Gallery Insert command on the Gallery menu places new styles into a stylesheet. A style is a definition of how you want the character, paragraph, or division to appear. The Gallery Insert form contains four fields. You access the Gallery Insert command from the Main menu by pressing Esc and typing G, then I.

```
COMMAND: Copy Delete Exit Format Help
         Insert Name Print Transfer Undo
Adds new style to style sheet
GALLERY         {}            ?                         Microsoft Word
```

Word provides many shortcuts for mouse users. The mouse commands associated specifically with this command appear in Table 22-1. Generic mouse movements and commands appear in Appendix E.

TABLE 22-1. MOUSE COMMANDS

Action	*Pointing To*	*Result*
Push Left Button	Menu Selection	Word presents the requested form or submenu or executes the requested command.
Push Left Button	Field	Word selects the field for change.
Push Left Button	Form Name	Word makes the requested changes and returns to the document.
Push Right Button	Fill in the Blank Field	Word provides a list of acceptable choices.
Push Right Button	Multiple Choice Field	Word makes the requested changes and returns to the document.
Push Right and Left Buttons	Anywhere Except the Form or Window	Word cancels the current operation and returns to Main menu.

The Key Code field contains the Alt key combination Word uses to identify the new style. For example, if you created a new paragraph style and typed SP in the Key Code field, then typing Alt-SP while in the document editing window would reformat the paragraph pointed to by the text cursor using the new style. Module 15 contains a detailed description of this process.

The Usage field selects one of three style types: character, paragraph, or division. Each Usage selection controls a different area of the document. The character style controls the appearance of individual characters. The paragraph style controls all aspects of individual paragraphs. This includes a default character style. The division style controls all aspects of the defined division. Module 20 contains a detailed description of the characteristics of each style type.

The Variant field selects one of the previously undefined style variants. A good way of remembering the purpose of the Variant field is to think of the Usage field as the category and the Variant field as the subcategory. Word allows a limited number of style variants per stylesheet. By assigning a specific variant to each style, you can keep track of the number of styles for each Usage type.

The Remark field provides an easy method for you to remember the purpose for a specific style. Word displays the remarks when you select a style using the Format Stylesheet menu (see Module 15).

APPLICATIONS

Use the Gallery Insert command to create styles for your documents. By using a stylesheet, you greatly reduce the effort required to reformat a document. Stylesheets also force each document to look the same, even if several operators typed it.

The Gallery Insert command always places a new style at the position pointed to by the cursor. By adjusting the cursor position to control style placement, you can make your stylesheets easier to use and edit. One way of using this feature is by placing all the standard styles first, the division styles second, the paragraph styles third, and the character styles last.

Be sure to use the Remarks field to completely identify a specific style. This allows other people to use your stylesheets with a minimum of confusion.

TYPICAL OPERATION

In this example you create styles using the Gallery Insert command. Begin this example at the Main menu.

1. Press **Esc**. Type **G**, then **I**. The Gallery Insert form appears.

```
INSERT key code: {}                          usage:(Character)Paragraph Division
        variant: 1                          remark:
Enter key code
GALLERY          {}                ?                          Microsoft Word
```

2. Type **SD**. Press **Tab** and select DIVISION by pressing **Spacebar**. Press **Tab** then **F1**. A listing of division variants appears.

```
Standard         1                2                3
4                5                6                7
8                9                10               11
12               13               14               15
16               17               18               19
20               21
```

```
INSERT key code: sd                          usage: Character Paragraph(Division)
        variant: Standard                   remark:
Enter variant or press F1 to select from list
GALLERY          {}                ?         CL               Microsoft Word
```

3. Press **Tab**. Type **Standard Division** and press **Enter**. Word enters the new division style into the stylesheet.

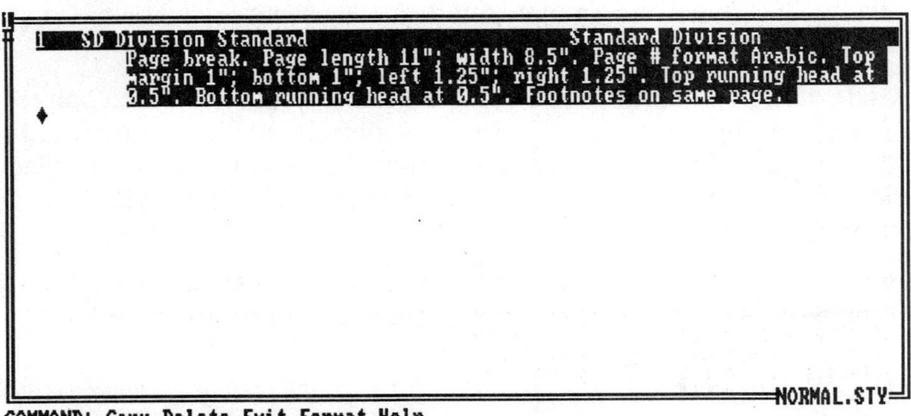

```
1   SD Division Standard                         Standard Division
        Page break. Page length 11"; width 8.5". Page # format Arabic. Top
        margin 1"; bottom 1"; left 1.25"; right 1.25". Top running head at
        0.5". Bottom running head at 0.5". Footnotes on same page.
♦
                                                              NORMAL.STY
COMMAND: Copy Delete Exit Format Help
         Insert Name Print Transfer Undo
Select style or press ESC to use menu
GALLERY          {}                ?                          Microsoft Word
```

4. Press **Down Arrow**. Type **I**. The Gallery Insert form appears.
5. Type **SP**. Press **Tab** and select PARAGRAPH by pressing **Spacebar**. Press **Tab** then **F1**. A listing of paragraph variants appears.

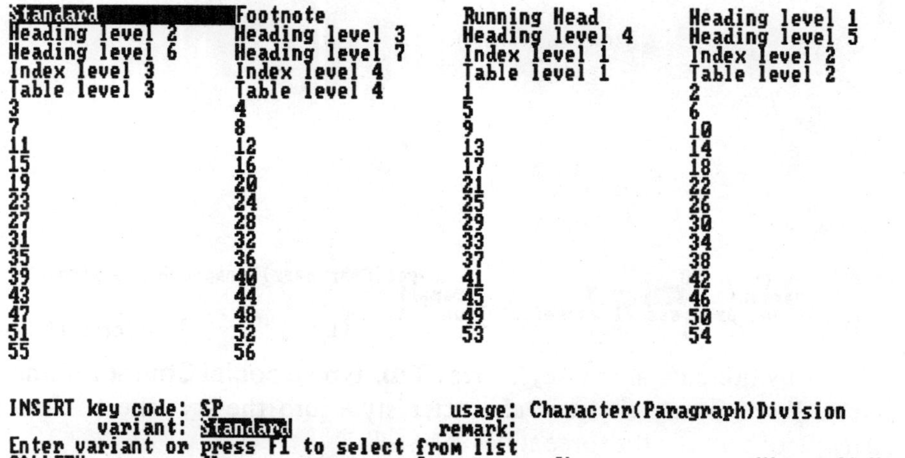

6. Press **Tab**. Type **Standard Paragraph** and press **Enter**. Word enters the new paragraph style into the stylesheet.

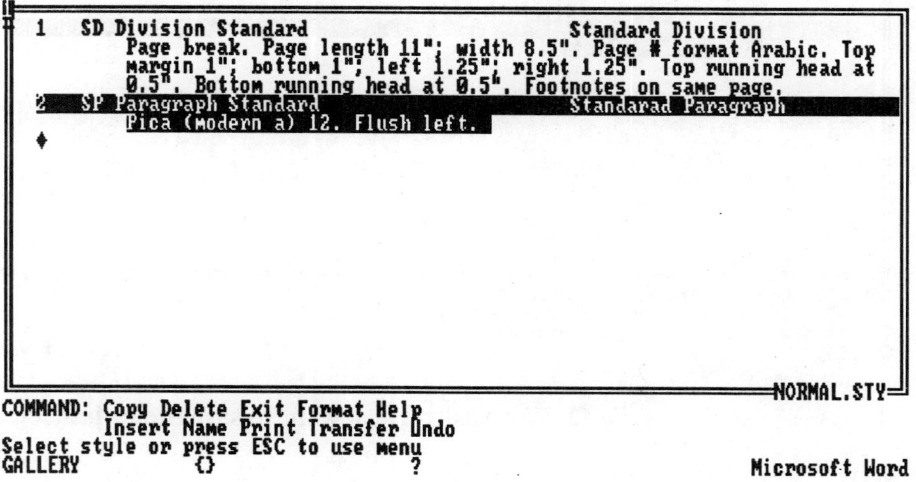

7. Press **Down Arrow**. Type **I**. The Gallery Insert form appears.
8. Type **SC**. Press **Tab** and select CHARACTER by pressing **Spacebar**. Press **Tab** then **F1**. A listing of character variants appears.

```
Page number              Line Number              Footnote ref             Summary Info
1                        2                        3                        4
5                        6                        7                        8
9                        10                       11                       12
13                       14                       15                       16
17                       18                       19                       20
21                       22                       23                       24
25
```

```
INSERT key code: SC                          usage:(Character)Paragraph Division
        variant: Page number                remark:
Enter variant or press F1 to select from list
GALLERY          {}                         ?         CL                 Microsoft Word
```

9. Select 1 by pressing arrow keys. Press **Tab**. Type **Special Character** and press **Enter**. Word enters the new character style into the stylesheet. Notice the differences between the three styles.

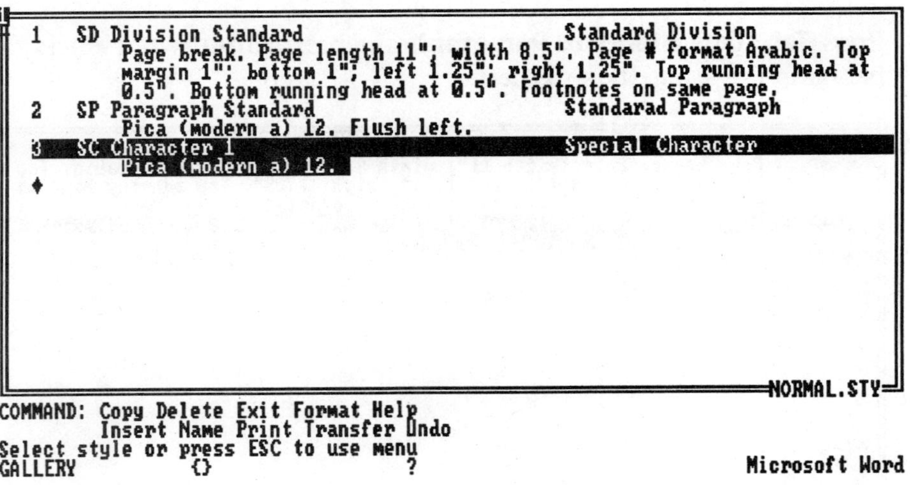

```
  1    SD Division Standard                                Standard Division
           Page break. Page length 11"; width 8.5". Page # format Arabic. Top
           margin 1"; bottom 1"; left 1.25"; right 1.25". Top running head at
           0.5". Bottom running head at 0.5". Footnotes on same page.
  2    SP Paragraph Standard                               Standarad Paragraph
           Pica (modern a) 12. Flush left.
  3    SC Character 1                                      Special Character
           Pica (modern a) 12.
  ♦
                                                                    NORMAL.STY
COMMAND: Copy Delete Exit Format Help
         Insert Name Print Transfer Undo
Select style or press ESC to use menu
GALLERY          {}                 ?                            Microsoft Word
```

10. Type **E**. Press **Esc**. Type **Q**. Word asks if you want to save the stylesheet.

```
QUIT:

Enter Y to save style sheet, N to lose edits, or Esc to cancel █
Pg1 Li1 Co1      {}                 ?                            Microsoft Word
```

11. Type **N**. The DOS prompt appears.

12. Turn to Module 25 to continue the learning sequence.

Module 23
GALLERY NAME

DESCRIPTION

The Gallery Name command allows you to change three parameters of every style: key code, variant, and remark. This command works in conjunction with the Gallery Copy command to produce new styles quickly and easily. You access this command from the Main menu by pressing Esc and typing G, then N.

```
GALLERY: Copy Delete Exit Format Help
         Insert Name Print Transfer Undo
Changes key code, variant, and remark for selected style
                  {}             ?                        Microsoft Word
```

The Gallery Name form contains three fields. The Key Code field tells Word what one- or two-key combination you wish to use. The Variant field describes the unique variation of paragraph, division, or character this style represents. The Remark field allows you to add a comment describing the style's purpose or features. Word adds this field so you can quickly identify the purpose of the styles in a stylesheet created by another person.

Word provides many shortcuts for mouse users. The mouse commands associated specifically with this form appear in Table 23-1. Generic mouse movements and commands appear in Appendix E.

TABLE 23-1. MOUSE COMMANDS

Action	*Pointing To*	*Result*
Push Left Button	Menu Selection	Word presents the requested form or submenu or executes the requested command.
Push Left Button	Field	Word selects the field for change.
Push Left Button	Form Name	Word makes the requested changes and returns to the document.
Push Right Button	Fill in the Blank Field	Word displays a list of acceptable choices.

Action	*Pointing To*	*Result*
Push Right and Left Buttons	Anywhere Except the Form or Window	Word cancels the current operation and returns to Main menu.

APPLICATIONS

The Gallery Name command allows you to rename the styles in a stylesheet. Use this command in conjunction with the Gallery Copy command to quickly create new styles.

TYPICAL OPERATION

In this example you create a new style entry using the Gallery Copy command and rename it using the Gallery Name command. Begin this example at the Main menu with LINCOLN.DOC loaded in the current window.

1. Press **Esc**. Type **G**. The Gallery menu appears.
2. Select T1 by pressing arrow keys. Press **C**. The contents of the T1 style appear in the scrap.
3. Press **Ctrl-PgDn**. Press **Ins**. A copy of the original T1 styles appears in the position pointed to by the cursor.
4. Select the new copy of the T1 style by pressing **Up Arrow**. Press **N**. The Gallery Name form appears.

```
        Elite (modern c) 10/24. Flush left, Left indent 1", right indent
        1", space after 1 li (keep in one column).
 11  N3 Paragraph 5                          Large Block Type-In
        EliteD (modern d) 10/24 Bold. Flush left, Left indent 1", right
        indent 1", space after 1 li (keep in one column).
 12  B  Character 1                          Bold Elite Character
        EliteD (modern d) 10 Bold.
 13  T1 Paragraph 7                          Table of Contents Heading
        Elite (modern c) 10/12 Bold Underlined. Flush left, space after 1
        li. Tabs at: 1.5" (left flush), 6.5" (right flush).
 14  T2 Paragraph 8                          Table of Contents Text
        Elite (modern c) 10/12. Flush left, Left indent 1.5" (first line
        indent -1.5"), space after 1 li. Tabs at: 1.5" (left flush), 6.5"
        (right flush).
 15  T1 Paragraph Heading level 1            Centered, Bold, All Caps
        Pica (modern a) 12 Bold Uppercase. Centered, space after 1 li (keep
        with following paragraph).
 ♦
                                                           WORDWARE.STY
NAME key code: T1            variant: Heading level 1
       remark: Centered, Bold, All Caps
Enter one or two letter key code for style
               {Paragraph He...} ?                         Microsoft Word
```

5. Type **H3**. Press **Tab**. Press **F1**. Word displays a listing of paragraph variants.

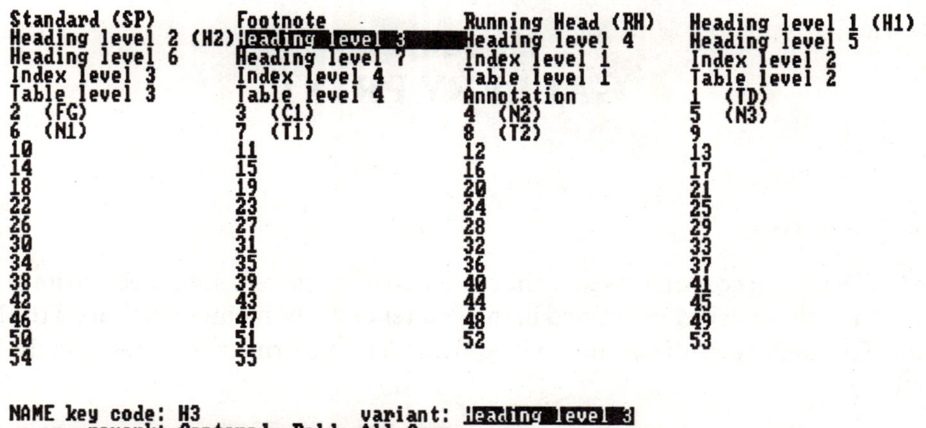

6. Select Heading Level 3 by pressing arrow keys. Press **Tab**. Type **Another Copy of T1**. Press **Enter**. The new version of T1 appears with variant, key code, and remark redefined.

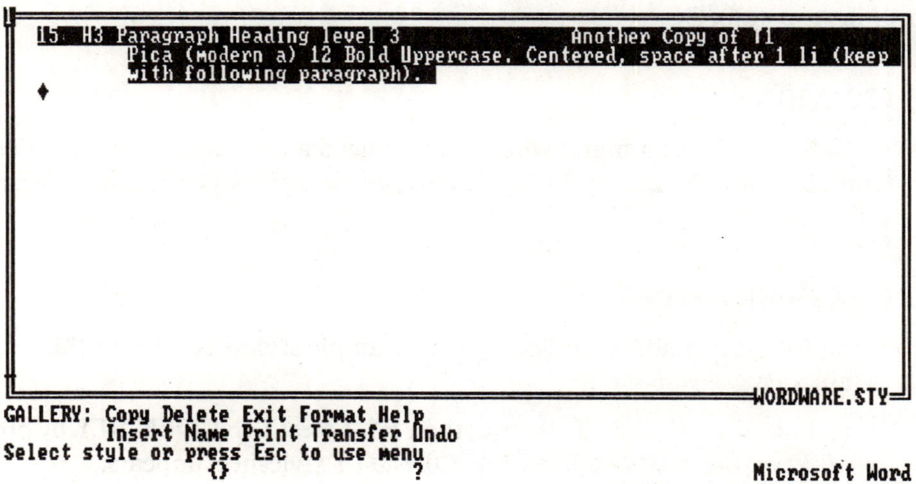

7. Type **T**, then **S**. Word saves the stylesheet.
8. Type **E**. The Main menu appears.
9. Turn to Module 18 to continue the learning sequence.

Module 24
GALLERY PRINT

DESCRIPTION

The Gallery Print command sends the contents of the current stylesheet to the printer. It uses the printer driver contained in the Printer Options menu selection on the Main menu. The Gallery Print command is equivalent to the Printer command on the Print menu.

```
COMMAND: Copy Delete Exit Format Help
         Insert Name Print Transfer Undo
Prints the contents of current style sheet
GALLERY          {}             ?          CL              Microsoft Word
```

Word provides many shortcuts for mouse users. There are no mouse commands associated specifically with this command. Generic mouse movements and commands appear in Appendix E.

APPLICATIONS

Use the Gallery Print command whenever you need a hard copy of your stylesheet. This is an exceptionally easy way to get an overall view of a stylesheet larger than one screen.

TYPICAL OPERATION

In this example you create a hard copy of the sample stylesheet. Begin this example at the Main menu.

1. Press **Esc**. Type **G**, then **T**, then **L**, then **F1**. Select LINCOLN.STY by pressing arrow keys. Press **Enter**. The LINCOLN.STY stylesheet appears.
2. Type **P**. Word Prints the contents of the stylesheet. Notice the Gallery version of print does not operate like the Main menu version of print.
3. Type **E**, then **N**. The Main menu appears.
4. Turn to Module 5 to continue the learning sequence.

Module 25
GALLERY TRANSFER

DESCRIPTION

The Gallery Transfer menu contains many commands for sending data to or getting data from files on disk. This data includes only stylesheet information. The Transfer menu on the Main menu controls document and glossary data transfers. You access the Gallery Transfer command from the Main menu by pressing Esc and typing G, then T.

```
COMMAND: Copy Delete Exit Format Help
         Insert Name Print Transfer Undo
Manages style sheet files (loads, saves, etc)
GALLERY         {}        ?                        Microsoft Word
```

Word provides many shortcuts for mouse users. The mouse commands associated specifically with this menu and commands appear in Table 25-1. Generic mouse movements and commands appear in Appendix E.

TABLE 25-1. MOUSE COMMANDS

Action	*Pointing To*	*Result*
Push Left Button	Menu Selection	Word presents the requested form or submenu or executes the requested command.
Push Left Button	Field	Word selects the field for change.
Push Left Button	Form Name	Word makes the requested changes and returns to the document.
Push Right Button	Fill in the Blank Field	Word provides a list of acceptable choices. When requesting filename choices, Word provides the list in the current directory. To get a list of the files in another directory, change the Gallery Transfer Options entry or select the appropriate drive/directory entry in the file listing.

Action	*Pointing To*	*Result*
Push Right Button	Multiple Choice Field	Word makes the requested changes and returns to the document when pointing to any dialogue box selection.
Push Right and Left Buttons	Anywhere Except the Form or Window	Word cancels the current operation and returns to Main menu.

LOAD The Gallery Transfer Load command retrieves a stylesheet file from disk. Word presents a form asking for the document name and a selection allowing the user to open the stylesheet as read only. If you open the stylesheet as read only, Word does not allow you to change its contents. You can obtain a listing of Word stylesheet files in the current directory by pressing F1 while in the document name field.

SAVE The Gallery Transfer Save command places a copy of the current stylesheet on disk. This allows you to retrieve the stylesheet at a future date for further editing. If you edit the current stylesheet and try to exit from the Main menu to DOS without saving it, Word prompts you to save it before quitting. You can switch between the Gallery and Main menu without saving the stylesheet.

CLEAR The Gallery Transfer Clear command removes the current stylesheet from memory and places Word in its startup condition. Before clearing the stylesheet from memory, Word checks if you changed it. If you changed the stylesheet, Word asks if you want to save it.

DELETE The Gallery Transfer Delete command removes a file from disk. You can obtain a listing of all the files on disk by pressing the F1 key. Word asks you to double check the filename before actually deleting the file. Word does not allow you to remove some default files (for example NORMAL.STY).

MERGE The Gallery Transfer Merge command places the contents of a stylesheet on disk in the position pointed to by the on-screen cursor. This allows you to combine stylesheets together.

OPTIONS The Gallery Transfer Options form contains a field for changing the default disk drive and directory. This affects the selection list Word presents whenever you press the F1 key in a form asking for a filename.

RENAME The Gallery Transfer Rename command changes the name of a file saved on disk. You can obtain a listing of all the files on disk by pressing the F1key.

APPLICATIONS

You use the Gallery Transfer menu to access Word's stylesheet file manipulation commands. As described above, these commands allow you to change filenames, load a stylesheet into memory, and save a stylesheet in memory to disk. They also perform other file manipulations required during a word processing session.

TYPICAL OPERATION

In this example you use all the commands on the Gallery Transfer menu. Begin this example at the Main menu with nothing loaded.

1. Press **Esc**. Type **G**, then **T**. The Gallery Transfer menu appears.

```
TRANSFER: Load Save Clear Delete Merge Options Rename

Loads named style sheet to view/edit.
GALLERY          {}                ?                            Microsoft Word
```

2. Type **O**. The Gallery Transfer Options form appears.

```
TRANSFER OPTIONS setup: C:\MW\0017

Enter drive or directory
GALLERY          {}                ?                            Microsoft Word
```

3. Press **Esc**. Type **I**. The Gallery Insert form appears.
4. Type **SD** and press **Tab**. Select DIVISION by pressing **Spacebar**. Press **Tab**, then **F1**. Select STANDARD by pressing arrow keys. Press **Tab**. Type **Standard Division** and press **Enter**. Word creates a division definition.

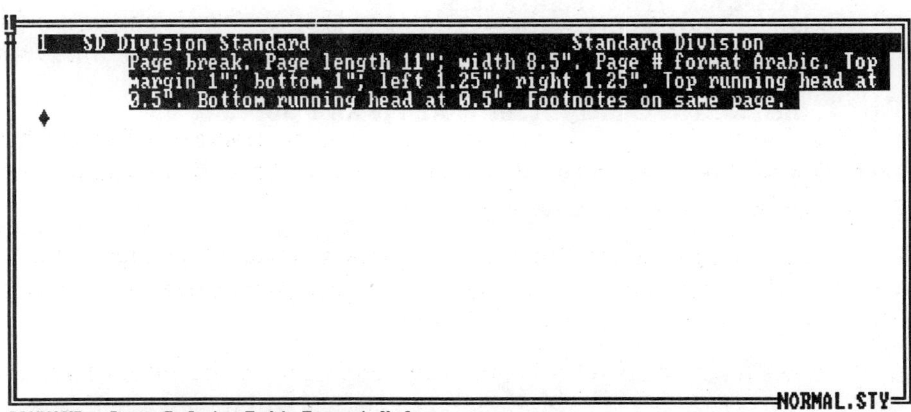

5. Type **T**, then **S**. The Gallery Transfer Save form appears.

```
TRANSFER SAVE style sheet name: C:\MW\0017\NORMAL.STY

Enter filename
GALLERY          {}              ?          CL              Microsoft Word
```

6. Press **Enter**. Word saves the stylesheet as NORMAL.STY.
7. Type **T**, then **C**. Word clears the Gallery edit area.
8. Press **Esc**. Type **I**. Type **SP** and press **Tab**. Select PARAGRAPH by pressing **Spacebar**. Press **Tab**, then **F1**. Select STANDARD by pressing arrow keys. Press **Tab**. Type **Standard Paragraph** and press **Enter**. Word creates a paragraph definition.

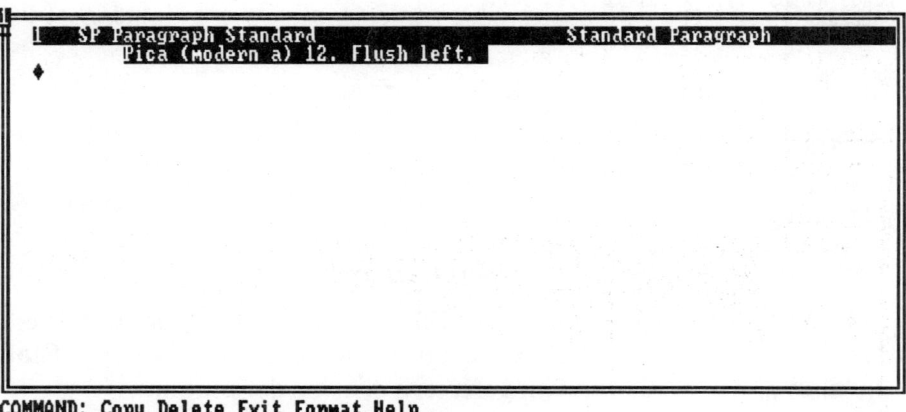

9. Type **T**, then **M**. The Gallery Transfer Merge form appears.

```
TRANSFER MERGE style sheet name: █

Enter filename or press F1 to select from list
GALLERY          {}              ?          CL              Microsoft Word
```

10. Press **F1**. Word displays a listing of stylesheet files available in the current directory.

```
NORMAL.STY




TRANSFER MERGE style sheet name: NORMAL.STY

Enter filename or press F1 to select from list (17809408 bytes free)
GALLERY         {}              ?         CL              Microsoft Word
```

11. Select NORMAL.STY by pressing arrow keys. Press **Enter**. Word places the previously defined stylesheet at the position currently pointed to by the cursor.

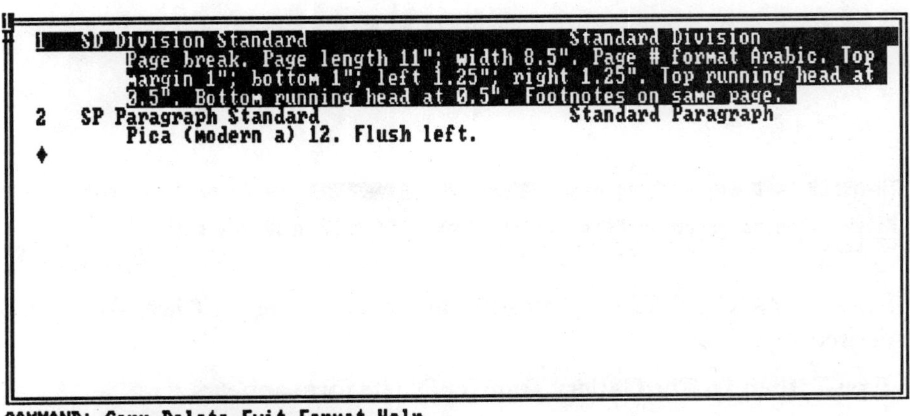


```
COMMAND: Copy Delete Exit Format Help
         Insert Name Print Transfer Undo
Select style or press ESC to use menu
GALLERY         {}              ?         CL              Microsoft Word
```

12. Type **T**, then **S**. Type **NORMAL.STY** and press **Enter**. Word asks if you want to overwrite the current file.

```
TRANSFER SAVE style sheet name: NORMAL.STY

Enter Y to overwrite file █
GALLERY         {}              ?         CL              Microsoft Word
```

13. Type **N**. The Gallery menu appears.
14. Type **T**, then **S**. Type **LINCOLN.STY** and press **Enter**. Word saves the stylesheet as LINCOLN.STY.
15. Type **T**, then **C** to clear the gallery window. Type **T**, then **L**. The Gallery Transfer Load form appears.

```
TRANSFER LOAD style sheet name: █                         read only: Yes(No)

Enter filename or press F1 to select from list
GALLERY          {}                    ?          CL                Microsoft Word
```

16. Press **F1**. Word displays a listing of stylesheet files available in the current directory.

```
LINCOLN.STY          NORMAL.STY






TRANSFER LOAD style sheet name: LINCOLN.STY               read only: Yes(No)

Enter filename or press F1 to select from list (17778688 bytes free)
GALLERY          {}                    ?                            Microsoft Word
```

17. Select LINCOLN.STY by pressing arrow keys. Press **Enter**. Word loads the desired stylesheet.
18. Type **T**, then **D**. The Gallery Transfer Delete form appears.

```
TRANSFER DELETE filename: █

Enter filename or press F1 to select from list
GALLERY          {}                    ?          CL                Microsoft Word
```

19. Press **F1**. Word displays a listing of all files in the current directory.

```
EPSONRX.PRD          MW365756.TMP        NORMAL.GLY          PLAIN.TXT
LINCOLN.DOC          NEW.PRD             NORMAL.STY          TEMP.
LINCOLN.STY          NORMAL.BAK          PLAIN.PRD           TTY.PRD









TRANSFER DELETE filename: EPSONRX.PRD

Enter filename or press F1 to select from list (17770496 bytes free)
GALLERY          {}              ?             CL              Microsoft Word
```

20. Select NORMAL.BAK by pressing arrow keys. Press **Enter**. Word asks if you really want to delete the file.

```
TRANSFER DELETE filename: NORMAL.BAK

Enter Y to confirm deletion of file
GALLERY          {}              ?             CL              Microsoft Word
```

21. Type **Y**. Word deletes the file.
22. Type **E**. Word asks if you want to attach the stylesheet to the current document.

```
EXIT:

Enter Y to attach style sheet, N to Ignore, or Esc to cancel
GALLERY          {}              ?                             Microsoft Word
```

23. Type **N**. The Main menu appears.
24. Turn to Module 20 to continue the learning sequence.

Module 26
GALLERY UNDO

DESCRIPTION

The Gallery Undo command allows you to reverse deletions and other actions you perform on stylesheet entries. This is especially useful when you accidentally remove a style. Word allows you to recover it as long as you perform no other gallery functions between the deletion and the restoration. You access this command from the Main menu by pressing Esc and typing G, then U.

```
GALLERY: Copy Delete Exit Format Help
         Insert Name Print Transfer Undo
Reverses effect of previous style revision
              {}          ?          CL               Microsoft Word
```

Word provides many shortcuts for mouse users. There are no mouse commands associated specifically with this command. Generic mouse movements and commands appear in Appendix E.

APPLICATIONS

Use the Gallery Undo command to reverse any change to your stylesheet. Word only stores one action, so you can only undo one action. This command works on all types of formatting changes, insertions, and deletions.

TYPICAL OPERATION

In this example you use the Gallery Undo command to recover an erased style and remove formatting changes to an existing style. Begin this example at the Main menu with LINCOLN.DOC loaded in the current window.

1. Press **Esc**. Type **G**, then **D**. Word deletes the first stylesheet entry.

```
 1   SP Paragraph Standard                         Standard Paragraph
        Pica (modern a) 12/18. Justified, space before 1 li.
 2   T1 Paragraph Heading level 1                  Gettysburg Heading
        Pica (modern a) 12 Bold Uppercase. Centered (keep with following
        paragraph).
 3   IT Character 1                                Italic Characters
        Pica (modern a) 12 Italic.
 4   H2 Paragraph Heading level 2                  Bold, Left Justified
        Pica (modern a) 12/18 Bold. Flush left, space before 1 li (keep
        with following paragraph).
 ♦
                                                              LINCOLN.STY
GALLERY: Copy Delete Exit Format Help
         Insert Name Print Transfer Undo
Copies selected style(s) to scrap
                 {Division Sta...} ?          CL               Microsoft Word
```

2. Type **U**. Word undeletes the first stylesheet entry.

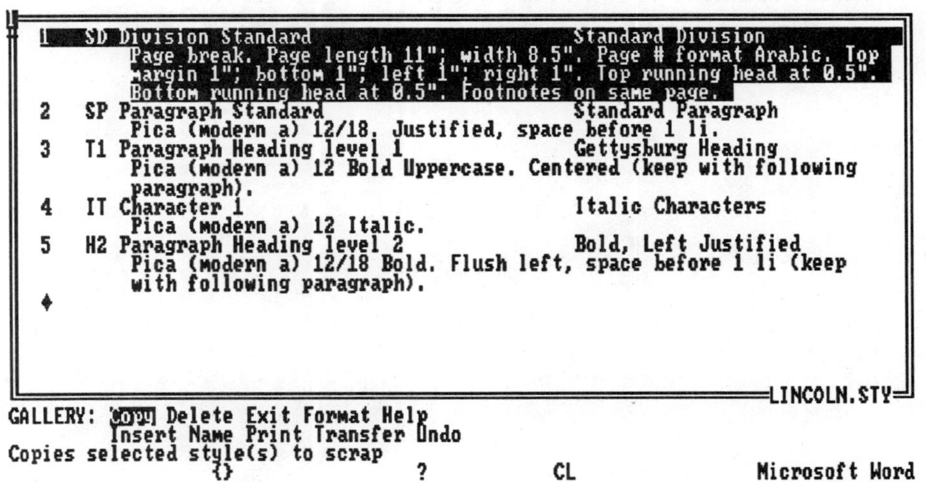

```
 1   SD Division Standard                          Standard Division
        Page break. Page length 11"; width 8.5". Page # format Arabic. Top
        margin 1"; bottom 1"; left 1"; right 1". Top running head at 0.5".
        Bottom running head at 0.5". Footnotes on same page.
 2   SP Paragraph Standard                         Standard Paragraph
        Pica (modern a) 12/18. Justified, space before 1 li.
 3   T1 Paragraph Heading level 1                  Gettysburg Heading
        Pica (modern a) 12 Bold Uppercase. Centered (keep with following
        paragraph).
 4   IT Character 1                                Italic Characters
        Pica (modern a) 12 Italic.
 5   H2 Paragraph Heading level 2                  Bold, Left Justified
        Pica (modern a) 12/18 Bold. Flush left, space before 1 li (keep
        with following paragraph).
 ♦
                                                              LINCOLN.STY
GALLERY: Copy Delete Exit Format Help
         Insert Name Print Transfer Undo
Copies selected style(s) to scrap
                 {}               ?          CL               Microsoft Word
```

3. Type **F**, then **M**. Select the Top field by pressing **Tab**. Type **2**. Select the Bottom field by pressing **Tab**. Type **2**. Press **Enter**. Word changes the style format.

```
 1   SD Division Standard                         Standard Division
        Page break. Page length 11"; width 8.5". Page # format Arabic. Top
        margin 2"; bottom 2"; left 1"; right 1". Top running head at 0.5".
        Bottom running head at 0.5". Footnotes on same page.
 2   SP Paragraph Standard                        Standard Paragraph
        Pica (modern a) 12/18. Justified, space before 1 li.
 3   T1 Paragraph Heading level 1                 Gettysburg Heading
        Pica (modern a) 12 Bold Uppercase. Centered (keep with following
        paragraph).
 4   IT Character 1                               Italic Characters
        Pica (modern a) 12 Italic.
 5   H2 Paragraph Heading level 2                 Bold, Left Justified
        Pica (modern a) 12/18 Bold. Flush left, space before 1 li (keep
        with following paragraph).
 ♦
                                                              LINCOLN.STY
GALLERY: Copy Delete Exit Format Help
        Insert Name Print Transfer Undo
Select style or press Esc to use menu
               {}              ?           CL              Microsoft Word
```

4. Type **U**. Word changes the style format to its original state. Type **E** to exit Gallery.
5. Turn to Module 29 to continue the learning sequence.

Module 27
HELP

DESCRIPTION

The Help command provides information about different Word functions. You access Help using one of three methods. The first method is context sensitive help from within a menu or in the document. Word presents a help screen showing the information pertinent to whatever the program is doing. You access this command by pressing Alt-H. The second method is through the Help command on the Main menu. This takes you to a help screen explaining how to use Help. Whenever you use the first or second methods, Word provides a menu for moving around in Help. The third method is using the direction arrows to highlight various commands on a menu. Word provides a quick summary of the menu function on the message line.

```
COMMAND: Copy Delete Format Gallery Help Insert Jump Library
         Options Print Quit Replace Search Transfer Undo Window
Provides quick reference information and lessons
Pg1 Li1 Co1      {}                 ?          CL                Microsoft Word
```

There are eight commands on the Help menu. The Exit command terminates the current Help session and returns you to the Main menu. The Next command displays the next help screen. The Previous command displays the previous help screen. The Basics command displays a help screen describing how to use Help. The Index command presents a listing of help topics for you to choose from. The Tutorial command starts the appropriate learning session for the current help topic. The Keyboard command presents a listing of keyboard specific speeed key actions for manipulating your document. The Mouse command presents a listing of mouse movements for manipulating your document.

APPLICATIONS

Use the Help command whenever you need information about a Word function or menu selection.

TYPICAL OPERATION

This example shows you how to use the Help command. It provides examples on how to access Help using all three methods described above. Begin this example at the DOS prompt.

1. Type **WORD** and press **Enter**. The Word introductory screen then the Main menu appear.

2. Press **Alt-H**. The Help menu appears.

```
HELP: Exit Next Previous Basics
      Index Tutorial Keyboard Mouse
Returns to location or menu where Help was requested
Pg1 Li1 Co1       {}            ?                                Microsoft Word
```

3. Type **E** to exit. The Main menu appears.

4. Press **Esc**. Notice the message line contains a description of the Copy command.

```
COMMAND: Copy Delete Format Gallery Help Insert Jump Library
         Options Print Quit Replace Search Transfer Undo Window
Copies selected text to scrap or to a named glossary entry
Pg1 Li1 Co1       {}            ?          CL                    Microsoft Word
```

5. Press **Right Arrow**. Notice the description changes to explain the Delete command.

6. Type **H**. The Help menu appears. Notice the help given tells how to use the help program rather than the edit help screen previously shown.

```
                              Help
HELP    Screen 1 of 3
Every Help screen lists name of topic and number of screens related to
topic in upper-left corner.

To get Help on a    1. Use direction keys to move highlight to command
command or command     or field you want help on.
field               2. Hold down Alt key while you press H (Alt+H).

To browse in Help   1. Press Escape key (Esc), then press H.
                    2. Press N (next) or P (previous) to view Help
                       information.

To view Help Index  1. Start Help (Press Esc, H, or Alt+H).
                    2. Press I to choose Index from Help menu.

                          Tutorial: Getting Quick Help
                          Using: Ch. 6, "Getting Help"
HELP: Exit Next Previous Basics
      Index Tutorial Keyboard Mouse
Returns to location or menu where Help was requested
Pg1 Li1 Co1       {}            ?                                Microsoft Word
```

7. Type **N**. The next help screen appears.

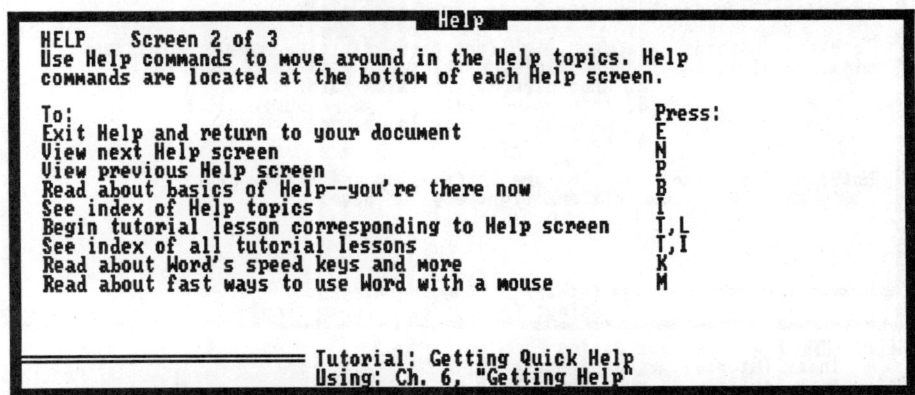

8. Type **P**. The previous help screen appears.
9. Type **I**. An alphabetical listing of help screens appears.

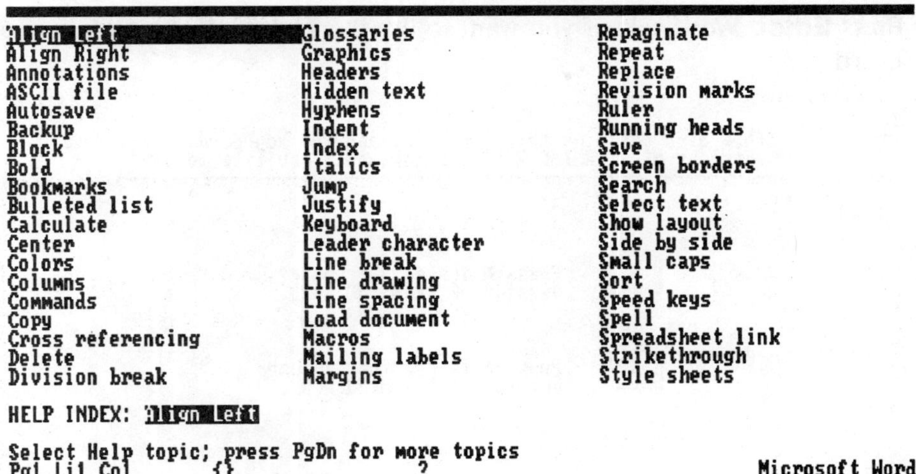

10. Highlight Margins using the arrow keys. Press **Enter**. The Format Division Margins help screen appears.

```
                                  Help
FORMAT DIVISION MARGINS    Screen 1 of 3
Specifies amount of space between edge of page and outer edge of text.
Includes: body text, running heads, graphics, etc.

To change margins    1. Move highlight above division mark of division
within a division       containing margins you want to change.
                     2. Choose Format Division Margins.
                     3. In command fields, type measurements for all
                        margins you want to change.
                     4. Press Enter.

Note: Word's default margins are 1" from top and bottom of page,
      and 1.25" from left and right edge of page.


                      Tutorial: Changing Margins
                      Using: Ch. 9, "Page Formatting"
HELP: Exit Next Previous Basics
      Index Tutorial Keyboard Mouse
Returns to location or menu where Help was requested
Pg1 Li1 Co1       {}          ?                        Microsoft Word
```

11. Type **T**. The Tutorial menu appears.

```
TUTORIAL: Lesson Index

Displays Learning Word lesson
Pg1 Li1 Co1       {}          ?                        Microsoft Word
```

12. Press **Enter**. Word asks if you want to use the keyboard or mouse version of Learn.

```
This disk contains both the mouse and the keyboard
versions of LEARNING WORD.  Which would you like to use?

      [M]    Press M to see the mouse
             version of LEARNING WORD.

      [K]    Press K to see the keyboard
             version of LEARNING WORD.
```

13. Press **K**. Word asks if you have a color screen.

14. Type **Y** or **N** depending on whether you have a color screen. Word presents a tutorial on margins.

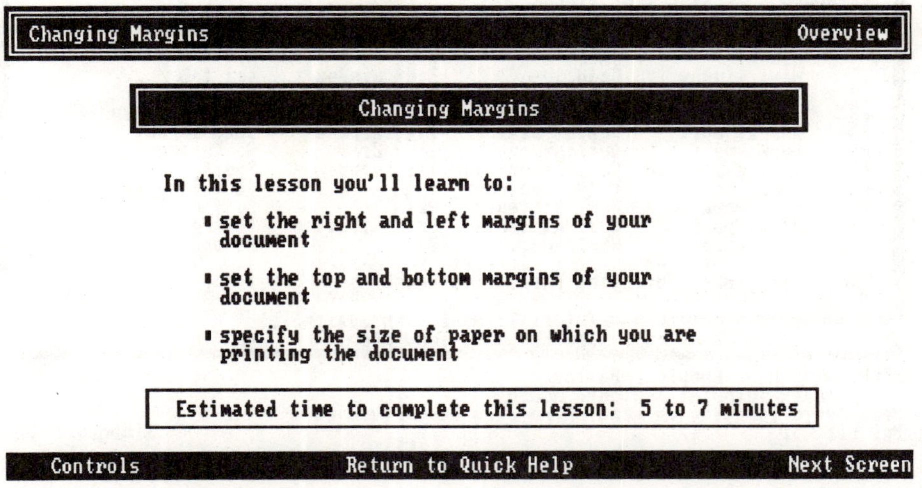

Changing Margins — Overview

Changing Margins

In this lesson you'll learn to:

- set the right and left margins of your document
- set the top and bottom margins of your document
- specify the size of paper on which you are printing the document

Estimated time to complete this lesson: 5 to 7 minutes

Controls — Return to Quick Help — Next Screen

15. Press **Ctrl-Q**. Word returns you to the help screen.
16. Type **T**, then **I**, then **K**. The tutorial index screen appears.

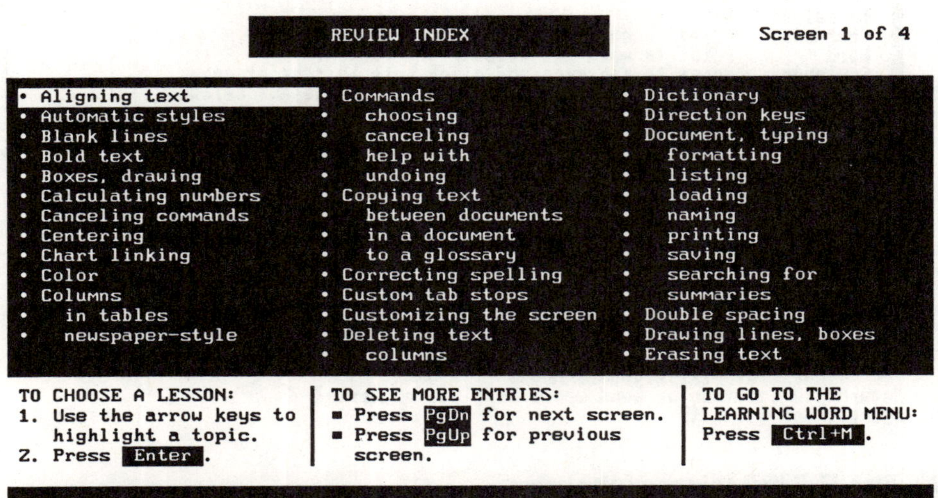

REVIEW INDEX — Screen 1 of 4

- Aligning text
- Automatic styles
- Blank lines
- Bold text
- Boxes, drawing
- Calculating numbers
- Canceling commands
- Centering
- Chart linking
- Color
- Columns
-   in tables
-   newspaper-style
- Commands
-   choosing
-   canceling
-   help with
-   undoing
- Copying text
-   between documents
-   in a document
-   to a glossary
- Correcting spelling
- Custom tab stops
- Customizing the screen
- Deleting text
-   columns
- Dictionary
- Direction keys
- Document, typing
-   formatting
-   listing
-   loading
-   naming
-   printing
-   saving
-   searching for
-   summaries
- Double spacing
- Drawing lines, boxes
- Erasing text

TO CHOOSE A LESSON:
1. Use the arrow keys to highlight a topic.
2. Press Enter.

TO SEE MORE ENTRIES:
- Press PgDn for next screen.
- Press PgUp for previous screen.

TO GO TO THE LEARNING WORD MENU:
Press Ctrl+M.

17. Press **Ctrl-Q**. Word returns you to the help screen.
18. Type **B**. The how to use help screen appears.

19. Type **K**. The Keyboard help screen appears.

```
                              Help
KEYBOARD    Screen 1 of 11
Speed function keys (when pressed alone or with Shift, Ctrl, or Alt):

      Alone            Shift            Ctrl             Alt
F1    Next window      Undo             Zoom window      Set tab
F2    Calculate        Outline view     Header           Footer
F3    Glossary         Record macro     Step mode        Copy to scrap
F4    Repeat edit      Repeat search    Toggle case      Show layout
F5    Overtype         Outline org.     Line draw        Go to page
F6    Ext. selection   Col. selection   Thesaurus        Spell
F7    Prev. word       Prev. sentence   Load             Show line breaks
F8    Next word        Next sentence    Print            Font name
F9    Prev. para.      Current line     Print preview    Text/graphics
F10   Next para.       Whole doc.       Save             Record style

(See next screen for speed formatting keys.)

=========================== Tutorial: No lesson available
                            See Keyboard Template
HELP: Exit Next Previous Basics
      Index Tutorial Keyboard Mouse
Returns to location or menu where Help was requested
Pg1 Li1 Co1        {}           ?                          Microsoft Word
```

20. Type **M**. The Mouse help screen appears.

```
                              Help
MOUSE     Screen 1 of 9

To select:   Do this:
Character    Point to character and click left button.
Word         Point to word and click right button.
Sentence     Point to sentence and click both buttons at once.
Line         Point in selection bar to left of line and click
             left button.
Paragraph    Point in selection bar to left of paragraph and click
             right button.
Document     Point anywhere in selection bar and click both buttons.
Text block   Point to first character and hold down left button;
             drag to last character and release button.
Column       Point to one corner and click left button; press
             Shift+F6; then point to opposite corner and click
             left button.

=========================== Tutorial: Selecting Text
                            Using: Ch. 4, "Scrolling, Selecting Text..."
HELP: Exit Next Previous Basics
      Index Tutorial Keyboard Mouse
Returns to location or menu where Help was requested
Pg1 Li1 Co1        {}           ?                          Microsoft Word
```

21. Type **E**. The Main menu appears.

22. Press **Esc** then type **Q**. The DOS prompt appears.

23. Turn to Module 40 to continue the learning sequence.

Module 28
INSERT

DESCRIPTION

The Insert command on the Main menu places text contained in the glossary or scrap at the position pointed to by the text cursor. The glossary is an area of multiple text string storage Word provides for each document. You can save the glossary to disk for future use. You can obtain a listing of the current glossary contents by pressing F1 while in the Insert form.

```
COMMAND: Copy Delete Format Gallery Help Insert Jump Library
         Options Print Quit Replace Search Transfer Undo Window
Inserts text from scrap or glossary; runs macros
Pg1 Li1 Co1      {}                  ?                    Microsoft Word
```

Besides any text strings you place in the glossary, Word provides six standard entries. The page entry places the current page number at the page marker position. The date entry places the current date at the date marker position. The time entry places the current time at the time marker position. Word automatically updates the date and time each time you edit the document. The dateprint and timeprint entries place a non-changing time and date at the position pointed to by the text cursor. The footnote entry places a footnote at the position pointed to by the text cursor.

The scrap contains a single text string displayed on the bottom line of the display between two curly brackets ({ }). When the scrap is empty, Word displays the curly brackets only. If the text length exceeds the available display area, Word displays the first seven letters, then three dots, then the last six letters. This acts as a reminder of the scrap contents. Word allows you to use the Ins key to move highlighted text from the scrap to the position pointed to by the text cursor as an alternative to using the Insert command.

Word provides many shortcuts for mouse users. There are no mouse commands associated specifically with this command. Generic mouse movements and commands appear in Appendix E.

APPLICATIONS

Use the Insert command to place the contents of the glossary or scrap at the position pointed to by the text cursor. Besides the six standard glossary entries described above, Word allows you to store standard text strings of your own in the glossary. Saving these strings to disk allows you to use them in macros.

Use the Ins key to reduce the time required to make multiple copies of the scrap contents. By placing a text string in the scrap, you can reduce your overall editing time in tables and other documents requiring repetitions of the same text.

TYPICAL OPERATION

In this example you use the Insert command to insert text from both the glossary and scrap. It also shows how to use the Ins key and one of the six standard glossary fields. Begin this example at the Main menu.

1. Select the F of Forescore by pressing arrow keys. Press **F6**. Highlight the entire paragraph by pressing arrow keys. Press **Del**. Word removes the first paragraph. Notice the deleted paragraph appears in the scrap.

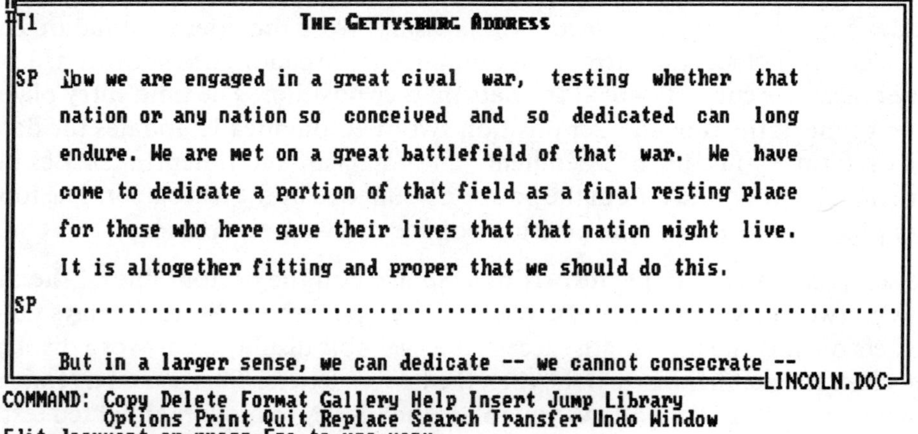

2. Press **Esc**. Type **I**. The Insert form appears.

```
INSERT from: {}

Enter glossary name or press F1 to select from list
Pg1 Li2 Co1       {Foresco...ual.¶}  ?                     Microsoft Word
```

3. Press **Enter**. Word places the contents of the scrap at the position pointed to by the text cursor. Notice Word does not empty the scrap.

```
T1                      THE GETTYSBURG ADDRESS

SP  Forescore and seven years ago our fathers brought forth  on  this
    continent a new nation, conceived in liberty and dedicated to the
    proposition that all men are created equal.

SP  Now we are engaged in a great cival  war,  testing  whether  that
    nation or any nation so  conceived  and  so  dedicated  can  long
    endure. We are met on a great battlefield of that  war.  We  have
    come to dedicate a portion of that field as a final resting place
    for those who here gave their lives that that nation might  live.
                                                           LINCOLN.DOC
COMMAND: Copy Delete Format Gallery Help Insert Jump Library
         Options Print Quit Replace Search Transfer Undo Window
Edit document or press Esc to use menu
Pg1 Li5 Co1      {Foresco...ual.¶}  ?                    Microsoft Word
```

4. Position the text cursor at the beginning of the title by pressing arrow keys. Press **Enter**, then **Up Arrow**. Press **Alt-S**. Type **P**. Type **PAGE:** . Press **Esc**. Type **I**. The Insert form appears.

5. Press **F1**. Word presents a list of default glossary fields.

```
page                                  footnote
date                                  dateprint
time                                  timeprint




INSERT from: page

Enter glossary name or press F1 to select from list
Pg1 Li1 Co7      {Foresco...ual.¶}  ?                    Microsoft Word
```

6. Select PAGE by pressing arrow keys. Press **Enter**. Word places a page number marker at the position pointed to by the cursor.

```
SP  PAGE: (page)█
T1                    THE GETTYSBURG ADDRESS

SP  Forescore and seven years ago our fathers brought forth  on  this
    continent a new nation, conceived in liberty and dedicated to the
    proposition that all men are created equal.

SP  Now we are engaged in a great cival  war,  testing  whether  that
    nation or any nation so  conceived  and  so  dedicated  can  long
    endure. We are met on a great battlefield of that  war.  We  have
                                                           LINCOLN.DOC
COMMAND: Copy Delete Format Gallery Help Insert Jump Library
         Options Print Quit Replace Search Transfer Undo Window
Edit document or press Esc to use menu
Pg1 Li1 Co13     {Foresco...ual.¶}  ?          CL            Microsoft Word
```

7. Press **Ins**. Word places the contents of the scrap at the position pointed to by the cursor.

```
SP  PAGE:  (page)Forescore   and   seven   years   ago   our   fathers
    brought forth on  this  continent  a  new  nation,  conceived  in
    liberty and dedicated to the proposition that all men are created
    equal.

SP  █
T1                    THE GETTYSBURG ADDRESS

SP  Forescore and seven years ago our fathers brought forth  on  this
    continent a new nation, conceived in liberty and dedicated to the
                                                           LINCOLN.DOC
COMMAND: Copy Delete Format Gallery Help Insert Jump Library
         Options Print Quit Replace Search Transfer Undo Window
Edit document or press Esc to use menu
Pg1 Li5 Co1      {Foresco...ual.¶}  ?          CL            Microsoft Word
```

8. Press **Esc**. Type **U**. Word removes the new text.
9. Press **Esc**. Type **T**, then **S**. The Transfer Save form appears.
10. Press **Enter**. Word displays a file save message. The Main menu appears.
11. Turn to Module 4 to continue the learning sequence.

Module 29
JUMP

DESCRIPTION

The Jump command allows you to move quickly from one section of a document to another. Word allows you to jump to another page, footnote, annotation, or bookmark. You access this command by pressing Esc and typing J at the Main menu.

```
JUMP to: Page Footnote Annotation bookmarK

Moves to specified page
P1 D1 C1          {2}          ?          CL          MR     Microsoft Word
```

PAGE The Jump Page command allows you to jump to another page. If you select a page that does not exist, Word takes you to the top of the last page in the document. The Jump Page form contains a single field. The Number field allows you to enter the desired page number.

FOOTNOTE The Jump Footnote command allows you to jump from a footnote reference to its associated text and back. If you select the reference, Word finds the associated text. If the text cursor does not currently point to a footnote, Word finds the next footnote in the text.

ANNOTATION The Jump Annotation is similar to the Jump Footnote command. Instead of finding footnote references, this command finds annotation references and their associated text. If the text cursor does not currently point to an annotation reference, Word finds the next annotation reference in the text.

BOOKMARK The Jump Bookmark command allows you to find previously placed bookmarks. By pressing F1 in the Name field, you can obtain a listing of current bookmarks. If you type a bookmark name that does not exist in the current document, Word displays an error message.

APPLICATIONS

Use the Jump command to find various sections in your document. Use the Jump Page command to find any page in your document quickly, or to find the top of the last page. Use the Jump Footnote command to find a footnote, then its reference. By finding the reference area, you can locate any footnote within your document. Select the reference, then use the Jump Footnote command to find it. Use the Jump Annotation command the same way you would the Jump Footnote command except on annotation references. Use the Jump Bookmark command to find a previously placed bookmark. Bookmarks are an editor's dream. By using bookmarks, you can quickly find several areas of a document that require rewording by the originator.

TYPICAL OPERATION

In this example you use the Jump command to locate several elements previously placed in the sample document. Begin this example at the Main menu with LINCOLN.DOC loaded in the current window.

1. With the cursor at the top of the file, press **Esc**. Type **J**, then **F**. Word finds the first footnote in the text.

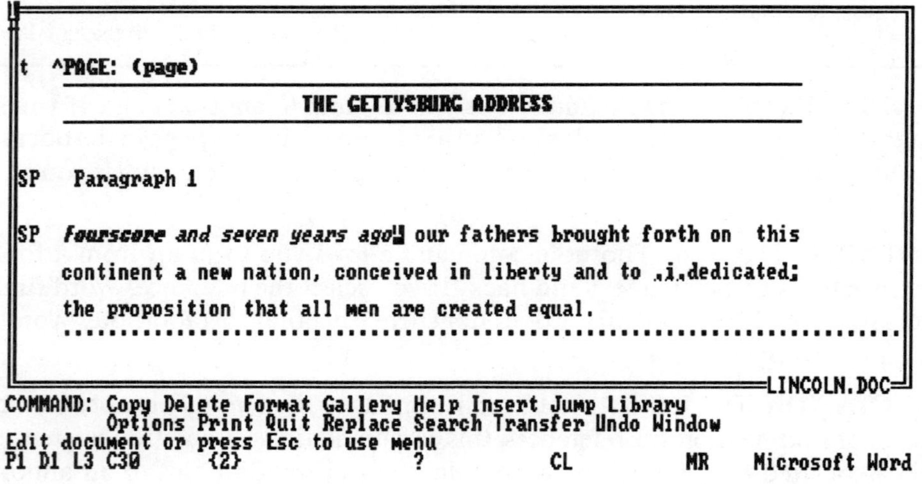

2. Press **Esc**. Type **J**, then **F**. Word finds the text associated with the first footnote.

```
*  1  87 years ago.

* | 2INITIALS, 5/27/89, 11:08 AM

SP ♦
```

3. Press **Esc**. Type **J**, then **F**. Word jumps back to the first footnote.
4. Press **Esc**. Type **J**, then **P**. The Jump Page form appears.

5. Type **2**. Press **Enter**. Word finds the top of the second page.

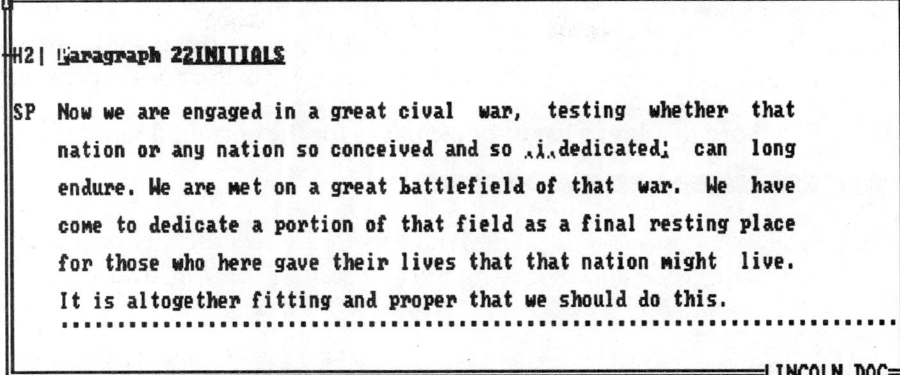

```
H2| Paragraph 22INITIALS

SP  Now we are engaged in a great cival  war,  testing  whether  that
    nation or any nation so conceived and so .i.dedicated;  can  long
    endure. We are met on a great battlefield of that  war.  We  have
    come to dedicate a portion of that field as a final resting place
    for those who here gave their lives that that nation might  live.
    It is altogether fitting and proper that we should do this.
    ....................................................................
                                                            LINCOLN.DOC
```

6. Press **Esc**. Type **J**, then **A**. Word selects the first annotation reference.

```
H2| Paragraph 22INITIALS

SP  Now we are engaged in a great cival  war,  testing  whether  that
    nation or any nation so conceived and so .i.dedicated;  can  long
    endure. We are met on a great battlefield of that  war.  We  have
    come to dedicate a portion of that field as a final resting place
    for those who here gave their lives that that nation might  live.
    It is altogether fitting and proper that we should do this.
    ....................................................................
                                                            LINCOLN.DOC
```

7. Press **Esc**. Type **J**, then **A**. Word finds the first annotation text.

```
* | 2INITIALS 5/27/89 11:08 AM
SP  ♦

                                                            LINCOLN.DOC
```

8. Press **Esc**. Type **J**, then **K**. The Jump Bookmark form appears.

```
JUMP BOOKMARK name: █

Enter bookmark name or press F1 to select from list
Co29              {7}              ?          CL          MR    Microsoft Word
```

9. Press **F1**. Word displays a list of bookmarks for the current document.

```
JUMP BOOKMARK name: PARA1

Enter bookmark name or press F1 to select from list
Co29              {7}              ?          CL          MR    Microsoft Word
```

10. Press **Enter**. Word finds the first paragraph heading (the point where you placed the first bookmark).

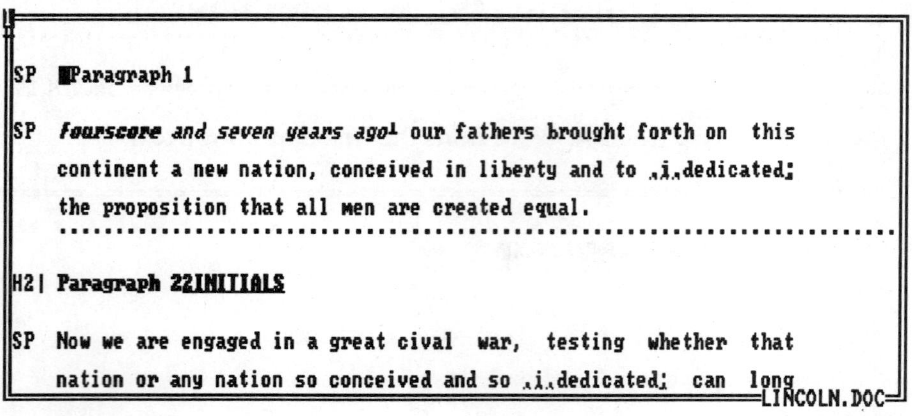

11. Turn to Module 30 to continue the learning sequence.

Module 30
LIBRARY AUTOSORT

DESCRIPTION

The Library Autosort command places selected text in a specified order. Normally, you use this command to sort the entries in a table; for example, a list of names and addresses. You access this command by pressing Esc and typing L, then A.

```
LIBRARY: Autosort Document-retrieval Hyphenate Index Link Number Run Spell
         Table thEsaurus
Sorts selected text
Pg1 Li1 Co1      {·}          ?           CL                  Microsoft Word
```

The Library Autosort form contains four fields. The By field determines how Word looks at numbers. When you select Alphanumeric, Word sorts the text by special characters, then numbers, then letters. Otherwise, Word sorts by numbers only. The Sequence field determines the order Word uses to sort the text. If you select Ascending, Word places 1 before 9 and A before Z. The Case field determines if Word differentiates between upper and lowercase letters. If you select Yes, Word places A before a. There are two methods of selecting text to sort. If you select a specific column of a table as the sort key, then the Column Only field contains Yes. If you want Word to take all the text in a row in account for sorting purposes, set the Column Only field to No.

Word provides many shortcuts for mouse users. The mouse commands associated specifically with this form appear in Table 30-1. Generic mouse movements and commands appear in Appendix E.

TABLE 30-1. MOUSE COMMANDS

Action	*Pointing To*	*Result*
Push Left Button	Menu Selection	Word presents the requested form or submenu or executes the requested command.
Push Left Button	Field	Word selects the field for change.
Push Left Button	Form Name	Word makes the requested changes and returns to the document.

Action	*Pointing To*	*Result*
Push Left Button with Column Select Mode On (Shift-F6, CS Appears On Status Line)	Upper Left Corner of Column in Window.	Word selects the column starting at the upper left corner selected to the lower right corner mouse dragged to with left button pushed.
Push Right Button	Multiple Choice Field	Word makes the requested changes and returns to the document.
Push Right and Left Buttons	Anywhere Except the Form or Window	Word cancels the current operation and returns to Main menu.

APPLICATIONS

Use the Library Autosort command to reduce the work required to create an ordered list or table. By typing the list or table without regard to order, you reduce the initial data time.

TYPICAL OPERATION

In this example you create a list and sort it using the Library Autosort command. Begin this example at the Main menu with nothing loaded in the current window. (Press Esc and type T, then C, then A to clear the display.)

1. Type **again** and press **Enter**. Type **Again** and press **Enter**. Type **zero** and press **Enter**. Type **123** and press **Enter**. Type **456** and press **Enter**. Type **sugar** and press **Enter**. Type **%123** and press **Enter**. Type **&123** and press **Enter**. Type **Like** and press **Enter**. Type **Mouse** and press **Enter**. Type **Rose** and press **Enter**. Type **rose** and press **Enter**. Press **Ctrl-PgUp**, then **F6**, then **Ctrl-PgDn**. Press **Esc**. Type **L**, then **A**. The Library Autosort form appears.

```
LIBRARY AUTOSORT by: Alphanumeric Numeric   sequence:(Ascending)Descending
                case: Yes(No)              column only: Yes(No)
Select option
Pg1 Li13 Co1      {3}            ?                    EX      Microsoft Word
```

2. Select the Case field by pressing **Tab**. Select Yes by pressing **Spacebar**. Press **Enter**. Word sorts the entries.

```
*    %123
*    &123
*    123
*    456
*    Again
*    again
*    Like
*    Mouse
*    Rose
*    rose
*    sugar
*    zero
*    ♦
COMMAND: Copy Delete Format Gallery Help Insert Jump Library
         Options Print Quit Replace Search Transfer Undo Window
Edit document or press Esc to use menu
Pg1 Li12 Co5      {3}          ?                        Microsoft Word
```

3. Press **Esc**. Type **L**, then **A**. Select Numeric by pressing **Spacebar**. Press **Tab**. Select Descending by pressing **Spacebar**. Press **Enter**. Word sorts only the numeric entries in reverse order. Notice Word highlights only the numeric entries.

```
*    456
*    %123
*    &123
*    123
*    Again
*    again
*    Like
*    Mouse
*    Rose
*    rose
*    sugar
*    zero
*    ♦
COMMAND: Copy Delete Format Gallery Help Insert Jump Library
         Options Print Quit Replace Search Transfer Undo Window
Edit document or press Esc to use menu
Pg1 Li4 Co4       {4}          ?        CL              Microsoft Word
```

4. Press **Ctrl-PgUp**, then **F6**, then **Ctrl-PgDn**. Press **Esc**. Type **L**, then **A**. Select Alphanumeric by pressing **Spacebar**. Press **Enter**. Word sorts all the entries in descending order.

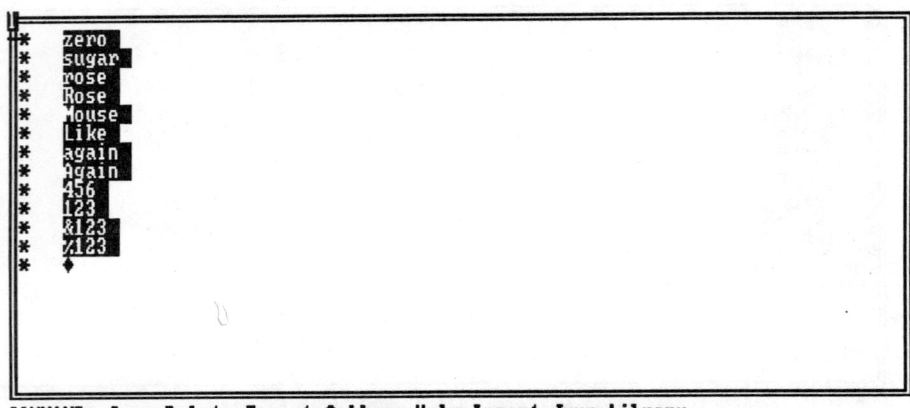

5. Press **Esc**. Type **L**, then **A**. Select the Sequence field by pressing **Tab**. Press **Spacebar** to select ascending. Select the Case field by pressing **Tab**. Press **Spacebar** to select no. Press **Enter**. Word sorts the entries in ascending order. Notice Word does not observe differences between upper and lowercase letters.

6. Press **Esc**. Type **T**, then **C**, then **A**. Type **N** to lose your changes. Word clears the example from the display.

7. Turn to Module 32 to continue the learning sequence.

Module 31
LIBRARY DOCUMENT-RETRIEVAL

DESCRIPTION

The Library Document-Retrieval command helps you maintain the documents you create. You can sort the displayed documents using any of the summary sheet fields. Other options allow you to print, copy, delete, or load a document. This command uses a unique method of selecting more than one document to perform print, copy, and delete functions. By highlighting the document name and pressing Spacebar, you select or deselect a file. Word shows file selection by placing an asterisk on the left side of the filename. You access the Library Document-Retrieval command by pressing Esc and typing L, then D.

```
LIBRARY: Autosort Document-retrieval Hyphenate Index Link Number Run Spell
         Table thEsaurus
Retrieves documents based on contents or summary information
Pg1 Li7 Co1        {·with·...window} ?                           Microsoft Word
```

Word provides many shortcuts for mouse users. The mouse commands associated specifically with this command and associated forms appear in Table 31-1. Generic mouse movements and commands appear in Appendix E.

TABLE 31-1. MOUSE COMMANDS

Action	*Pointing To*	*Result*
Push Left Button	Menu Selection	Word presents the requested form or submenu or executes the requested command.
Push Left Button	Field	Word selects the field for change.
Push Left Button	Form Name	Word makes the requested changes and returns to the document.
Push Right Button	Multiple Choice Field	Word makes the requested changes and returns to the document.
Push Right Button	Fill in the Blank Field	Word displays a list of acceptable choices.
Push Right and Left Buttons	Anywhere Except the Form or Window	Word cancels the current operation and returns to Main menu.

QUERY The Library Document-Retrieval Query command changes the summary sheet fields Word uses to qualify documents for display. By placing a parameter in one or more fields, you can limit the number of files Word displays. In addition to the standard summary sheet fields, this form contains a Path field used to determine the directory Word searches.

EXIT The Library Document-Retrieval Exit command returns you to the Main menu. Using this command, you can look at the documents available in the current query directory without performing any actions on them.

LOAD The Library Document-Retrieval Load command places the selected file in the current window. You may load only one document at a time. Word asks if you want to save the stylesheet and document if it detects changes to them before loading the new document. As with the Transfer Load command on the Main menu, Word presents a form asking for the document name and if you want to open it as read only.

PRINT The Library Document-Retrieval Print command allows you to print all the selected files in batch mode (in other words, without loading the document or any user intervention). Word uses the current options and print driver selection in the Print Options form. You can choose to print the document, the summary sheet, or both when using this command. If you try to print without selecting any files, Word displays an error message.

UPDATE The Library Document-Retrieval Update command allows you to change the summary sheet information for the selected document. You may change the information for only one document at a time. Word presents the same summary sheet form discussed as part of the Transfer Save command (Module 45).

VIEW The Library Document-Retrieval View command allows you to display three different levels of information about the documents in the current subdirectory. The first field of the Library Document-Retrieval form selects the level. The first level is filename only. The second level is the filename, title, and one other piece of summary sheet information (whatever you choose as the sort field). The third level displays the entire summary sheet for the selected document. The Library Document-Retrieval View form contains a second field for sorting the documents. Word allows you to sort by any of the listed summary sheet fields.

COPY The Library Document-Retrieval Copy command allows you to move the contents of a document to another drive or directory. The first field contains the name of the destination drive and directory. The second field asks if you want the files in the source directory deleted as Word copies them to the destination. The third field determines if Word copies the stylesheets associated with the selected documents to the new directory.

DELETE The Library Document-Retrieval Delete command removes the selected files from the current directory. Before Word actually deletes the files, it asks if you are sure you want them deleted.

APPLICATIONS

Use the Library Document-Retrieval command and its associated subcommands to maintain the directory containing your files. Using this command saves time and effort loading, printing, deleting, and copying files. By judiciously entering file selection criteria using a combination of the Library Document-Retrieval View and Library Document-Retrieval Query commands, you can minimize the work required to find a document. This command is also convenient for finding old, unneeded files, then deleting them using the Library Document-Retrieval Delete command.

TYPICAL OPERATION

In this example you use the Library Document-Retrieval command to perform various subdirectory maintenance related tasks. Begin this example at the Main menu.

NOTE

> Due to differences in directory names or individual machines, the path appearing in this example may not match the one displayed on your screen. However, your filenames should match the ones appearing in the screen shots. Whenever you see the term PATHNAME, type your pathname in the field.

1. Press **Esc**. Type **L**, then **D**. The Library Document-Retrieval display appears.

```
DOCUMENT-RETRIEVAL: Query Exit Load Print Update View Copy Delete

Press Spacebar to mark-unmark file, Ctrl+Spacebar to mark all, or Esc for menu
                                    ?                                Microsoft Word
```

2. Type **Q**. The Library Document-Retrieval Query form appears.

```
QUERY path: C:\MW\0017
  author:
  operator:
  keywords:
  creation date:                          revision date:
  document text:
  case: Yes(No)                           marked files only: Yes(No)
Enter search directories separated by commas or press F1 to select from list
                                    ?       CL                       Microsoft Word
```

3. Type **PATHNAME/*.*** in the Path field. Press **Enter**. A listing of all files in the current directory appears. Note that Word added the *.* filename designator to the path entry in the upper left corner of the display.

```
Path: C:\MW\0017\*.*
 C:\MW\0017\EPSONRX.PRD                C:\MW\0017\NORMAL.GLY
 C:\MW\0017\LINCOLN.BAK                C:\MW\0017\NORMAL.STY
 C:\MW\0017\LINCOLN.CMP                C:\MW\0017\PLAIN.PRD
 C:\MW\0017\LINCOLN.DOC                C:\MW\0017\PLAIN.TXT
 C:\MW\0017\LINCOLN.STY                C:\MW\0017\SPECIALS.CMP
 C:\MW\0017\NEW.PRD                    C:\MW\0017\TTY.PRD
```

```
DOCUMENT-RETRIEVAL: Query Exit Load Print Update View Copy Delete

Press Spacebar to mark-unmark file, Ctrl+Spacebar to mark all, or Esc for menu
                                    ?                                Microsoft Word
```

4. Type **Q**. Select the Author field by pressing **Tab**. Type **YOUR NAME** and press **Enter**. Notice Word reduces the number of files to the two including YOUR NAME in the summary sheet.

```
Path: C:\MW\0017\*.*
 C:\MW\0017\LINCOLN.BAK                C:\MW\0017\LINCOLN.DOC
```

```
DOCUMENT-RETRIEVAL: Query Exit Load Print Update View Copy Delete

Press Spacebar to mark-unmark file, Ctrl+Spacebar to mark all, or Esc for menu
                                    ?           CL                   Microsoft Word
```

5. Type **U**. The Library Document-Retrieval Update Summary form appears.

```
UPDATE SUMMARY filename: C:\MW\0017\LINCOLN.BAK
   title: Lincoln's Gettysburg Address            version number: 1.0
   author: Your Name                              creation date: 04/13/89
   operator: Your Name                            revision date: 05/28/89
   keywords: Lincoln Gettysburg
   comments: This is Lincoln's Gettysburg Address
Enter full filename or press F1 to select from list
                                    ?           CL                   Microsoft Word
```

6. Press **Esc**. Type **V**. The Library Document-Retrieval View form appears.

```
VIEW: Short Long Full
      Sort by:(Directory)Author Operator Revision_date Creation_date Size
Select option
                                    ?          CL              Microsoft Word
```

7. Select Long by pressing **Spacebar**. Press **Tab** to select the Sort By field. Select Author by pressing **Spacebar**. Press **Enter**. Word displays a long view of the document listing. Notice the long view contains the author name as the second value listed.

```
Path: C:\MW\0017\*.*                         author       title
 C:\MW\0017\LINCOLN.BAK                      Your Name    Lincoln's Gettysburg Addr
 C:\MW\0017\LINCOLN.DOC                      Your Name    Lincoln's Gettysburg Addr

DOCUMENT-RETRIEVAL: Query Exit Load Print Update View Copy Delete

Press Spacebar to mark-unmark file, Ctrl+Spacebar to mark all, or Esc for menu
                                    ?          CL              Microsoft Word
```

8. Type **V**. Select Full by pressing **Spacebar**. Select the Sort By field by pressing **Tab**. Select Creation Date by pressing **Spacebar**. Press **Enter**. Word displays a full view of the summary sheet for the first file. Note the files appear in creation date order.

```
Path: C:\MW\0017\*.*
 C:\MW\0017\LINCOLN.BAK                C:\MW\0017\LINCOLN.DOC

filename: C:\MW\0017\LINCOLN.BAK                   char count: 1797
title: Lincoln's Gettysburg Address                version number: 1.0
author: Your Name                                  creation date: 04/13/89
operator: Your Name                                revision date: 05/28/89
keywords: Lincoln Gettysburg
comments: This is Lincoln's Gettysburg Address

DOCUMENT-RETRIEVAL: Query Exit Load Print Update View Copy Delete

Press Spacebar to mark-unmark file, Ctrl+Spacebar to mark all, or Esc for menu
                                    ?          CL              Microsoft Word
```

9. Press **Spacebar** to select LINCOLN.BAK. Type **C**. The Library Document-Retrieval Copy form appears.

```
COPY marked files to drive/directory: █
     delete files after copy: Yes(No)          copy style sheets: Yes(No)
Enter path or press F1 to select from list
                                   ?                              Microsoft Word
```

10. Press **Esc**. Type **D** to select the Library Document-Retrieval Delete command. Word asks if you want to delete the file.

```
Path: C:\MW\0017\*.*
*C:\MW\0017\LINCOLN.BAK                 C:\MW\0017\LINCOLN.DOC

filename: C:\MW\0017\LINCOLN.BAK                     char count: 1797
title: Lincoln's Gettysburg Address                  version number: 1.0
author: Your Name                                    creation date: 04/13/89
operator: Your Name                                  revision date: 05/28/89
keywords: Lincoln Gettysburg
comments: This is Lincoln's Gettysburg Address
DELETE:
Enter Y to confirm deletion of marked files █
                                   ?          CL                  Microsoft Word
```

11. Type **Y**. Word deletes the marked file.
12. Type **E** to select the Library Document-Retrieval Exit command. The Main menu appears.
13. Press **Esc**. Type **L**, then **D** to select the Library Document-Retrieval command. Type **P**. The Library Document-Retrieval Print form appears.

```
PRINT marked files: Summary Document Both
Select option
                                   ?          CL                  Microsoft Word
```

14. Select Both by pressing **Spacebar**. Press **Enter**. Word prints the document and summary sheet.
15. Type **L**. Word loads LINCOLN.DOC and returns to the Main menu.
16. Turn to Module 36 to continue the learning sequence.

Module 32
LIBRARY HYPHENATE

DESCRIPTION

The Library Hyphenate command automatically hyphenates words to improve the appearance of your document. It does this by reducing the white space between words when using justified paragraph alignment. If you add hyphenation and later add text that negates the need for the hyphen, Word automatically removes it by using an optional hyphen. Optional hyphens print only at the end of a line of text. You access this command by pressing Esc and typing L, then H at the Main menu. You can create optional hyphens manually by pressing Ctrl and typing hyphen. The optional hyphen does not appear unless Word positions it at the end of a line, or you select All in the Options Show Hidden Text field.

```
LIBRARY: Autosort Document-retrieval Hyphenate Index Link Number Run Spell
         Table thEsaurus
Hyphenates all or selected portion of document
P1 D1 C1           {}                 ?           CL          MR    Microsoft Word
```

The Library Hyphenate form contains two fields. The Confirm field determines if Word automatically hyphenates words or asks you if you want the word hyphenated first. The Hyphenate Caps field determines if Word hyphenates words containing capital letters.

Word provides many shortcuts for mouse users. The mouse commands associated specifically with this form appear in Table 32-1. Generic mouse movements and commands appear in Appendix E.

TABLE 32-1. MOUSE COMMANDS

Action	*Pointing To*	*Result*
Push Left Button	Menu Selection	Word presents the requested form or submenu or executes the requested command.
Push Left Button	Field	Word selects the field for change.
Push Left Button	Form Name	Word makes the requested changes and returns to the document.

Action	*Pointing To*	*Result*
Push Right Button	Multiple Choice Field	Word makes the requested changes and returns to the document.
Push Right and Left Buttons	Anywhere Except the Form or Window	Word cancels the current operation and returns to Main menu.

APPLICATIONS

Use the Library Hyphenate command to improve the appearance of your document. When using justified text, hyphens can reduce the amount of white space appearing between letters. If you use left justified text, hyphens can make the right edge appear less ragged. By using the arrows during hyphenation, you can select the exact point where Word hyphenates the word.

TYPICAL OPERATION

In this example you use the Library Hyphenate command to improve the appearance of the sample document. Begin this example at the Main menu with LINCOLN.DOC loaded in the current window.

1. Press **Ctrl-PgUp**. Press **Esc**. Type **L**, then **H**. The Library Hyphenate form appears.

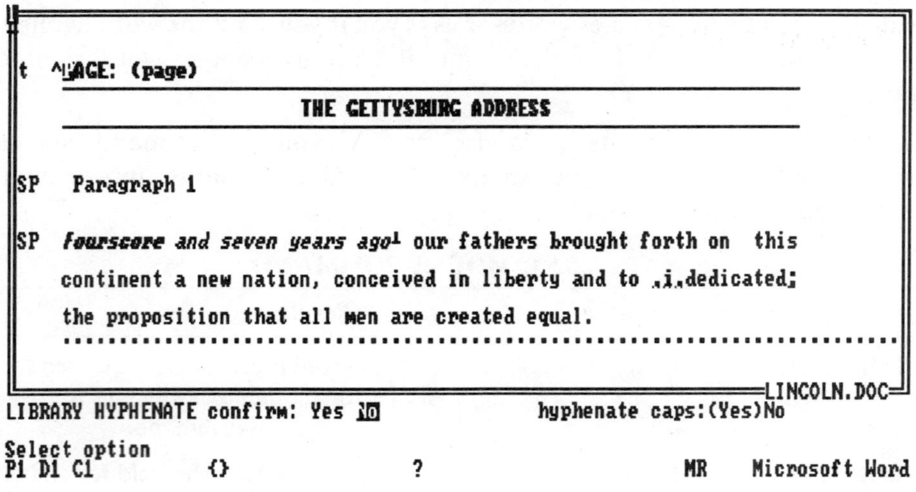

2. Press **Spacebar** to select Yes in the Confirm field. Press **Enter**. Word finds the first word to hyphenate.

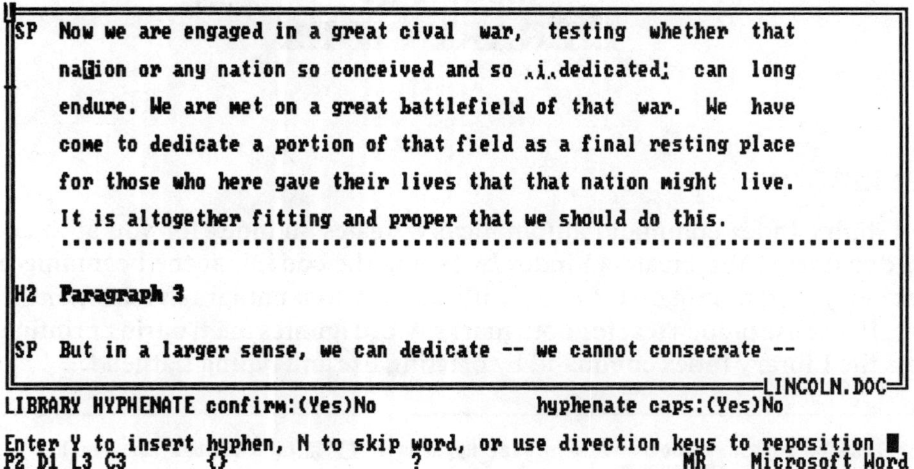

```
SP  Now we are engaged in a great cival  war,  testing  whether  that
    nation or any nation so conceived and so  dedicated,  can  long
    endure. We are met on a great battlefield of that  war.  We  have
    come to dedicate a portion of that field as a final resting place
    for those who here gave their lives that that nation might  live.
    It is altogether fitting and proper that we should do this.
    ....................................................................

H2  Paragraph 3

SP  But in a larger sense, we can dedicate -- we cannot consecrate --
                                                            LINCOLN.DOC
LIBRARY HYPHENATE confirm:(Yes)No              hyphenate caps:(Yes)No

Enter Y to insert hyphen, N to skip word, or use direction keys to reposition
P2 D1 L3 C3        {}               ?                   MR    Microsoft Word
```

3. Type **Y**. Word finds the second word to hyphenate.
4. Press **Right Arrow** to position the cursor between the n and the f of unfinished. Type **Y**. Word finds the third word to hyphenate.
5. Type **Y**. Word goes back to the top of the document.
6. Press **Esc**. Type **T**, then **S**. Press **Enter**. Word saves the document.
7. Turn to Module 35 to continue the learning sequence.

Module 33
LIBRARY INDEX

DESCRIPTION

The Library Index command automatically creates an index for you at the end of your document. You create an index by typing the code .i. at the beginning of the index entry. You terminate the entry with a semicolon, paragraph mark, or division mark. If you use hidden text for both marks, Word ignores them during printing. You access the Library Index command by pressing Esc and typing L, then I.

```
LIBRARY: Autosort Document-retrieval Hyphenate Index Link Number Run Spell
         Table thEsaurus
Compiles index from coded entries
Pg1 Li1 Co1        {several·}        ?                       Microsoft Word
```

The Library Index form contains four fields that describe how to format the index. The Entry/Page # Separated By field tells Word what characters to place between the entry and the page number on which it appears. The Cap Main Entries field tells Word to use all uppercase lettering for first level entries, even if they are lowercase in the text. The Indent Each Level entry tells Word how much to indent each level if you don't use a stylesheet. The Use Stylesheet field tells Word to use the formatting characteristics contained in the stylesheet. To use this feature, you must have a paragraph style using the Index Level variant. Word provides five levels of indexing.

Word supplies two methods for marking index entries. You can manually add the .i. code at the beginning and appropriate end code to each entry, or use a macro to assist you. The Word-supplied Index_Entry.Mac macro provides a good basis for creating your own custom macro. You can also use the Index_Entry.Mac macro by itself by highlighting the entry and pressing Ctrl-IE.

The macro must be loaded on your disk to be active. Load MACRO.GLY by pressing Esc, typing T, then G, then L. Press F1 for a list, highlight MACRO.GLY with arrow keys, and press Enter.

Word provides many shortcuts for mouse users. There are no mouse commands associated specifically with this command. Generic mouse movements and commands appear in Appendix E.

APPLICATIONS

Use the Library Index command to create indexes for your document automatically. After you insert or delete text, use the Library Index command to quickly recreate the index. Using the Word-supplied Index_Entry.Mac macro greatly reduces the work required to create the index.

TYPICAL OPERATION

In this example you create an index for LINCOLN.DOC using the Word-supplied Index_Entry.Mac macro. Begin this example at the Main menu with LINCOLN.DOC loaded in the current window.

1. Press **Ctrl-PgUp** to place the cursor at the beginning of the document. Press **F10** three times to select the first paragraph. Press **Right Arrow** then **Ctrl-Shift-Enter**. Word creates a page break after the first paragraph.

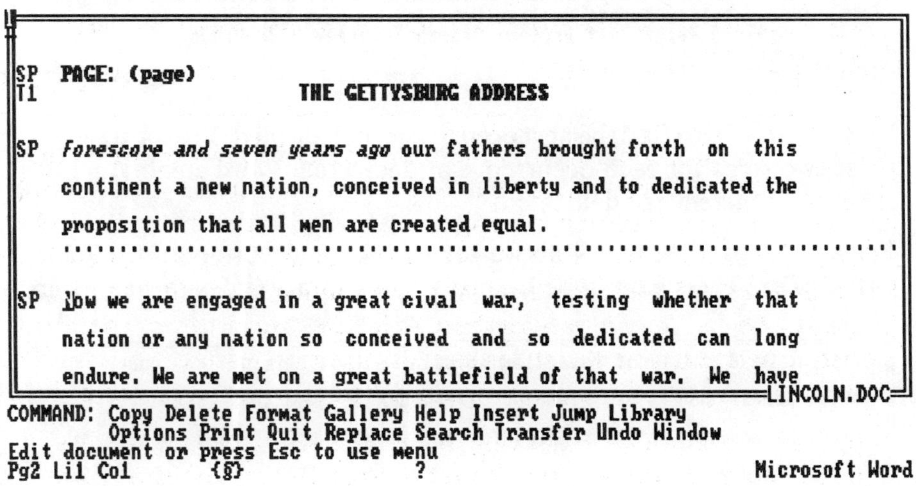

2. Press **Ctrl-PgUp**. Press **Esc**. Type **S**, then **dedicated**. Press **Enter**. Word finds the first occurrence of dedicated.

3. Press **Esc**. Type **O**. Select the Show Hidden Text field by pressing arrow keys. Press **Spacebar** for yes, then **Enter**. Press **Ctrl-IE**. Word creates the index entry for the first occurrence of dedicated.

```
SP  PAGE: (page)
T1                        THE GETTYSBURG ADDRESS

SP  Forescore and seven years ago our fathers brought forth  on  this
    continent a new nation, conceived in liberty and to .i.dedicated;
    the proposition that all men are created equal.
    ..........................................................................

SP  Now we are engaged in a great cival  war,  testing  whether  that
    nation or any nation so  conceived  and  so  dedicated  can  long
    endure. We are met on a great battlefield of that  war.  We  have
                                                              LINCOLN.DOC
COMMAND: Copy Delete Format Gallery Help Insert Jump Library
         Options Print Quit Replace Search Transfer Undo Window
End of macro
Pg1 Li4 Co66       {dedicated}       ?                        Microsoft Word
```

4. Press **Shift-F4** to find the next occurrence of dedicated. Press **Ctrl-IE**. Perform these two steps for each occurrence of dedicated. Word creates an index entry for each occurrence of dedicated.

5. Perform steps 2, 3, and 4 above for the words devotion and freedom. Press **Ctrl-PgDn**. Press **Esc**. Type **L**, then **I**. The Library Index form appears.

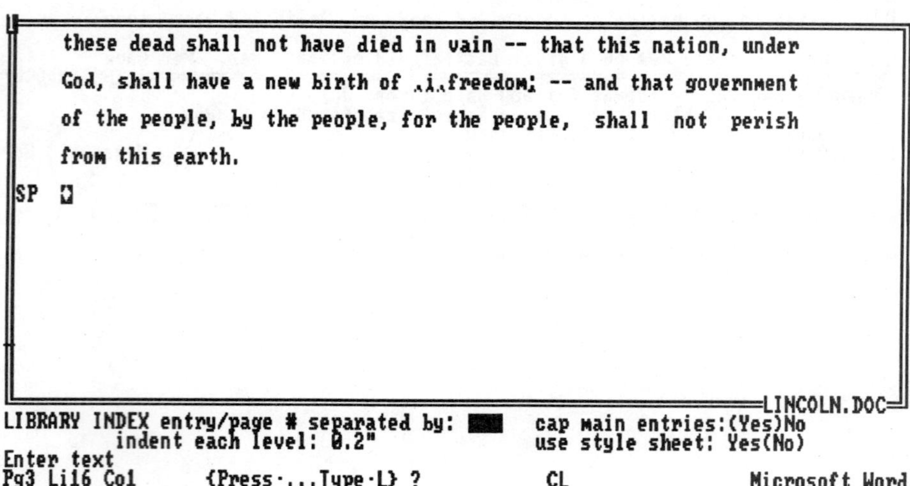

```
    these dead shall not have died in vain -- that this nation, under
    God, shall have a new birth of .i.freedom; -- and that government
    of the people, by the people, for the people,  shall  not  perish
    from this earth.

SP
                                                              LINCOLN.DOC
LIBRARY INDEX entry/page # separated by:        cap main entries:(Yes)No
          indent each level: 0.2"               use style sheet: Yes(No)
Enter text
Pg3 Li16 Col      {Press·...Type·L} ?         CL              Microsoft Word
```

6. Press **Enter**. Word generates the index.

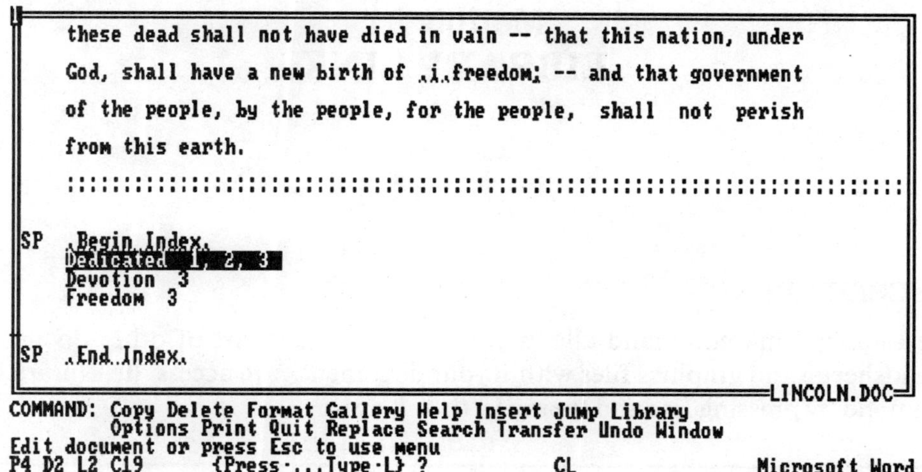

7. Press **Esc**. Type **T**, then **S**. Press **Enter**. Word saves the document.
8. Turn to Module 38 to continue the learning sequence.

Module 34
LIBRARY LINK

DESCRIPTION

The Library Link command allows you to place all or part of other documents, spreadsheets, and graphics files within your document. You access the Library Link command by pressing Esc and typing L, then L again.

```
LIBRARY: Autosort Document-retrieval Hyphenate Index Link Number Run Spell
         Table thEsaurus
Lets you import a portion of a spreadsheet or an image from another program
Pg1 Li7 Co1        {·with·...window} ?                          Microsoft Word
```

Word provides many shortcuts for mouse users. The mouse commands associated specifically with this form appear in Table 34-1. Generic mouse movements and commands appear in Appendix E.

TABLE 34-1. MOUSE COMMANDS

Action	*Pointing To*	*Result*
Push Left Button	Menu Selection	Word presents the requested form or submenu or executes the requested command.
Push Left Button	Field	Word selects the field for change.
Push Left Button	Form Name	Word makes the requested changes and returns to the document.
Push Right Button	Multiple Choice Field	Word makes the requested changes and returns to the document.
Push Right Button	Fill in the Blank Field	Word displays a list of acceptable choices.
Push Right and Left Buttons	Anywhere Except the Form or Window	Word cancels the current operation and returns to Main menu.

DOCUMENT The Library Link Document command allows you to place all or part of documents created by Word within your document. The Library Link Document form contains two fields. The Filename field contains the name of the file you wish to import. You can obtain a listing of documents by pressing F1. The Bookmark field tells Word what text within the document to import. If you do not specify a particular bookmark, Word imports the entire document. To obtain a listing of bookmarks in the target file, press F1.

This command differs from the Graphic command in that Word automatically places the text in your document so you actually see it. To update the text as you change the referenced documents, highlight the entire document, and use the Library Link Document command. If you press Enter without entering a filename, Word looks through the document for files to update. The document reference appears as hidden text at the beginning of the imported document. Another hidden text paragraph marks the end of the imported document.

GRAPHICS The Library Link Graphics command allows you to import graphics into your Word document. Word accepts graphics files using Lotus PIC, PC Paintbrush PCX or PCC, Microsoft Pageview, Hewlett-Packard Graphics Language (HPGL), Postscript (EPS), TIFFB, TIFFG, various print files (graphics screens sent to a file instead of a printer), Capture File (Word utility for capturing screens), or Windows Clipboard formats. Unlike the spreadsheet and document files, Word only places a reference to the graphic within your document. You can change the position of the graphic by changing the position of the hidden text reference. You don't see the actual picture unless you print the document or use print preview.

The Library Link Graphics form contains seven fields. The Filename field tells Word the name of the file you wish to import. Pressing F1 in the field provides a list of files in the current default directory.

The File Format field tells Word what type of graphic file you wish to import. Pressing F1 in this field allows you to select the correct format if Word does not automatically recognize it.

The Alignment in Frame field allows you to select where Word places the graphic within the frame. By pressing F1 you can obtain a listing of acceptable choices: centered, left, or right. Word defaults to the centered selection. The Graphics Width and Graphics Height fields determine the size of the graphic frame. By pressing F1 you can obtain suggestions on sizes to make the graphic. The Graphics Width field F1 selections always contain two choices: same size as the current text frame, and actual drawing size. Word does not require you use one of these two choices, it offers them as suggestions. When you place a size in the Graphics Width field, Word automatically changes the F1 choices in the Graphics Height field to match. The Graphics Height field F1 selections include three choices: same size as the frame width, the size required to preserve the aspect ratio of the drawing, or the original drawing size. As with the Graphics Width field, Word offers these choices as suggestions, not absolute requirements.

The Space Before and Space After fields tell Word how much space in inches to place before and after the graphic. This measurement prevents text from encroaching on the area reserved for the graphic.

SPREADSHEET The Library Link Spreadsheet command allows you to place all or part of a spreadsheet within a Word document. Word accepts spreadsheets from Lotus 1-2-3™, Multiplan™, or Microsoft Excel™ for Windows™. The Library Link Spreadsheet form contains two fields. The Filename field identifies the particular spreadsheet you wish to import. By pressing F1 you can obtain a listing of spreadsheets. The Area field tells Word which section of the spreadsheet you wish to import. If you do not select a specific area, Word imports the entire spreadsheet. By pressing F1 in the Area field, you can obtain a listing of named areas in the spreadsheet. You may specify not only named areas, but a specific range of cells by typing the coordinates of the upper left and lower right corners (for example A1:D17). As with the Link Library Document command, Word places a copy of the spreadsheet in your document. You update spreadsheet links by highlighting the entire document, pressing Esc, typing L, then L, then S, and pressing Enter. Word looks for all the spreadsheet references throughout the text and updates them automatically.

APPLICATIONS

Use the Library Link command and its associated subcommands to reduce the work required to create a composite document. For example, if several people work on a document at the same time, you could create a master document containing nothing but a heading and document links. Then as each document reaches completion, you can quickly update the entire document using the Library Link Document command.

Another use of this set of commands is when you want to combine graphics and text together. For example, a report containing a spreadsheet and associated graph with amplifying text is easy to create using the Library Link Spreadsheet and Library Link Graphics commands. You can add the amplifying text directly after importing the spreadsheet and graph.

By combining the font-handling capabilities and the Library Link Graphics command, you can create complex documents with the appearance usually associated with low-end desktop publishing programs.

TYPICAL OPERATION

In this example you use the Library Link Document command to create a new document from the sample document. Begin this example at the Main menu with LINCOLN.DOC loaded in the current window.

1. Select Paragraph 1 by pressing arrow keys. Highlight both the heading and text of paragraph 1 by pressing **F6**, then arrow keys. Press **Esc**. Type **F**, then **K**. Type **PARA1** and press **Enter**. Word asks if you want to overwrite the current bookmark.
2. Type **Y**. Word creates a new bookmark.
3. Press **Esc**. Type **T**, then **C**, then **A**. Word asks if you want to save your changes.
4. Type **Y**. Word saves the document, then clears the screen.
5. Press **Esc**. Type **L**, then **L** again. The Library Link menu appears.

```
LIBRARY LINK: Document Graphics Spreadsheet

Lets you import a bookmarked region from another document
Pg1 Li7 Co1         {2}                ?          CL                 Microsoft Word
```

6. Type **D**. The Library Link Document form appears.

```
LIBRARY LINK DOCUMENT filename: █                              bookmark:

Enter filename or press F1 to select from list
Pg1 Li7 Co1         {3}                ?          CL                 Microsoft Word
```

7. Press **F1**. Word presents a listing of available documents. Select LINCOLN.DOC using arrow keys.
8. Press **Tab** to select the Bookmark field. Press **F1**. Word presents a list of bookmarks in LINCOLN.DOC.

```
PARA1                                         PARA2
PARA3













LIBRARY LINK DOCUMENT filename: C:\MW\0017\LINCOLN.DOC      bookmark: PARA1

Enter bookmark name or press F1 to select from list
Pg1 Li7 Co1         {3}                ?          CL                 Microsoft Word
```

9. Press **Enter**. Word places a reference in the new document. Notice Word included both the text and the associated footnote.

```
*   .D.C:\MW\0017\LINCOLN.DOC.PARA1
    Paragraph 1
*   Fourscore and seven years ago1 our fathers brought forth on this
    continent a new nation, conceived in liberty and to .i.dedicated:
    the proposition that all men are created equal.
*   .D.
*   ♦
*   1    87 years ago.
*   ◘

COMMAND: Copy Delete Format Gallery Help Insert Jump Library
         Options Print Quit Replace Search Transfer Undo Window
Edit document or press Esc to use menu
Pg1 Li7   Co1    {5}         ?                          Microsoft Word
```

10. Press **Esc**. Type **T**, then **S**, then **NEW**. Press **Enter**. Word saves the new document.
11. Press **Esc**. Type **T**, then **L**, then **LINCOLN**. Press **Enter**. Word loads LINCOLN.DOC.
12. Select the footnote reference in the first paragraph by pressing arrow keys. Press **Esc**. Type **F**, then **M**, then **O**. Press **Spacebar** to turn off the revision marks and press **Enter**. Press **Del**. Word removes the footnote and reference.
13. Press **Esc**. Type **T**, then **S**. Press **Enter**. Word saves the document.
14. Press **Esc**. Type **T**, then **L**, then **NEW**. Press **Enter**. Word loads the new document.
15. Press **F6**, then **PgDn** to select the entire document. Press **Esc**. Type **L**, then **L**, then **D**. Press **Enter**. Word asks if you want to update the document link.

```
LIBRARY LINK DOCUMENT filename:                       bookmark:

Enter Y to update link, N to skip and continue, or Esc to cancel █
Pg1 Li11   Co4   {♦¶♦→8...ago.¶}   ?        CL            Microsoft Word
```

16. Type **Y**. Word updates the document link to reflect the loss of the footnote in the sample document.

```
* .D.C:\MW\0017\LINCOLN.DOC.PARA1
   Paragraph 1
* Fourscore and seven years ago our fathers brought forth on this
  continent a new nation, conceived in liberty and to .i.dedicated;
  the proposition that all men are created equal.
* .D.
*

COMMAND: Copy Delete Format Gallery Help Insert Jump Library
         Options Print Quit Replace Search Transfer Undo Window
Edit document or press Esc to use menu
Pg1 Li12   Co1     {♦¶♦→8...ago.¶}   ?          CL              Microsoft Word
```

17. Turn to Module 47 to continue the learning sequence.

Module 35
LIBRARY NUMBER

DESCRIPTION

The Library Number command automatically numbers or renumbers an outline or other numbered list (paragraphs). Normally, Word uses the style found in the *Chicago Manual of Style* for numbering purposes. In this scheme, roman numerals appear first, capital letters next, arabic numbers next. Word provides the means for you to select the numbering method used. Simply provide Word an example of the method you like at the beginning of the outline or document. Word does not number paragraphs beginning with a hyphen (-), asterisk (*), or bullet (•, Alt-254 on numeric keypad). In outline view, Word does not number body text. You access the Library Number command by pressing Esc and typing L, then D.

```
LIBRARY: Autosort Document-retrieval Hyphenate Index Link Number Run Spell
         Table thEsaurus
Numbers headings in outline or selected paragraphs in document
Pg1 Li7 Col       {-4}             ?                        Microsoft Word
```

Word provides many shortcuts for mouse users. There are no mouse commands associated specifically with this command. Generic mouse movements and commands appear in Appendix E.

The Library Number form contains two fields. The first field determines if you update or remove the numbering. If you select remove, Word deletes all numbering at the beginning of headings in outline view or paragraphs in document view. The Restart Sequence field determines if Word restarts at 1 when you select a subsection of a document for renumbering.

APPLICATIONS

Using the Library Number command allows you to automatically number all or part of your document. This feature is especially useful when working on large, complex documents or outlines. By automatically renumbering a document, you ensure the sequence remains intact even when you remove paragraphs or headings.

TYPICAL OPERATION

In this example you use the Library Number command to number an outline. Begin this example at the Main menu with nothing loaded.

1. Press **Shift-F2**. Word switches to outline view.
2. Type **Heading 1** and press **Enter**. Press **Alt-0** to go to the next level. Type **Subheading 1** and press **Enter**. Type **Subheading 2** and press **Enter**. Press **Alt-9** to go to the previous level. Type **Heading 2** and press **Enter**. Press **Alt-0**. Type **Subheading 3** and press **Enter**. Type **Subheading 4** and press **Esc**. Type **L**, then **N**. The Library Number form appears.

```
LIBRARY NUMBER: Update Remove            restart sequence:(Yes)No

Select option
Level 1          {·4}            ?                        Microsoft Word
```

3. Press **Enter**. Word numbers the document.

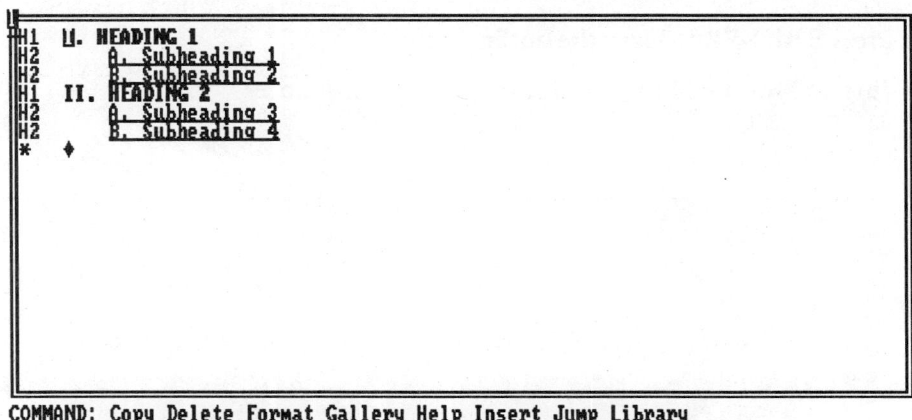


```
COMMAND: Copy Delete Format Gallery Help Insert Jump Library
         Options Print Quit Replace Search Transfer Undo Window
Edit document or press Esc to use menu
Level 1          {·4}            ?                        Microsoft Word
```

4. Press **Ctrl-PgUp**. Press **Del** three times to remove the current numbering. Type **1**. Press **Down Arrow** to select the first subheading. Press **Del** three times. Type **1.1**. Press **Esc**. Type **L**, then **N**. Press **Enter**. Word renumbers the document.

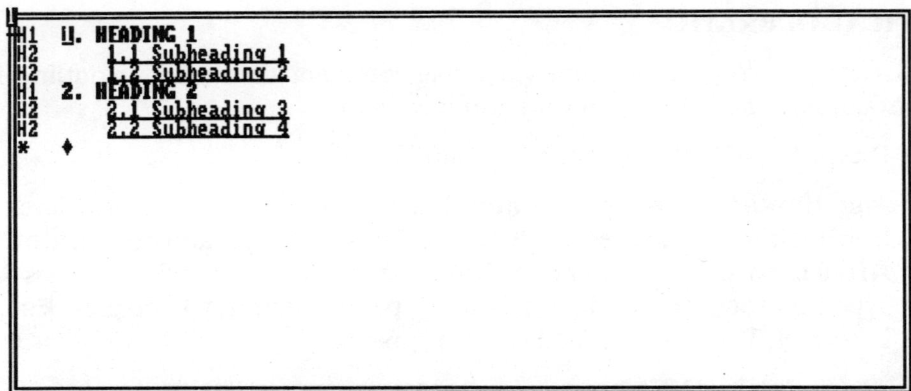

5. Press **Esc**. Type **L**, then **N**. Select Remove by pressing **Spacebar**. Press **Enter**. Word removes the heading numbers.
6. Press **Shift-F2** to leave the outline view.
7. Turn to Module 31 to continue the learning sequence.

Module 36
LIBRARY RUN

DESCRIPTION

The Library Run command allows you to execute other programs from inside Word. For example, if you wanted to execute a DOS command, you could use the Library Run command to create another copy of COMMAND.COM in memory. You would then see the usual DOS prompt. To get back to Word, you would type EXIT and press Enter. To access the Library Run command press Esc and type L, then R.

```
LIBRARY: Autosort Document-retrieval Hyphenate Index Link Number Run Spell
         Table thEsaurus
Runs DOS or OS/2 commands without quitting Word
Pg1 Li7 Co1        {·with·...window} ?                        Microsoft Word
```

Word provides many shortcuts for mouse users. There are no mouse commands associated specifically with this command. Generic mouse movements and commands appear in Appendix E.

APPLICATIONS

Use the Library Run command whenever you need to perform some task outside of Word without actually leaving Word. If you use the Library Run command, any documents, stylesheets, or glossaries loaded into memory are there when you return. This command saves time by eliminating the need to reload Word each time you need to perform a simple task. Since Word retains all your work in memory, the amount of memory left to execute programs when using the Library Run command is small. Therefore, you should only use this command to execute small utility programs or DOS commands.

TYPICAL OPERATION

In this example you use the Library Run command to execute a few DOS commands, then return to Word. Begin this example at the Main menu.

1. Press **Esc**. Type **L**, then **R**. The Library Run form appears. Notice Word suggests you execute a copy of COMMAND. You do not need the .COM extension since only .COM, .EXE, and .BAT files execute.

```
LIBRARY RUN: COMMAND

Enter DOS or OS/2 command
Pg1 Li7 Co1      {2}          ?          CL                Microsoft Word
```

3. Press **Enter**. The DOS prompt appears.

```
The IBM Personal Computer DOS
Version 3.10 (C)Copyright International Business Machines Corp 1981, 1985
             (C)Copyright Microsoft Corp 1981, 1985

C:\MW\WORD>
```

NOTE

If you get the message "Bad command or file name. Press a key to resume Word." Press any key. Press Esc and type L, then R. Type /COMMAND. Press Enter. You should see the DOS prompt appear.

4. Type **DIR** and press **Enter**. DOS produces a listing of files in the current directory.

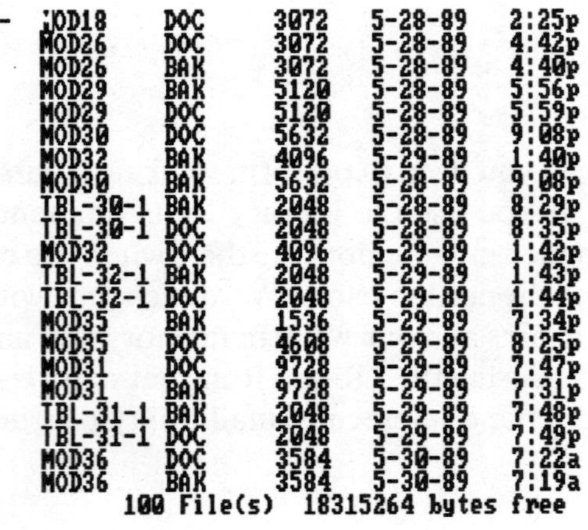

```
MOD18     DOC    3072   5-28-89   2:25p
MOD26     DOC    3072   5-28-89   4:42p
MOD26     BAK    3072   5-28-89   4:40p
MOD29     BAK    5120   5-28-89   5:56p
MOD29     DOC    5120   5-28-89   5:59p
MOD30     DOC    5632   5-28-89   9:08p
MOD32     BAK    4096   5-29-89   1:40p
MOD30     BAK    5632   5-28-89   9:08p
TBL-30-1  BAK    2048   5-28-89   8:29p
TBL-30-1  DOC    2048   5-28-89   8:35p
MOD32     DOC    4096   5-29-89   1:42p
TBL-32-1  BAK    2048   5-29-89   1:43p
TBL-32-1  DOC    2048   5-29-89   1:44p
MOD35     BAK    1536   5-29-89   7:34p
MOD35     DOC    4608   5-29-89   8:25p
MOD31     DOC    9728   5-29-89   7:47p
MOD31     BAK    9728   5-29-89   7:31p
TBL-31-1  BAK    2048   5-29-89   7:48p
TBL-31-1  DOC    2048   5-29-89   7:49p
MOD36     DOC    3584   5-30-89   7:22a
MOD36     BAK    3584   5-30-89   7:19a
        100 File(s)  18315264 bytes free

C:\MW\WORD>
```

5. Type **EXIT** and press **Enter**. Word displays the message "Press a key to resume Word."

6. Press any key. The Word display returns. The Main menu appears.

7. Turn to Module 34 to continue the learning sequence.

Module 37
LIBRARY SPELL

DESCRIPTION

The Library Spell command checks the spelling of words within your document. It begins at the current cursor position and checks until it reaches the end of your document. If you began the spelling check at a point after the beginning of the document, Word asks if you want to continue the spelling check at the top. If you answer yes, Word checks the document spelling until it reaches the current cursor position. To access the Library Spell command, press Esc and type L, then S. You can also access the spelling checker by pressing Alt-F6.

```
LIBRARY: Autosort Document-retrieval Hyphenate Index Link Number Run Spell
         Table thEsaurus
Runs DOS or OS/2 commands without quitting Word
Pg1 Li7 Co1        {·with·...window} ?                         Microsoft Word
```

If the Library Spell command finds an error in your document, it presents a window, showing the incorrect word, and a menu to assist you in correcting the word or adding it to one of the three dictionaries. The Library Spell menu contains six selections. These selections include: Correct, Add, Exit, Ignore, Options, and Undo.

```
SPELL: Correct Add Exit Ignore Options Undo

Select correction for unknown word and press Enter, or press Esc to use menu
Pg1 Li3 Co9        {1}               ?                            LINCOLN.DOC
```

CORRECT The Library Spell Correct form contains two fields. The Correct field contains the word you want Word to replace the incorrect spelling with. You can select a new word by pressing the arrow keys. The Remember Correction field allows Word to update automatically all words with the same misspelling in your document when you select Yes.

ADD The Library Spell Add form allows you add a correctly spelled word to one of the three dictionaries. Word uses the standard dictionary everytime you use the Library Spell command. The user dictionary contains words that affect a group of documents, but not necessarily all the documents you create. The document dictionary contains words used only in this particular document.

EXIT The Library Spell Exit command allows you to stop the current spell checking session and return to the Main menu. Word does not return you to the place you originally started the spell check. Instead, it places the text cursor at the last word checked by the spelling checker.

IGNORE The Library Spell Ignore command tells Word to pass the incorrectly spelled word. Word ignores the word for the rest of the spelling session; however, the spell checker will reflag the word during the next spell checking session.

OPTIONS The Library Spell Options form controls the spelling checker configuration. The Dictionary field contains the name of the user dictionary. You can press F1 to obtain a listing of dictionary files. The Lookup field determines how thoroughly Word searches for alternative spellings. If you select Complete, Word attempts to find every possible alternative in the standard dictionary. The Ignore All Caps field controls whether Word checks the spelling of acronyms and other capitalized words. The Alternatives field controls whether Word automatically presents a list of alternative spellings for you. The default setting for this field is AUTO. The Check Punctuation field determines if Word checks the punctuation as well as the spelling of your document. Whenever Word finds an abnormal capitalization or other punctuation error, it asks if you want it corrected.

UNDO The Undo command reverses the effects of a previous spelling correction. Unlike the Undo command on the Main menu, the spelling checker allows you to undo all your spelling corrections if necessary.

Word provides many shortcuts for mouse users. There are no mouse commands associated specifically with this command. Generic mouse movements and commands appear in Appendix E.

APPLICATIONS

Use the spelling checker to determine the accuracy of the spelling and punctuation in your document. By making sure the words in your document are correctly spelled, you enhance its appearance as well.

TYPICAL OPERATION

In this example you use the Library Spell command to check the spelling of LINCOLN.DOC. Begin this example at the Main menu with LINCOLN.DOC loaded in the current window.

1. Press **Esc**. Type **L**, then **S**. The Library Spell checking dictionaries message appears. The spelling checker finds the misspelled word, Forescore. The Library Spell menu appears.

2. Type **O**. The Library Spell Options form appears.

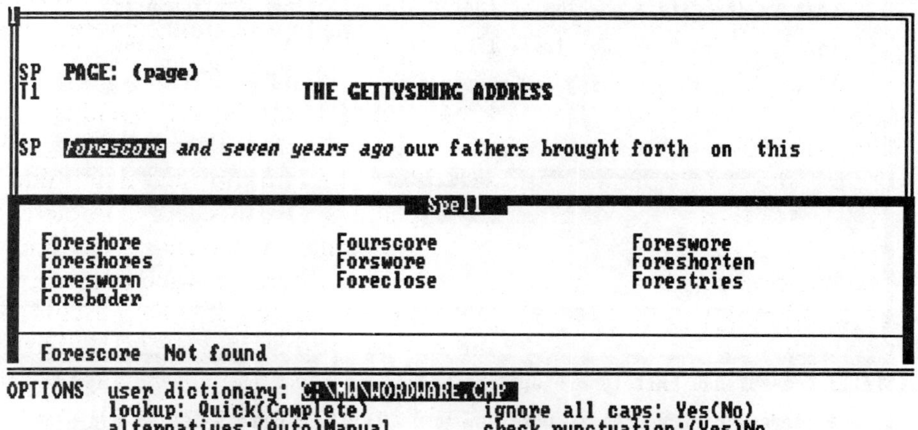

```
SP  PAGE: (page)
T1                        THE GETTYSBURG ADDRESS

SP  Forescore and seven years ago our fathers brought forth  on  this

                                   Spell
  Foreshore                 Fourscore                 Foreswore
  Foreshores                Forswore                  Foreshorten
  Foresworn                 Foreclose                 Forestries
  Foreboder

  Forescore  Not found
OPTIONS  user dictionary: C:\MW\WORDWARE.CMP
         lookup: Quick(Complete)           ignore all caps: Yes(No)
         alternatives:(Auto)Manual         check punctuation:(Yes)No
Enter filename of user dictionary or press F1 to select from list
Pg1 Li3 Co9        {loading·}       ?                          LINCOLN.DOC
```

3. Press **F1**. Word displays a list of dictionary files.

```
C:\MW\*.CMP
0009.CMP            UPDAT-AM.CMP       [0018]          [WORD]
COAST.CMP           UPDICT.CMP         [0019]          [A:]
DCDOCDCT.CMP        WORDWARE.CMP       [0023]          [B:]
HIGHFREQ.CMP        [..]               [0024]          [C:]
MAINDICT.CMP        [0008]             [0025]          [D:]
SPECIALS.CMP        [0009]             [COAST]         [E:]
SPECIFIC.CMP        [0017]             [DOC]
```

```
OPTIONS  user dictionary: 0009.CMP
         lookup: Quick(Complete)           ignore all caps: Yes(No)
         alternatives:(Auto)Manual         check punctuation:(Yes)No
Enter filename of user dictionary or press F1 to select from list
Pg1 Li3 Co9        {loading·}       ?                          LINCOLN.DOC
```

4. Select SPECIALS.CMP by pressing arrow keys. Press **Enter**. The Library Spell menu reappears.
5. Type **I**. Word searches for the next incorrect spelling or punctuation.

```
come to dedicate a portion of that field as a final resting place
for those who here gave their lives that that nation might  live.
It is altogether fitting and proper that we should do this.

                              Spell

 that  is repeated

SPELL: Correct Add Exit Ignore Options Undo

Select correction for unknown word and press Enter, or press Esc to use menu
Pg1 Li10 Co45       {Press·}         ?                          LINCOLN.DOC
```

6. Type **U**. Word returns to the previous misspelling.
7. Type **C**. The Library Spell Correct form appears.

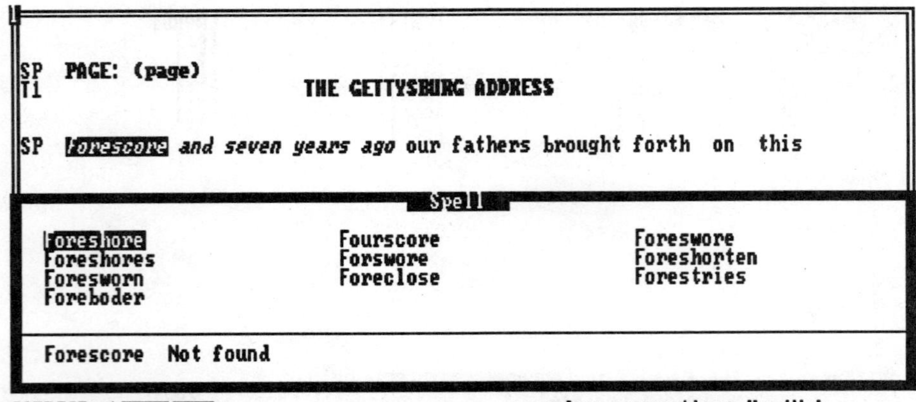

8. Select Fourscore by pressing arrow keys. Press **Enter**. Word corrects the misspelling and searches for the next misspelling.
9. Type **U** to undo the correction. Press **A**. The Library Spell Add form appears.

```
ADD word to: Standard User Document

Select dictionary
Pg1 Li3 Co9       {ur}            ?                              LINCOLN.DOC
```

10. Select Document by pressing **Right Arrow**. Press **Enter**. Word adds the word to the document dictionary.
11. Type **E**. Word returns to the Main menu and displays the number of misspellings and words checked.

```
    come to dedicate a portion of that field as a final resting place
    for those who here gave their lives that that nation might  live.
    It is altogether fitting and proper that we should do this.
.......................................................................
SP  But in a larger sense, we can dedicate -- we cannot consecrate --
    we cannot hallow -- this ground. The brave men, living  and  dead
    who struggled here, have consecrated it, far above our poor power
    to add or detract. The world will little note, nor long remember,
    what we say here, but it can never forget what they did here.  It
    is for us  the  living,  rather  to  be  dedicated  here  to  the
                                                          LINCOLN.DOC
COMMAND: Copy Delete Format Gallery Help Insert Jump Library
         Options Print Quit Replace Search Transfer Undo Window
86 words checked, 2 unknown
Pg1 Li10 Co45      {ur}            ?                    Microsoft Word
```

12. Turn to Module 39 to continue the learning sequence.

Module 38
LIBRARY TABLE

DESCRIPTION

The Library Table command creates a table of contents from the outline or marked text in your document. You access the Library Table command by pressing Esc and typing L, then T.

```
LIBRARY: Autosort Document-retrieval Hyphenate Index Link Number Run Spell
         Table thEsaurus
Compiles table of contents from outline or coded entries
P1 D1 L1 C1         {·in·your·}      ?                       Microsoft Word
```

Word provides two methods for creating tables. The first method uses your document outline. To use this feature, you must define the paragraph style used for the outline with the Heading variant. Each heading level variant create a different level in the table. The other method works similar to the Library Index command. You begin by marking the starting and ending text. You can mark the beginning of the text with *.Letter.* The letter consists of any alpha character except d, g, i, p, and l. Word uses these characters for other purposes. You mark the end of the text with a semicolon, paragraph mark, or division mark.

The Library Table form contains six fields. The From field selects which method Word uses to generate the table. If you select Codes, Word looks at the Index Code field to determine which hidden text letter to look for. The Page Numbers field allows you to tell Word to include page numbers in the table listing. The Entry/Page Number Separated By field usually contains a control code (default tab). You can also use spaces or any other character you wish. The Indent Each Level field tells Word how much to index each table level when you don't use a spreadsheet. The Use Style Sheet field tells Word that you defined how you want the table formatted using a stylesheet.

Word provides many shortcuts for mouse users. There are no mouse commands associated specifically with this command. Generic mouse movements and commands appear in Appendix E.

APPLICATIONS

Use the Library Table command whenever you need to create any type of reference table. The most common tables created using this command include table of contents and table of illustrations. Using the Library Table command saves time in generating a table of contents as your text changes. You could also use this command to create lists of authorities and other reference tables.

TYPICAL OPERATION

In this example you create a table of contents using the outline method. Begin this example at the Main menu with LINCOLN.DOC loaded in the current window.

1. Press **Ctrl-PgUp** to advance the text cursor to the beginning of the document. Press **F10** three times to select the first paragraph. Press **Enter**. Word creates a new paragraph.
2. Press **Up Arrow**. Press **Esc**. Type **F**, then **P** to select the Format Paragraph command. Select Left in the Alignment field by pressing **Spacebar**. Press **Enter**. Word changes the paragraph format.
3. Press **Esc**. Type **F**, then **C** to select the Format Character command. Press **Spacebar** to select Yes in the Bold field. Press **Tab**, then **Spacebar** to select No in the Italics field. Press **Enter**. Word changes the character format.
4. Press **Esc**. Type **F**, then **S**, then **R** to record the new style. Type **H2**. Press **Tab** twice. Press **F1** to obtain a list of paragraph styles. Select Heading Level 2 by pressing arrow keys. Press **Tab**. Type **Bold, Left Justified**. Word creates a new paragraph style in the stylesheet. The Format Stylesheet Record form appears as shown below.

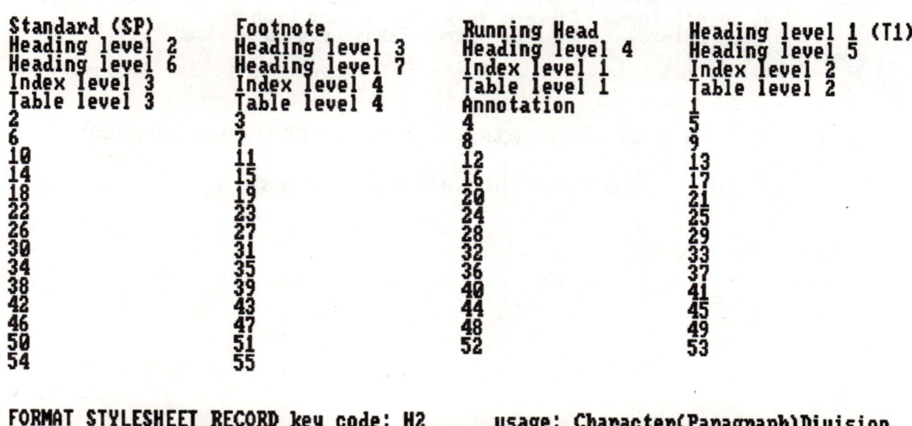

5. Press **Enter** and type **Paragraph 1**. Select the first letter of the second paragraph by pressing arrow keys. Press **Enter**, then **Up Arrow**. Press **Alt-H2**. Type **Paragraph 2**. Select the first letter of the third paragraph by pressing arrow keys. Press **Enter**, then **Up Arrow**. Press **Alt-H2**. Type **Paragraph 3**.
6. Press **Esc**. Type **L**, then **T**. The Library Table form appears.

```
LIBRARY TABLE from: Outline Codes          index code: C
       page numbers:(Yes)No                entry/page number separated by: ^t
       indent each level: 0.4"             use style sheet: Yes(No)
Select option
P3 D1 L1 C12       {.}              ?                                  Microsoft Word
```

7. Press **Spacebar** to select Outline. Select the Use Style Sheet field by pressing arrow keys. Press **Spacebar** to select Yes. Press **Enter**. Word generates a table of contents. Notice the hidden text indicating the beginning and end of each table. Notice the division indicator shows this is the third division.

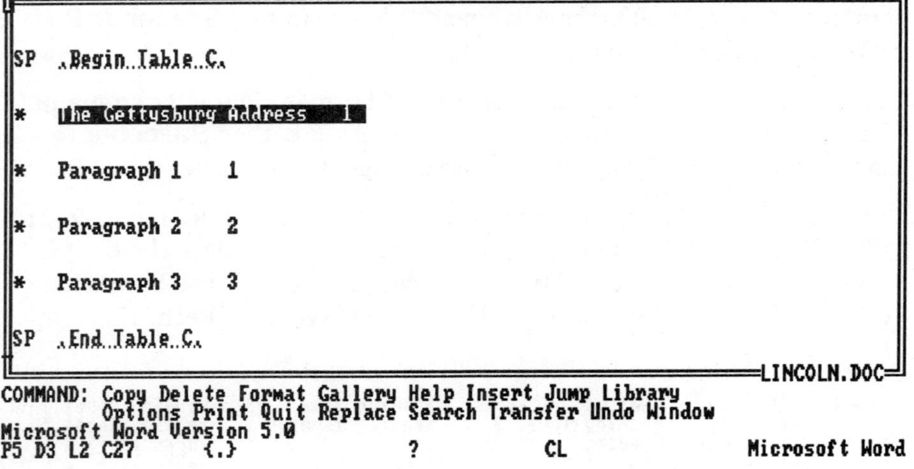

8. Press **Esc**. Type **T**, then **A**. Word saves the document and stylesheet.
9. Turn to Module 13 to continue the learning sequence.

Module 39
LIBRARY THESAURUS

DESCRIPTION

The Library Thesaurus command provides a list of words with similar meanings to the word you select by pointing to it with the text cursor (the base word). This command allows you to vary the language in a document without changing its meaning. You access the Library Thesaurus command by pressing Esc and typing L, then E. You can also press Ctrl-F6 to access the thesaurus without using the Library Thesaurus command.

```
LIBRARY: Autosort Document-retrieval Hyphenate Index Link Number Run Spell
         Table Thesaurus
Displays list of synonyms for selected word
Pg1 Li1 Co1        {You·b}        ?          CL                  Microsoft Word
```

If the thesaurus does not find the base word, Word presents a window containing a list of words with similar spellings. By highlighting the appropriate word and pressing Enter, you can find a listing of synonyms.

The Library Thesaurus menu contains four commands. The arrow symbols show you can highlight the displayed synonyms by pressing arrow keys. The Enter command replaces the original word with the word or group of words you highlight. (Sometimes the thesaurus will display phrases with similar meanings to your original word.) The Esc command returns you to the Main menu without replacing a word. Pressing Ctrl-F6 continues the synonym search using the word you highlight in the thesaurus window.

The thesaurus window contains three distinct sections. The base word appears in the upper left corner followed by a colon (:). The word usage appears in the leftmost column (for example, verb, noun, or adj). The list of synonyms appears to the right of the usage indication. Word groups the synonyms according to usage and general meaning. This makes it easier for you to find the correct synonym.

Word provides many shortcuts for mouse users. The mouse commands associated specifically with the Thesaurus command appear in Table 39-1. Generic mouse movements and commands appear in Appendix E.

TABLE 39-1. MOUSE COMMANDS

Action	*Pointing To*	*Result*
Push Left Button	Enter if Base Word Found	Word replaces the base word with the highlighted word.
Push Left Button	Enter if Base Word Not Found	Word finds the highlighted word in the thesaurus.
Push Left Button	Esc	Word leaves the thesaurus and returns to the Main menu without changing the base word.
Push Left Button	Ctrl-F6	Word finds synonyms for the highlighted word found in the thesaurus.
Push Left Button	Ctrl-PgUp	Word returns to the previous thesaurus window. (Finds the previous word.)
Push Right Button	Synonym	Word replaces the base word with the highlighted word.
Push Right and Left Buttons	Anywhere Except the Thesaurus Menu or Window	Word cancels the current operation and returns to Main menu.

APPLICATIONS

The Thesaurus command provides an elegant method of increasing the effectiveness and appearance of your document through the use of varied grammar. This command also allows you to find synonyms with a slightly different context than the highlighted word. You can use this as an aid to writing when you don't remember exactly what word you want to use. Finally, you can use synonyms of words to increase or decrease the line length when using fonts with justified margins. By changing the line length, you can reduce large open spaces that appear between words.

TYPICAL OPERATION

In this example you use the Thesaurus command to find synonyms for several words. You also see what happens when Word cannot find the base word in the thesaurus dictionary. Begin the example at the Main menu with LINCOLN.DOC loaded in the current window.

1. Select nation by pressing arrow keys. Press **Ctrl-F6**. The Library Thesaurus window appears.

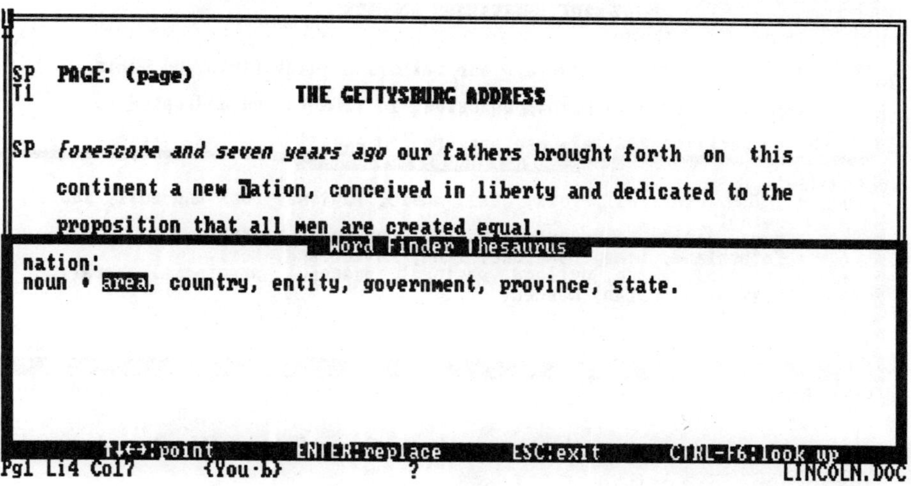

2. Highlight government by pressing arrow keys. Press **Enter**. Word substitutes the word government for nation.

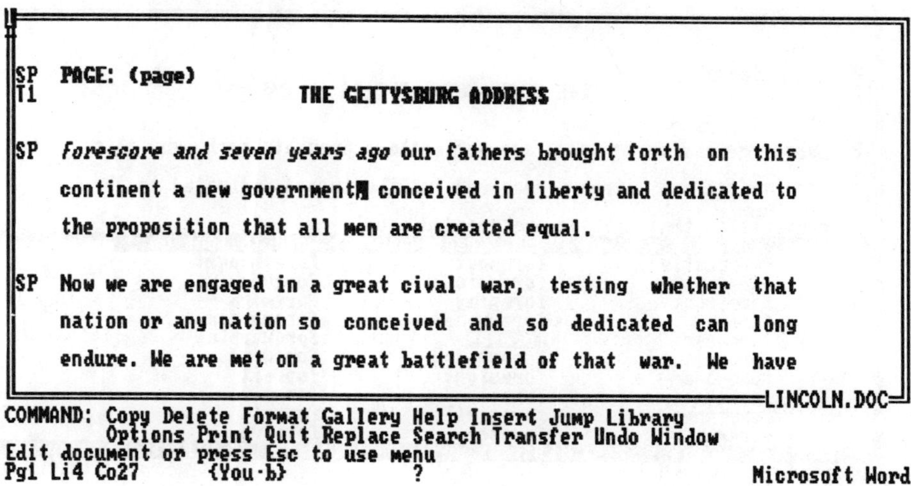

3. Press **Ctrl-F6**. The Library Thesaurus window appears.
4. Highlight country by pressing arrow keys. Press **Ctrl-F6**. The thesaurus finds synonyms for country. Notice that country has two different parts of speech uses.

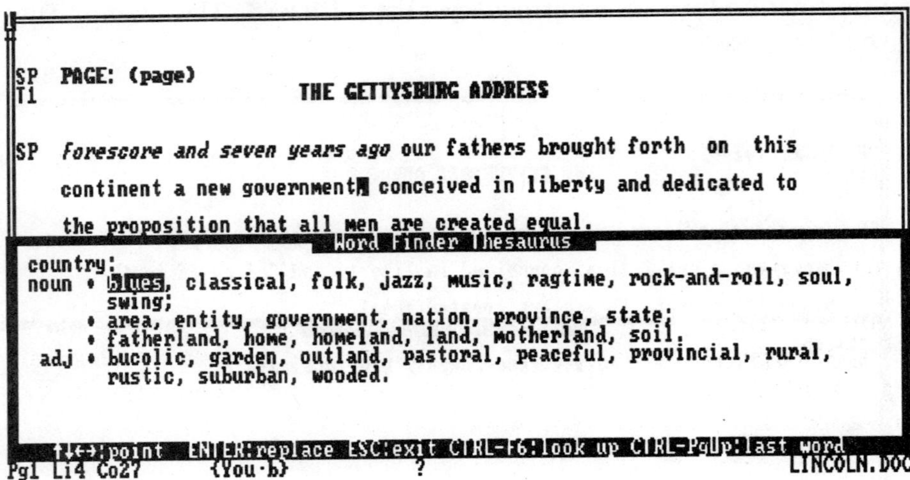

5. Highlight nation by pressing arrow keys. Press **Enter**. Word replaces the word government with nation.
6. Select Forescore by pressing arrow keys. Press **Ctrl-F6**. Word displays a word not found message.

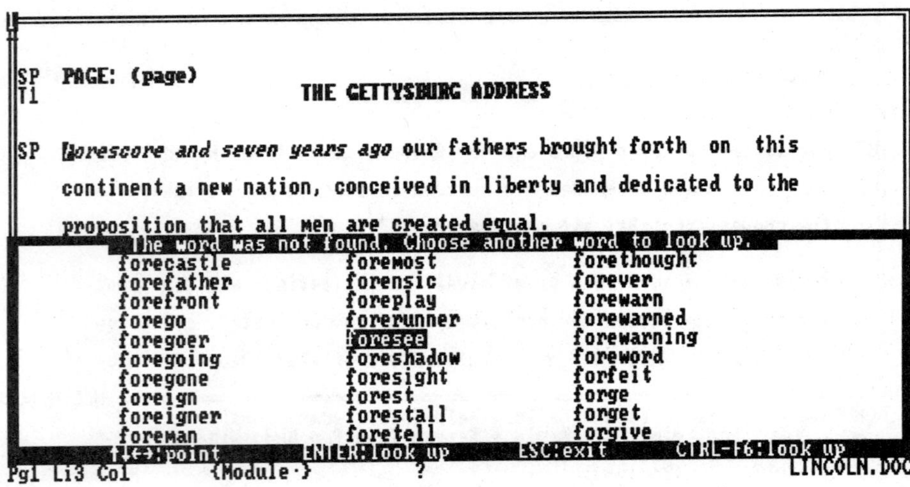

7. Highlight foreword by pressing arrow keys. Press **Enter**. The thesaurus finds synonyms of foreword. Notice Word allows you to back up to the previous screen by pressing Ctrl-PgUp.
8. Press **Esc**. The Main menu reappears.
9. Turn to Module 33 to continue the learning sequence.

Module 40
OPTIONS

DESCRIPTION

The Options command on the Main menu allows you to change many Word parameters. These parameters include display settings and miscellaneous equipment settings. Word splits these options into two groups: Window Options, which control window appearance, and General Options, which control all other features. You access the Options command by pressing Esc, then typing O.

```
COMMAND: Copy Delete Format Gallery Help Insert Jump Library
         Options Print Quit Replace Search Transfer Undo Window
Sets display and operation options; turns menu on/off
Pg1 Li1 Col      {}                ?                        Microsoft Word
```

WINDOW OPTIONS The For Window Number field determines which window (if more than one is active) any changes affect. Word allows you to use a maximum of eight windows. Word always defaults to the currently active window (the one with the number highlighted in the upper left corner). You can change the affected window by typing a different window number in the field.

The Show Hidden Text field determines if Word displays hidden text. When you select Yes, Word displays any text you formatted as hidden. Hidden text normally contains notes or other text you don't want to print.

The Show Ruler field determines if Word displays a ruler accross the top of the window. The ruler allows you to change tab stops and margins without using the Format command. It also shows you where text will appear when printed if you set Show Layout to Yes.

The Show Non-Printing Symbols field controls the display of control codes and contains three options. The first option, None, displays no control codes at all. The second and third options, Partial and All, display control codes used to format the text appearing on screen. All displays every control code used by Word to format the text. Partial displays only the paragraph, newline, and optional hyphen codes. Table 40-1 lists the control codes used in Word and describes their function.

TABLE 40-1. TEXT FORMATTING CONTROL CODES

Code	*Description*
¶	Paragraph Mark - Shows where you placed carriage returns in the document. Since Word automatically word wraps sentences within a paragraph, no mark appears at the end of each line.
↓	Newline Character - Shows where you added a new line of text to a document without using a carriage return.
-	Optional Hyphen Character - Shows where you added an optional hyphen to a document. Word splits words at the place marked by an optional hyphen when necessary.
⇹	Hidden Text Marker - Shows the position of a hidden note or comment.

The Show Layout field controls the screen text positioning. When you set Show Layout to Yes, Word shows the beginning and end of each line as it would appear when printed. This includes columns and other formatting features, but not graphics. This allows you to add optional hyphens as necessary to provide pleasing output. The disadvantage to using the Show Layout display is that some text scrolls off the right side of the screen when using larger paper or finer print. This reduces your ability to read the text as you type. The Show Layout option significantly slows screen updates and other Word functions.

The Show Line Breaks field performs a function like the Show Layout option. However, instead of showing all layout features, Word shows where each line will break when you select Yes. This means that columnar text will not appear in its printed format. This option does allow Word to update the screen quicker than the Show Layout option.

The Show Outline field places Word in the outline mode when you select Yes. In outline mode, you can view as much or little of the text as you like. You can also restructure your document quicker than in edit mode.

The Show Style Bar field determines if Word displays the style used by a paragraph or division on the left side of the window. By knowing what style your paragraph uses, you can make global changes to your document more easily by using the Gallery command.

GENERAL OPTIONS The Mute field determines if Word produces an audible tone when a keyboard or other error occurs. When you select Yes, Word sounds a tone for each mistake.

The Summary Sheet option interfaces with the Document-Retrieval option of the Library menu. When you select Yes, Word asks you for document details to place in a document database (only on new documents). When you use the document-retrieval function, you can ask for documents based on various parameters including date and time.

The Measure field determines the unit of measure Word uses when displaying text on screen. The In option displays characters relative to inches. The Cm option displays characters relative to centimeters. The P10 and P12 options display the characters relative to 10- and 12-pitch fonts respectively. Finally, the Pt option displays characters relative to the current proportionally spaced font point size.

The Display Mode field changes the type of presentation Word uses from graphics to text. On some computers, using a CGA or Monochrome Display Adapter (MDA), the screen updates faster using text mode. In text mode you can use colors on a CGA display. The graphics mode allows you to see some characters as they actually appear. For example, bold lettering appears bold and italic letters are italicized. When using an Enhanced Graphics Adapter (EGA), this option also lets you select the number of text lines Word displays. This allows you to display more of your document at one time.

The Paginate field allows you to select between manual and automatic pagination of your document. When you select Automatic, Word repaginates the document for you automatically. When you select Manual, Word waits until you select the Repaginate command on the Print menu before paginating your document.

The Colors field allows you to change the colors Word uses to paint the menus, window borders, and the window background. It also affects the message and status lines. Word changes the number of colors and how you can change them to reflect your display adapter type and the current display mode.

The Autosave field determines if Word saves your document automatically. The number you place in the field is the number of minutes between saves. If you use this option and you experience a computer or power failure, Word can recreate your document for you. If you type 0 in this field, Word does not automatically save your document.

The Autosave Confirm field determines if Word asks before it automatically saves your document. If you select Yes, Word will display a message on the message line before saving your document. When you select No, Word saves the document without asking.

The Show Menu field controls whether Word displays the Main menu at all times. Selecting No hides the Main menu, so you can see more text at one time. Word always displays the Main menu when you press Esc during an editing session.

The Show Borders field determines if Word provides a border around the text area. When using the keyboard exclusively, this option allows you to view more text. You must use a border when using a mouse; otherwise, you can't access the windows, positioning controls, or zoom command.

The Date Format field changes the method Word uses when inserting a live/static date into text. The two formats include month/day/year and day/month/year.

The Decimal Character field allows you to change the ASCII character Word uses for a decimal point.

The Time Format field changes the method Word uses when inserting a live/static time into text. When using the 24-hour option, 1 p.m. becomes 1300 (where the 00 portion equals the minutes).

The Default Tab Width field changes the spacing Word inserts between tabs when the current paragraph style does not define a spacing. Word ignores this field when you define the tab spacing for a paragraph.

The Line Numbers field allows you to display the current page line number pointed to by the cursor. Word places it in the lower left corner of the screen.

The Count Blank Space field changes the method Word uses to count lines of text in your document when you select Yes in the Line Numbers field. If you select Yes, Word counts both text and blank lines. For example, if you double spaced three lines of text, Word would count it as six when you select Yes. If you select No, Word counts only the actual lines of text without regard for spacing.

The Cursor Speed field determines how fast Word moves the cursor across the screen. This helps you compensate for the relative speed of different machines. The slowest speed is 0; the fastest speed is 9.

The Linedraw Character field changes the ASCII character Word uses in the Linedraw mode. When in Linedraw mode, you can use the cursor to draw boxes or other rectangular shapes. The ASCII character set provides several line thicknesses, double lines, and shaded line characters. Word uses all the appropriate characters associated with the selected character in this mode, even though you select the vertical character only.

The Speller Path field tells Word where to find the dictionary used with the spelling checker. Word sets this field automatically during installation.

Word allows you to use a mouse within the Options form. See Appendix E for general details on how to use a mouse with Word. Table 40-2 shows the mouse actions associated specifically with the Options command.

TABLE 40-2. MOUSE COMMANDS

Action	*Pointing To*	*Result*
Push Left Button	Field	Word selects the field for change.
Push Left Button	Form Name	Word makes the requested changes and returns to the document.
Push Right Button	Fill in the Blank Field	Word provides a list of acceptable choices. Word provides choices for the Menu Color and Linedraw Character entries only.
Push Right Button	Multiple Choice Field	Word makes the requested changes and returns to the document.
Push Right and Left Buttons	Anywhere Except the Form or Window	Word cancels the current operation and returns to Main menu.

APPLICATIONS

Use the Options command to change any of the parameters discussed in the description section of this module. These parameters include display settings and miscellaneous equipment settings. In most cases, you will change field entries on the Options form to suit personal tastes. For example, you can change the screen colors and cursor speed to meet your needs. In other instances you will change the field entries to achieve a desired effect in your document. For example, you can change the line thickness used as a border around a title.

TYPICAL OPERATION

In this example you learn how to change various Word settings using the Options command. Begin this example at the DOS prompt.

1. Type **WORD** and press **Enter**. The Word introductory screen then the Main menu appear.
2. Press **Esc** then type **O**. The Options form appears. Notice Word highlights the first option of the first field.

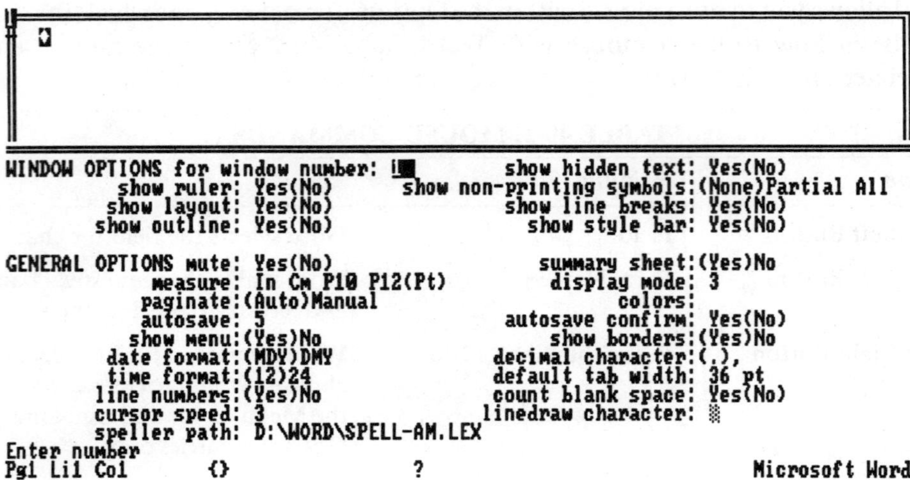

3. Select the Show Non-Printing Symbols field using the arrow keys. Press **Spacebar** twice. Notice the highlight moves to Partial, then to All.

4. Press **Enter**. Type **The Gettysburg Address** and press **Enter**. Notice Word places a dot symbol between each word to represent a space and a paragraph symbol to represent a carriage return.

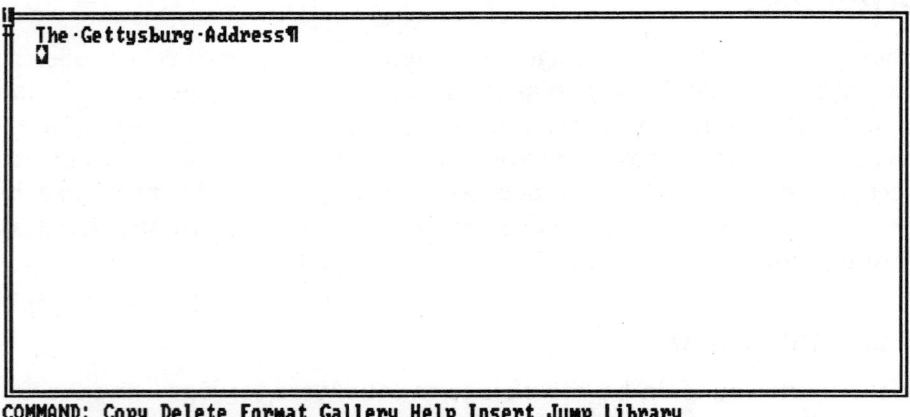

5. Press **Esc** then type **O**. The Options form appears.

6. Select the Show Non-Printing Symbols field using the arrow keys. Press **Spacebar** to select None, then press **Enter**. The control codes disappear.

7. Press **Esc** then type **O**. The Options form appears.

8. Select the Show Menu field using the arrow keys. Press **Spacebar** to select no, then press **Enter**. Word removes the Main menu from the display.

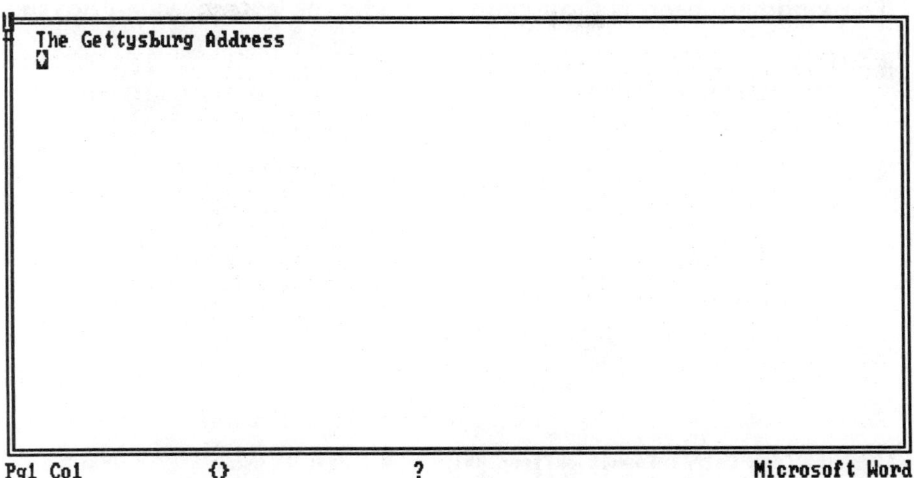

9. Press **PgDn**. Word beeps to indicate the end of document.
10. Press **Esc**. Notice the Main menu reappears.
11. Type **O**. The Options form appears.
12. Select the Show Menu field using the arrow keys. Press **Spacebar** to select yes. Select the Mute field using the arrow keys. Press **Spacebar** to select yes, then **Enter**. Press **PgDn**. Word does not beep to indicate the end of document.
13. Press **Esc** then type **O**. The Options form appears.
14. Select the Mute field using the arrow keys. Press **Spacebar**. Select the Show Ruler field using the arrow keys and press **Spacebar**. Select the Show Style Bar field using the arrow keys and press **Spacebar**. Press **Enter**. Word displays the ruler and style bar (the asterisks on the left side of each line of text).

```
L[········1········2········3········4········5········6····]····7···
*   The Gettysburg Address
*
```

15. Press **Esc** then type **O**. The Options form appears.
16. Select the Show Borders field using the arrow keys, press **Spacebar**, then **Enter**. The window appears without borders. Notice the text moved left two spaces.

```
▌   L[········1·········2·········3·········4·········5·········6····]····7····
-*   The Gettysburg Address
 *   ▯

COMMAND: Copy Delete Format Gallery Help Insert Jump Library
         Options Print Quit Replace Search Transfer Undo Window
Microsoft Word Version 5.0
Pg1 Co1           { }           ?                            Microsoft Word
```

17. Press **Esc** then type **O**. Select the Show Borders field using the arrow keys, press **Spacebar** to select yes, then **Enter**. The window appears with borders.
18. Press **Esc** then type **Q**. Word asks if you want to save your edits.

```
QUIT:

Enter Y to save changes to document, N to lose changes, or Esc to cancel ▮
Pg1 Co1           { }           ?                            Microsoft Word
```

19. Type **N**. The DOS prompt appears.
20. Turn to Module 45 to continue the learning sequence.

Module 41
PRINT

DESCRIPTION

The Print menu contains the eight output commands supplied by Word. These selections include provisions for sending output to the printer, display, or a file. The input comes from the glossary, keyboard, or current document. You access the Print command by pressing Esc, then typing P.

```
COMMAND: Copy Delete Format Gallery Help Insert Jump Library
         Options Print Quit Replace Search Transfer Undo Window
Prints, repaginates, sets printing options
Pg1 Li1 Col       {}           ?          CL                Microsoft Word
```

Word provides many shortcuts for mouse users. The mouse commands associated specifically with this command appear in Table 41-1. Generic mouse movements and commands appear in Appendix E.

TABLE 41-1. MOUSE COMMANDS

Action	*Pointing To*	*Result*
Push Left Button	Menu Selection	Word presents the requested form or submenu or executes the requested command.
Push Left Button	Field	Word selects the field for change.
Push Left Button	Form Name	Word makes the requested changes and returns to the document.
Push Right Button	Field	Word makes the requested changes and returns to the document.
Push Right and Left Buttons	Anywhere Except the Form or Window	Word cancels the current operation and returns to the Main menu.

PRINTER The Print Printer command sends the contents of the current document to the printer. Word prints the document exactly as formatted.

DIRECT The Print Direct command sends input from the keyboard directly to the printer. By using this command, you can send control codes or text directly to the printer. Word continues to send input from the keyboard until you press Esc.

FILE The Print File command sends the contents of the current document to a file. Word asks which file you would like to send the output to. If the file exists, Word asks if you want to overwrite it before beginning the print sequence. Unlike other fields asking for a filename, the Print File form does not allow you to use F1 to obtain a list of files in the current directory.

GLOSSARY The Print Glossary command sends the contents of the glossary (except the six standard entries) to the printer. Word prints the name and contents of each entry. The contents include any control codes included with the entry (for example page breaks).

MERGE The Print Merge command combines the contents of a data file with the current document. This provides an easy method of creating form letters. Word prints an error message and provides an audible signal each time it encounters an error in the data file. Appendix G shows how to create a form letter using Word.

OPTIONS The Print Options form provides access to various print functions. These include printer name, destination, and number of copies. The Printer field contains the filename for the Word print driver to use while printing. The Setup field contains the destination port for the printed output. Acceptable destinations include LPT1: through LPT3: and COM1: through COM2:. The Model field contains the actual printer model number. The Graphics Resolution field contains the number of dots per inch Word uses to print graphics. The higher the number, the better the quality of the graphic output. When you select a high resolution number, the printout time dramatically increases because the printer places more dots on the page. The Copies field tells Word how many copies of the document to print. Word does not place a limit on how many copies you request. The Draft field selects whether Word uses the final print output described by the stylesheet or the draft mode described by the printer definition file. The Hidden Text field selects whether Word prints the contents of hidden text paragraphs. The Summary Sheet field outputs the user provided summary to the printer when active. The summary is part of the save procedure when selected by the Commands menu. The Range field works with the Page Numbers field to define how much of the document Word prints. The Widow/Orphan Control field changes how Word prints paragraphs. A widow is a single sentence from a paragraph printed at the bottom of a page. An orphan is a single sentence from a paragraph printed at the top of a page. When active, the widow/orphan control keeps at least two sentences from a paragraph together. This makes a document look neater. The Queued field controls whether Word places a document into a print queue for printing or prints it directly. By placing the document in the print queue, you can resume working almost immediately after selecting print, although at reduced speed. The Paper Feed field controls dot matrix and laser printers. It selects where the printer retrieves paper for printing purposes. The Duplex field tells Word to print on both sides of the paper if the printer supports duplex printing. Some laser printers currently support duplex printing.

QUEUE The Print Queue command contains a submenu for controlling the print queue. The Continue command restarts printing at a previously paused point. The Pause command temporarily suspends printing. The Restart command restarts printing after a pause. Instead of restarting at the point of pause, Word restarts the document at the beginning of the print sequence. The Stop command stops Word from printing the current copy of the current document. If more copies or documents reside in the queue, Word begins printing the next item.

REPAGINATE The Print Repaginate command causes Word to redefine the page breaks. You can either tell Word where each page break should occur, or allow Word to create the page breaks automatically. You only need to use this command if you selected Manual in the Paginate field of the Options form; otherwise, Word automatically updates the pagination for you.

PREVIEW The Print Preview command allows you to see exactly how your document will appear before you print it. Word allows you to see up to two pages at a time. The Print Preview Exit command cancels preview mode and redisplays the Main menu. The Print Preview Jump command allows you to move quickly from one section of the document to another. You can also move one page at a time by pressing PgDn or PgUp. The Print Preview Options menu contains three commands. The Print Preview Options 1-Page command tells Word to display only one page at a time. The Print Preview Options 2-Page command tells Word to display two pages at a time. Word does not differentiate between odd and even pages using this option. The Print Preview Options Facing-Pages command tells Word to display two pages with the even page on the left side of the screen and the odd page on the right side of the screen. When you use this particular option, pressing PgUp or PgDn moves you two pages at a time through the document. When you display page 1 using this option, only page 1 appears on the right side of the screen. Word displays nothing of the left side of the screen.

APPLICATIONS

Use the Print menu whenever you need to output a document to the printer, display, or a file. Use the Direct command to control how the printed output appears. The Glossary command allows you to send text fragments and macros to the printer. Using the Merge command allows you to create form letters or other form documents (for example purchase orders or checks). Use the File command to send a document to a file rather than the printer.

The Print Preview command is a new enhancement to version 5.0 of Word. Use it to see the final document output. This is especially convenient when using a laser printer to produce a document with a large number of fonts or graphics.

TYPICAL OPERATION

In this example you exercise various print commands. Begin this example at the DOS prompt.

1. Type **WORD** and press **Enter** to start Word. Press **Esc**. Type **T**, then **L** to select the Transfer Load command. Press **F1**. Select LINCOLN.DOC using the arrow keys. Press **Enter**. The Gettysburg Address appears.
2. Type the following text.

   But in a larger sense, we can dedicate — we cannot consecrate — we cannot hallow — this ground. The brave men, living and dead who struggled here, have consecrated it, far above our poor power to add or detract. The world will little note, nor long remember, what we say here, but it can never forget what they did here. It is for us the living, rather to be dedicated here to the unfinished work which they who fought here have thus far so nobly advanced. It is rather, to be dedicated here to the great task remaining before us — that from these honored dead we take increased devotion to that cause for which they gave the last full measure of devotion — that we here highly resolve that these dead shall not have died in vain — that this nation, under God, shall have a new birth of freedom — and that government of the people, by the people, for the people, shall not perish from this earth.
3. Place the cursor on the first paragraph using the arrow keys. Press **F6**, then **Ctrl-PgDn**. Word selects all three paragraphs.

4. Press **Up Arrow** twice, then **Esc**. Type **F**, then **P**. Select the Line Spacing field using **Tab**. Type **3**. Select the Space After field using **Tab**. Type **3** and press **Enter**. Word changes the format of the three paragraphs.

```
resolve that these dead shall not have died in vain -- that this

nation, under God, shall have a new birth of freedom -- and that

government of the people, by the people, for the people, shall not

perish from this earth.


::::::::::::::::::::::::::::::::::::::::::::::::::::::::::::::::::::::::
*  ♦

                                                          LINCOLN.DOC
COMMAND: Copy Delete Format Gallery Help Insert Jump Library
         Options Print Quit Replace Search Transfer Undo Window
Edit document or press Esc to use menu
Pg1 Li24 Co1      {¶}              ?          CL        EX        Microsoft Word
```

5. Press **Esc**. Type **P**. Word displays the Print menu.

```
PRINT: Printer Direct File Glossary Merge Options Queue Repaginate preView

Prints document in the active window
Pg2 Li15 Co1      {}               ?                              Microsoft Word
```

6. Type **R**. The Print Repaginate form appears.

```
PRINT REPAGINATE confirm page breaks: Yes No

Select option
Pg1 Li24 Co1      {¶}              ?          CL        EX        Microsoft Word
```

7. Press **Spacebar** to select yes, then **Enter**. Word displays a page break position and asks if you want to place the page break there.

```
here, but it can never forget what they did here. It  is  for  us  the

living, rather to be dedicated here to the unfinished work which  they

who fought here have thus far so nobly advanced. It is rather,  to  be
.......................................................................

dedicated here to the great task remaining  before  us  --  that  from

these honored dead we take increased devotion to that cause for which

they gave the last full measure of devotion --  that  we  here  highly
                                                           LINCOLN.DOC
PRINT REPAGINATE confirm page breaks:(Yes)No

Enter Y to confirm or use direction keys
Pg2 Li1 Co1       {¶}                ?          CL             Microsoft Word
```

8. Press **Up Arrow** seven times. Type **Y**. The Main menu reappears. Notice Word places the page break at the desired position.

```
proper that we should do this.



.......................................................................

But in a larger sense, we can dedicate -- we cannot consecrate  --  we

cannot hallow -- this ground. The  brave  men,  living  and  dead  who

struggled here, have consecrated it, far above our poor power  to  add
                                                           LINCOLN.DOC
COMMAND: Copy Delete Format Gallery Help Insert Jump Library
         Options Print Quit Replace Search Transfer Undo Window
31 lines and 367 words counted
Pg2 Li1 Co1       {¶}                ?                         Microsoft Word
```

9. Place the cursor on the first paragraph using the arrow keys. Press **F6**, then **Ctrl-PgDn**. Word selects all three paragraphs.

10. Press **Up Arrow** twice, then **Esc**. Type **F**, then **P**. Select the Line Spacing field using **Tab**. Type **1**. Select the Space After field using **Tab**. Type **1**. Press **Enter**. Word changes the format of the three paragraphs.

NOTE

The following steps assume you have a printer connected to your computer and you have no print spooler installed. Your screen may appear slightly different than the ones shown due to printer configuration. To bypass this section proceed to step 25.

11. Press **Esc**. Type **P**, then **O**. The Print Commands form appears.

```
PRINT OPTIONS printer: EPSONRX                    setup: LPT1:
      model: RX-80                                graphics resolution: 240 dpi
      copies: 1                                   draft: Yes(No)
      hidden text: Yes(No)                        summary sheet: Yes(No)
      range:(All)Selection Pages                  page numbers:
      widow/orphan control:(Yes)No                queued: Yes(No)
      paper feed: Continuous                      duplex: Yes(No)
Enter printer name or press F1 to select from list
Pg2 Li15 Co1      {}               ?                          Microsoft Word
```

12. Select the Copies field using **Tab**. Type **2**. Select the Queued field using **Tab**. Press **Spacebar**, then **Enter**. The Print menu reappears.
13. Press **Enter**. The printer begins printing.
14. Press **Esc**. Type **P**, then **Q**. The Print Queue form appears.

```
PRINT QUEUE: Continue Pause Restart Stop

Resumes printing after Pause command
Pg2 Li14 Co1      {}               ?                 EX       Microsoft Word
```

15. Type **P**. The printer stops printing.
16. Press **Esc**. Type **P**, then **Q**, then **C**. The printer starts printing where it left off.
17. Press **Esc**. Type **P**, then **Q**, then **P**. The printer stops printing.
18. Press **Esc**. Type **P**, then **Q**, then **R**. The printer starts a new copy of the document.
19. Press **Esc**. Type **P**, then **Q**, then **S**. The printer stops printing. The printer starts the second copy of the document if not already started when you issued the stop command.
20. Press **Esc**. Type **C**. The Copy form appears.

```
COPY to: {}

Enter glossary name or press F1 to select from list
Pg2 Li14 Co1      {}               ?                          Microsoft Word
```

21. Type **TEMP**, then press **Enter**. The Main menu reappears.

22. Press **Esc**. Type **P**, then **G**. Word prints the glossary contents (the highlighted text). Notice Word adds the glossary name (TEMP) and any document control codes.

23. Press **Esc**. Type **P**, then **D**. The Print Direct form appears.

```
PRINT DIRECT:

Enter text
Pg2 Li14 Col     {}              ?                         Microsoft Word
```

24. Type **THIS IS A WAY OF SENDING INFORMATION OR CONTROL CHARACTERS DIRECTLY TO THE PRINTER**. Press **Enter** then **Esc**. Word sends the string directly to the printer. The Main menu reappears. Notice Word does not display the typed text on screen.

25. Press **Esc**. Type **P**, then **F**. Word asks for a filename.

```
PRINT FILE name: █

Enter filename
Pg2 Li14 Col     {}              ?                         Microsoft Word
```

26. Type **TEMP** and press **Enter**. Word displays a printing message but does not send the output to the printer.

27. Press **Esc**. Type **P**, then **V**. The Print Preview display appears.

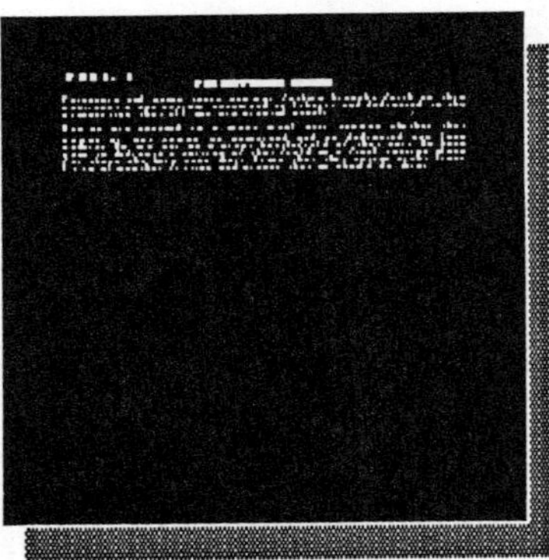

```
PRINT PREVIEW: Exit Jump Options Print

Use PgUp and PgDn to scroll through document
Pg1                           ?                              LINCOLN.DOC
```

28. Type **E**. The Main menu reappears.

29. Press **Esc**. Type **T**, then **S**. The Transfer Save form appears.

30. Press **Enter**. Word displays a file save message. The Main menu appears.
31. Press **Esc**. Type **Q**. Word asks if you want to save the glossary.

```
QUIT:

Enter Y to save glossary, N to lose edits, or Esc to cancel █
Pg2 Li14 Co1      {}                    ?                    Microsoft Word
```

32. Type **N**. The DOS prompt appears.
33. Turn to Module 19 to continue the learning sequence.

Module 42
QUIT

DESCRIPTION

The Quit command on the Main menu allows you to leave Word after an editing session. If you change the document, glossary, or style sheet and don't save it, Word asks if you want to save it before quitting. To quit from the keyboard, press Esc, then type Q. To use a mouse with this command, simply press the left mouse button while pointing to the Quit command with the mouse pointer.

```
COMMAND: Copy Delete Format Gallery Help Insert Jump Library
         Options Print Quit Replace Search Transfer Undo Window
Ends Word session
Pg1 Li1 Co1      {}              ?          CL              Microsoft Word
```

APPLICATIONS

Use the Quit command whenever you complete an editing session. Word always gives you the option to save all files before you quit.

TYPICAL OPERATION

In this example you quit from the Word Main menu using the keyboard. Begin at the DOS prompt.

1. Type **WORD** and press **Enter**. The Word introductory screen, then the Main menu appears.
2. Press **Esc**. Word highlights the first option of the Main menu.

```
COMMAND: Copy Delete Format Gallery Help Insert Jump Library
         Options Print Quit Replace Search Transfer Undo Window
Copies selected text to scrap or to a named glossary entry
Pg1 Li1 Co1      {}              ?                          Microsoft Word
```

3. Type **Q**. The DOS prompt appears.
4. Turn to Module 27 to continue the learning sequence.

Module 43
REPLACE

DESCRIPTION

The Replace command on the Main menu searches for a specific string and replaces it with another string. Word always begins searching at the position pointed to by the text cursor. A search and replace procedure always searches from the top of the document to the bottom.

```
COMMAND: Copy Delete Format Gallery Help Insert Jump Library
         Options Print Quit Replace Search Transfer Undo Window
Replaces specified text with new text
Pg1 Li1 Co1       {}            ?                        Microsoft Word
```

Word provides many shortcuts for mouse users. There are no mouse commands associated specifically with this command. Generic mouse movements and commands appear in Appendix E.

The Text field contains the character string Word looks for. The With Text field tells Word what to put in place of the search text. The Confirm field tells Word to ask about each replacement when you select YES; otherwise, Word automatically replaces all the matching strings. The Case field determines whether Word differentiates between upper and lowercase letters. Selecting NO means that Word will not differentiate between upper and lowercase letters. The Whole Word field determines if Word will look for partial matches. For example if you type JOIN for the text field, and select YES for the Whole Word field, Word will not stop if it sees JOINING.

APPLICATIONS

Use the Replace command whenever you need to remove or replace text. You can remove repetitive text by specifying a Text field without a With Text field. Word replaces the search text with nothing. The Confirm, Case, and Whole Word fields help you define exactly how you want Word to look for the specified text.

TYPICAL OPERATION

In this example you use the Replace command to search and replace text. This example also shows what happens when you ask Word to search for text that doesn't exist in the document. Begin this example at the Main menu with LINCOLN.DOC loaded in the current window.

1. Press **Esc**. Type **R**. The Replace form appears.

```
REPLACE text: █                              with text:
        confirm:(Yes)No  case: Yes(No) whole word: Yes(No)
Enter text
Pg1 Li1 Co1      {}                ?                         Microsoft Word
```

2. Type **THAT** in the Text field and press **Tab**. Type **THET** in the With Text field and press **Tab** twice. Press **Spacebar** for yes, then **Enter**. Word displays an error message, "Search text not found."

```
COMMAND: Copy Delete Format Gallery Help Insert Jump Library
         Options Print Quit Replace Search Transfer Undo Window
Search text not found
Pg1 Li1 Co1      {}                ?                         Microsoft Word
```

3. Press **Esc**. Type **R**. The Replace form appears. Notice Word retained the previous selections.

4. Press **Tab** three times, then **Spacebar**, then **Enter** to change the Confirm field from No to Yes. Word finds the first occurrence of the word THAT and asks if you want to replace it.

```
SP  PAGE: (page)
T1                    THE GETTYSBURG ADDRESS

SP  Forescore and seven years ago our fathers brought forth  on  this
    continent a new nation, conceived in liberty and dedicated to the
    proposition that all men are created equal.

SP  Now we are engaged in a great cival  war,  testing  whether  that
    nation or any nation so  conceived  and  so  dedicated  can  long
    endure. We are met on a great battlefield of that  war.  We  have
                                                          LINCOLN.DOC
REPLACE text: THAT                       with text: THET
        confirm:(Yes)No  case: Yes(No) whole word: Yes(No)
Enter Y to replace, N to ignore, or press Esc to cancel █
Pg1 Li5 Co16     {}                ?            CL           Microsoft Word
```

5. Type **Y**. Word replaces the word THAT with THET, then highlights the next occurrence of the word THAT. Notice Word uses the same case lettering you typed in.

```
SP  PAGE: (page)
T1                        THE GETTYSBURG ADDRESS

SP  Forescore and seven years ago our fathers brought forth  on  this
    continent a new nation, conceived in liberty and dedicated to the
    proposition THET all men are created equal.

SP  Now we are engaged in a great cival  war,  testing  whether  that
    nation or any nation so  conceived  and  so  dedicated  can  long
    endure. We are met on a great battlefield of that  war.  We  have
                                                          LINCOLN.DOC
REPLACE text: THAT                  with text: THET
        confirm:(Yes)No  case: Yes(No) whole word: Yes(No)
Enter Y to replace, N to ignore, or press Esc to cancel
Pg1 Li6 Co65     {}               ?          CL           Microsoft Word
```

6. Press **Esc**. The Main menu appears. Word lists how many replacements it made. Notice the second occurrence of the word THAT remains highlighted.

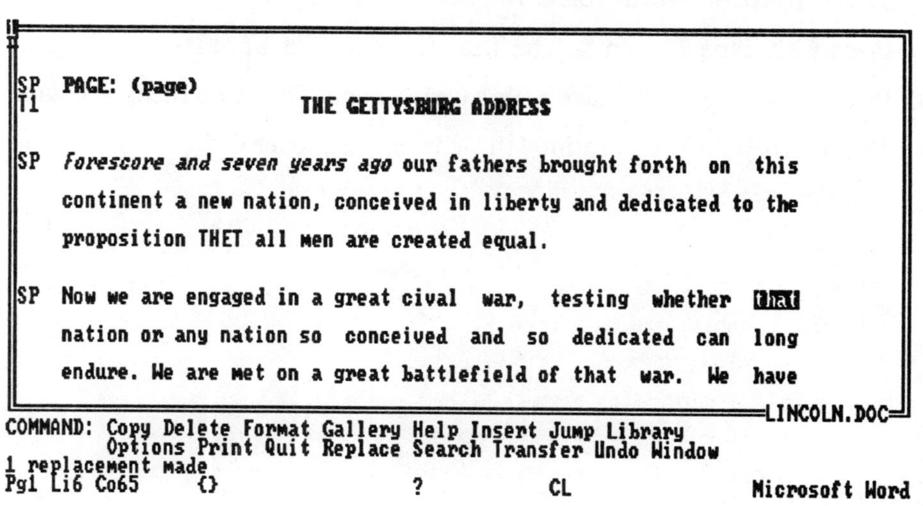

```
SP  PAGE: (page)
T1                        THE GETTYSBURG ADDRESS

SP  Forescore and seven years ago our fathers brought forth  on  this
    continent a new nation, conceived in liberty and dedicated to the
    proposition THET all men are created equal.

SP  Now we are engaged in a great cival  war,  testing  whether  that
    nation or any nation so  conceived  and  so  dedicated  can  long
    endure. We are met on a great battlefield of that  war.  We  have
                                                          LINCOLN.DOC
COMMAND: Copy Delete Format Gallery Help Insert Jump Library
         Options Print Quit Replace Search Transfer Undo Window
1 replacement made
Pg1 Li6 Co65     {}               ?          CL           Microsoft Word
```

7. Press **Left Arrow**, then **Esc**. Type **R**. Press **Tab** twice, then **Spacebar** to change the Confirm field from Yes to No. Press **Enter**. Word replaces all occurrences of THAT with THET.

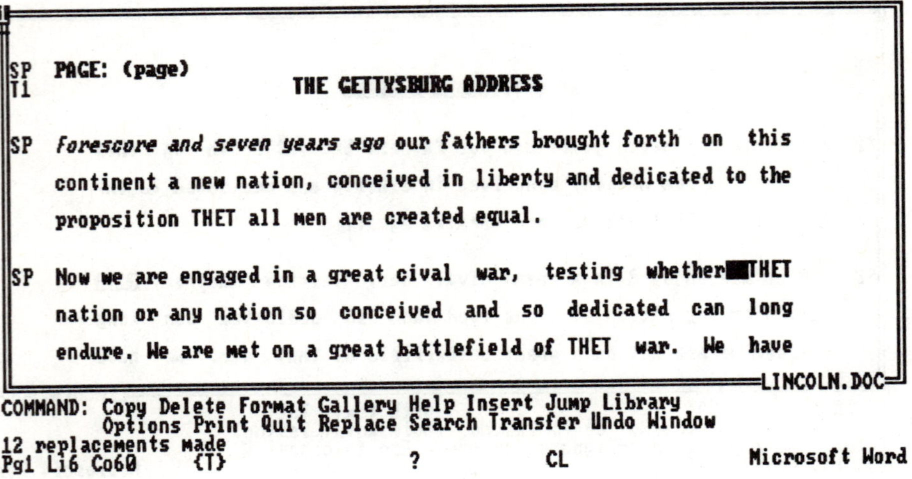

8. Press **Ctrl-PgUp**. Press **Esc**. Type **R**. Type **THET** and press **Tab**. Type **that** and press **Tab**. Press **Spacebar** to select no confirm, then **Tab**. Press **Spacebar** for yes, then **Enter**. Word replaces all occurrences of THET with that.
9. Press **Esc**. Type **T**, then **S**. The Transfer Save form appears.
10. Press **Enter**. Word displays a file save message. The Main menu appears.
11. Turn to Module 37 to continue the learning sequence.

Module 44
SEARCH

DESCRIPTION

The Search command on the Main menu looks for a specific string of characters within a document. When it finds the first occurrence of the string, it stops and highlights the area where the string appears. Word always searches in one direction only (either top to bottom, or bottom to top). A search always begins from the position pointed to by the text cursor. By pressing Shift-F4, you can search for the next occurrence of the string.

```
COMMAND: Copy Delete Format Gallery Help Insert Jump Library
         Options Print Quit Replace Search Transfer Undo Window
Searches for specified text, searching up or down from highlight position
Pg1 Li1 Co1      {}                 ?                          Microsoft Word
```

Word provides many shortcuts for mouse users. There are no mouse commands associated specifically with this command. Generic mouse movements and commands appear in Appendix E.

The Text field contains the character string Word looks for. The Direction field determines which way Word searches from the current text cursor position. Selecting UP causes Word to search from the bottom of the document to the top; otherwise, Word searches from the top of the document to the bottom. The Case field determines whether Word differentiates between upper and lowercase letters. Selecting NO means that Word will not differentiate between upper and lowercase letters. The Whole Word field determines if Word will look for partial matches. For example if you type JOIN for the text field and select YES for the Whole Word field, Word will not stop if it sees JOINING.

APPLICATIONS

Use the Search command whenever you need to find a particular word or sentence in your document. The Direction, Case, and Whole Word fields help you define exactly how you want Word to look for the specified text. By placing a peculiar word or string of characters within the text, you can find the place you stopped editing a document at the beginning of each editing session.

TYPICAL OPERATION

In this example you search for a specific word in the sample document. Begin this example at the Main menu with LINCOLN.DOC loaded in the current window.

1. Press **Esc**. Type **S**. The Search form appears.

```
SEARCH text: █
        direction: Up(Down) case: Yes(No) whole word: Yes(No)
Enter text
Pg1 Li1 Co1       {}                ?           CL                  Microsoft Word
```

2. Type **THAT** and press **Enter**. Word highlights the first occurrence of the word THAT. Notice that Word does not discriminate between THAT and that since the Case field selection equals NO.

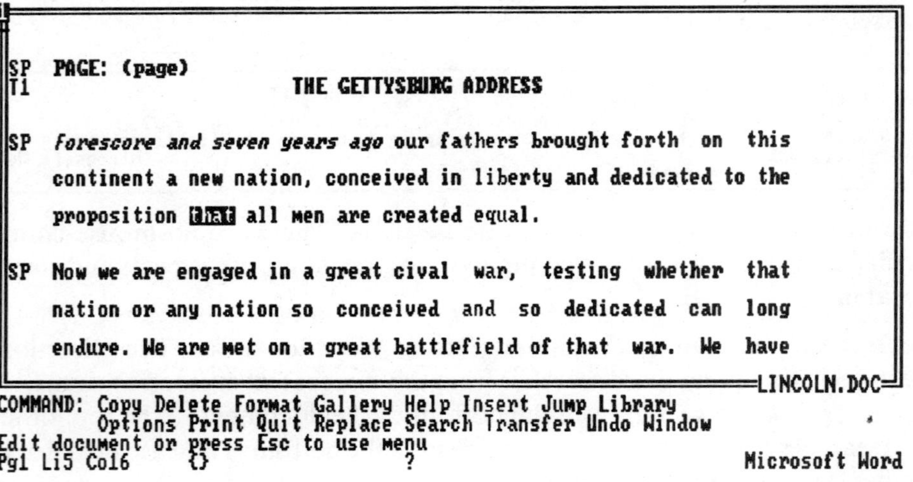

3. Press **Shift-F4**. Word highlights the next occurrence of the word THAT.
4. Turn to Module 43 to continue the learning sequence.

Module 45
TRANSFER

DESCRIPTION

The Transfer command contains many options for sending data to or getting data from files on disk. You access the Transfer command by pressing Esc then typing T.

```
COMMAND: Copy Delete Format Gallery Help Insert Jump Library
         Options Print Quit Replace Search Transfer Undo Window
Manages document files (loads, saves, etc); sets default drive/directory
Pg1 Li1 Co1      {}          ?          CL             Microsoft Word
```

Word provides many shortcuts for mouse users. The mouse commands associated specifically with this menu and options appear in Table 45-1. Generic mouse movements and commands appear in Appendix E.

TABLE 45-1. MOUSE COMMANDS

Action	*Pointing To*	*Result*
Push Left Button	Menu Selection	Word presents the requested form or submenu or executes the requested command.
Push Left Button	Field	Word selects the field for change.
Push Left Button	Form Name	Word makes the requested changes and returns to the document.
Push Right Button	Fill in the Blank Field	Word provides a list of acceptable choices. When requesting filename choices, Word provides the list in the current directory. To get a list of the files in another directory, change the Transfer Options entry or select the appropriate drive/ directory when in the files display.
Push Right Button	Multiple Choice Field	Word makes the requested changes and returns to the document.
Push Right and Left Buttons	Anywhere Except the Form or Window	Word cancels the current operation and returns to the Main menu.

LOAD The Transfer Load command retrieves a document file from disk. Word presents a form with two fields. The first field asks for the document name. The second field contains a selection allowing the user to open the document as read only. When you open a document as read only, Word does not allow you to change its contents. This feature is useful on networks; several people can view a file at the same time. You can obtain a listing of Word files in the current directory by pressing F1 while in the Filename field.

SAVE The Transfer Save command places a copy of the current document on disk. This allows you to retrieve the document at a future date for further editing. If you edit the current document and try to exit without saving it, Word prompts you before quitting to ask if you want to save it. The Filename field contains the name of the document. The Format field selects the format Word uses to store the document. Normally, you select the Word format which stores the document exactly as you created it. The Text Only option allows you to store document text only. Text Only With Line Breaks stores the text and the carriage returns at the end of each line. This allows you to retain the document margins. Before you use either of these options, Word asks if you want to lose document formatting. The Rich Text Format (RTF) option stores the document in such a way that any program able to read RTF documents will retain the Word formatting. Using this storage technique allows you to send your work to other word processors, even other machines.

CLEAR The Transfer Clear command contains two options. The first command, All, removes all documents from memory, detaches any stylesheets attached to the current window by the Format Stylesheet Attach command, clears all glossary entries, and places Word in its startup condition. The glossary contains Word macros and text scraps. The second command, Window, removes the current document from memory, detaches any attached stylesheets, and places Word in its startup condition. Before clearing any of the documents from memory, Word checks if you changed any of the documents and asks if you want to save them.

DELETE The Transfer Delete command removes a file from disk. You can obtain a listing of all the files on disk by pressing the F1 key. Word asks you to double check the filename before actually deleting the file.

MERGE The Transfer Merge command places the contents of a file on disk in the position pointed to by the on-screen cursor. This allows you to combine documents. For example, if a group of people worked on parts of a document, you could combine them for final editing and printing.

OPTIONS The Transfer Options form allows you to change the default disk drive and directory. Normally, Word uses the current directory as the default. You can override this default by typing a pathname in the Setup field and selecting the Yes option of the Save Between Sessions field. Word uses the default drive and directory as the source for file listings when you press the F1 key in a field asking for a filename.

RENAME The Transfer Rename command changes the name of a file saved on disk. You can obtain a listing of all the files on disk by pressing the F1 key.

GLOSSARY The Transfer Glossary menu provides the means of manipulating the Word glossary. The Transfer Glossary Load command allows you to place previously saved macros and text scraps into memory. This new glossary replaces the previous one. You can remove the current glossary by using the Transfer Glossary Clear command. The Transfer Glossary Save command allows you to save text segments and macro definitions in a disk file. The Transfer Glossary Merge command allows you to combine the current glossary with one saved on disk.

ALLSAVE The Allsave command performs the functions of three commands: Transfer Save, Transfer Glossary Save, and Gallery Save. It places copies of the current document, stylesheet, and glossary on disk.

APPLICATIONS

You use the Transfer menu to access Word's file manipulation commands. As described above, these options allow you to change filenames, load a file into memory, and save a file in memory to disk. They also perform other file manipulations required during a word processing session.

The Transfer menu also contains a submenu for performing some of the same file operations on glossary files. Glossary files contain permanently defined macro definitions such as time and date, user-defined macros for text manipulation, and text scraps of often typed paragraphs or phrases. An example of a user-defined macro is a letter-starting macro. This macro would type the company name and address contained in a text scrap, add the current date from the date macro, and add the customer name and address as well. The same macro could also attach the stylesheet to a document and format the paragraphs as required. Appendix H shows you how to create macros. Appendix I contains some sample macros for you to try and modify.

TYPICAL OPERATION

In this example you use the various Transfer menu options to manipulate disk files. Begin this example at the DOS prompt.

1. Type **WORD** and press **Enter**. The Word introductory screen, then the Main menu appear.

2. Type **The Gettysburg Address**. Press **Enter**. Press **Esc** then type **T**. The Transfer menu appears.

```
TRANSFER: Load Save Clear Delete Merge Options Rename Glossary Allsave

Loads named document
Pg1 Co1          {}               ?                            Microsoft Word
```

3. Type **S**. The Transfer Save form appears.

```
TRANSFER SAVE filename: █
                format:(Word)Text-only Text-only-with-line-breaks RTF
Enter filename
Pg1 Co1          {}               ?                            Microsoft Word
```

4. Type **LINCOLN** and press **Right Arrow**. Press **Spacebar** to select the Text Only option, then press **Enter**. Word asks if you want to lose document formatting.

```
TRANSFER SAVE filename: LINCOLN
                format: Word(Text-only)Text-only-with-line-breaks RTF
Enter Y to confirm loss of formatting █
Pg1 Co1          {}               ?          CL                Microsoft Word
```

5. Type **N**. Word cancels the save operation and displays the Transfer Save form.

6. Type **LINCOLN** and press **Enter**. The Summary Information form appears.

```
SUMMARY INFORMATION
   title: █                                  version number:
   author:                                    creation date: 4/13/89
   operator:                                  revision date: 4/13/89
   keywords:
   comments:
Enter text
Pg1 Li2 Co1     {}               ?          CL                Microsoft Word
```

7. Type **Lincoln's Gettysburg Address** and press **Tab**. Type **1.0** and press **Tab**. Type **Your Name** and press **Tab** twice. Type **Your Name** and press **Tab** twice. Type **Lincoln Gettysburg** and press **Tab**. Type **This is Lincoln's Gettysburg Address**. The Summary form appears as shown below.

```
SUMMARY INFORMATION
   title: Lincoln's Gettysburg Address       version number: 1.0
   author: Your Name                          creation date: 4/13/89
   operator: Your Name                        revision date: 4/13/89
   keywords: Lincoln Gettysburg
   comments: This is Lincoln's Gettysburg Address█
Enter text
Pg1 Li2 Co1     {}               ?                            Microsoft Word
```

8. Press **Enter**. Word saves the file then displays the number of characters in the file. The Main menu appears.
9. Press **Esc**. Type **T**, then **C**. The Transfer Clear menu appears.

```
TRANSFER CLEAR: All Window

Clears all documents, glossaries, style sheets
Pg1 Li1 Co1      {}                    ?          CL               Microsoft Word
```

10. Press **Enter**. Word clears the edit area.
11. Press **Esc**. Type **T**, then **L**. The Transfer Load form appears.

```
TRANSFER LOAD filename: █                          read only: Yes(No)

Enter filename or press F1 to select from list
Pg1 Li2 Co1      {}                    ?          CL               Microsoft Word
```

12. Press **F1**. A list of word processing files in the current directory appears.

```
LINCOLN.DOC









TRANSFER LOAD filename: LINCOLN.DOC               read only: Yes(No)

Enter filename or press F1 to select from list (17276928 bytes free)
Pg1 Li2 Co1      {}                    ?          CL               Microsoft Word
```

13. Select LINCOLN.DOC using the arrow keys. Press **Enter**. Word loads the file and displays the number of characters loaded. The Main menu appears.
14. Press **Esc**. Type **T**, then **D**. The Transfer Delete form appears.

```
TRANSFER DELETE filename: █

Enter filename or press F1 to select from list
Pg1 Li2 Co1      {}                    ?          CL               Microsoft Word
```

15. Press **F1**. Word displays a list of files. Notice the list differs from the list displayed in the Transfer Load form.

```
EPSONRX.PRD          NEW.PRD            PLAIN.TXT          TTY.PRD
LINCOLN.DOC          PLAIN.PRD




TRANSFER DELETE filename: EPSONRX.PRD

Enter filename or press F1 to select from list (17264640 bytes free)
Pg1 Li2 Co1      {}                   ?          CL              Microsoft Word
```

16. Select PLAIN.PRD using the arrow keys. Press **Enter**. Word asks you to confirm file deletion by pressing Y.

```
TRANSFER DELETE filename: PLAIN.PRD

Enter Y to confirm deletion of file █
Pg1 Li2 Co1      {}                   ?                          Microsoft Word
```

17. Type **N** to cancel the deletion. The Main menu appears.
18. Press **Esc**. Type **T**, then **D**. The Transfer Delete form appears.
19. Press **F1**. Word displays a list of files. Notice that Word did not delete PLAIN.PRD.
20. Select LINCOLN.DOC using the arrow keys and press **Enter**. Word displays an error message.

```
COMMAND: Copy Delete Format Gallery Help Insert Jump Library
         Options Print Quit Replace Search Transfer Undo Window
Cannot delete file
Pg1 Li2 Co1      {}                   ?          CL              Microsoft Word
```

21. Press **Esc**. Type **T**, then **O**. The Transfer Options form appears.

```
TRANSFER OPTIONS setup: C:\MW\0017
          save between sessions: Yes(No)
Enter path or press F1 to select from list
Pg1 Co1          {}                ?          CL                  Microsoft Word
```

22. Press **Esc**. Word does not change the default directory. The Main menu appears.
23. Press **Esc**. Type **T**, then **R**. The Transfer Rename form appears.

```
TRANSFER RENAME filename: C:\MW\0017\LINCOLN.DOC

Enter new name for file
Pg1 Li2 Co1      {}                ?          CL                  Microsoft Word
```

24. Type **LINCOLNS** then press **Enter**. Word changes the name of the document on disk and on screen.

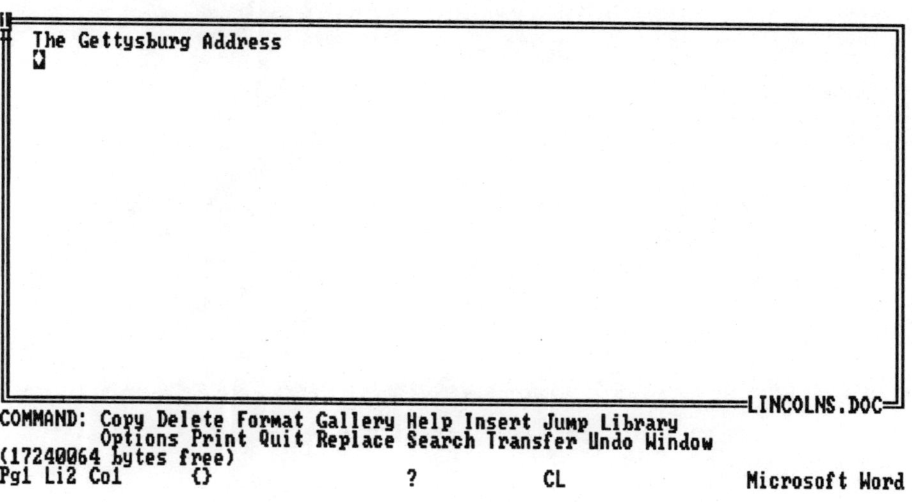

25. Press **Esc**. Type **T**, then **R**. The Transfer Rename form appears.
26. Type **LINCOLN** then press **Enter**. Word changes the name of the document on disk and on screen.
27. Press **Esc**. Type **T**, then **G**. The Transfer Glossary menu appears.

```
TRANSFER GLOSSARY: Load Save Merge Clear

Loads named glossary
Pg1 Co1          {}                ?          CL                  Microsoft Word
```

28. Type **S**. The Transfer Glossary Save form appears.

```
TRANSFER GLOSSARY SAVE filename: C:\MW\0017\NORMAL.GLY

Enter filename
Pg1 Li2 Co1      {}                 ?           CL                  Microsoft Word
```

29. Press **Enter**. Word displays a file save message. The Main menu appears.
30. Press **Esc**. Type **Q**. The DOS prompt appears.
31. Turn to Module 8 to continue the learning sequence.

Module 46
UNDO

DESCRIPTION

The Undo command on the Main menu reverses any changes you make to a document. It stores only the most recent change. For example, if you delete a text segment, then decide you need it back, you can use the Undo command to recover it. However, if you decide you need the text segment back after performing another action (changing a paragraph format for example), the Undo command will not recover it for you. The Undo command works not only on restoring text; it restores the format of reformatted characters, paragraphs, or divisions. It also removes added text. If you decide the change was correct, you can restore the change by using the Undo command as well.

```
COMMAND: Copy Delete Format Gallery Help Insert Jump Library
         Options Print Quit Replace Search Transfer Undo Window
Undoes last edit or command
Pg1 Li1 Co1       {}               ?          CL                  Microsoft Word
```

Word provides many shortcuts for mouse users. There are no mouse commands associated specifically with this command. Generic mouse movements and commands appear in Appendix E.

APPLICATIONS

Use the Undo command whenever you want to restore previous document conditions. This includes any type of document change; however, the Undo command works only on the most recent document change.

TYPICAL OPERATION

In this example you experiment using the Undo command to restore various changes to the sample document. This includes deleting text, changing the format of a paragraph, and adding text. Begin this example at the Main menu.

1. Select the F of Forescore by pressing arrow keys. Press **F6**. Highlight the entire paragraph by pressing arrow keys. Press **Del**. Word removes the first paragraph. Notice the title retains the formatting of the deleted paragraph and the deleted paragraph appears in the scrap.

```
SP  THE GETTYSBURG ADDRESS

SP  Now we are engaged in a great cival  war,  testing  whether  that
    nation or any nation so  conceived  and  so  dedicated  can  long
    endure. We are met on a great battlefield of that  war.  We  have
    come to dedicate a portion of that field as a final resting place
    for those who here gave their lives that that nation might  live.
    It is altogether fitting and proper that we should do this.
SP  ..................................................................
                                                           LINCOLN.DOC
COMMAND: Copy Delete Format Gallery Help Insert Jump Library
         Options Print Quit Replace Search Transfer Undo Window
Edit document or press Esc to use menu
Pg1 Li1 Co23     {¶Fores...equal.}  ?                   Microsoft Word
```

2. Press **Esc**. Type **U**. Word replaces the paragraph. Notice the title appears correctly formatted and the scrap is empty.

```
T1                        THE GETTYSBURG ADDRESS

SP  Forescore and seven years ago our fathers brought forth  on  this
    continent a new nation, conceived in liberty and dedicated to the
    proposition that all men are created equal.

SP  Now we are engaged in a great cival  war,  testing  whether  that
    nation or any nation so  conceived  and  so  dedicated  can  long
    endure. We are met on a great battlefield of that  war.  We  have
    come to dedicate a portion of that field as a final resting place
    for those who here gave their lives that that nation might  live.
                                                           LINCOLN.DOC
COMMAND: Copy Delete Format Gallery Help Insert Jump Library
         Options Print Quit Replace Search Transfer Undo Window
Edit document or press Esc to use menu
Pg1 Li4 Co44     {}                 ?        CL         Microsoft Word
```

3. Press **Alt-T**. Type **1**. Word reformats the paragraph to match the title.

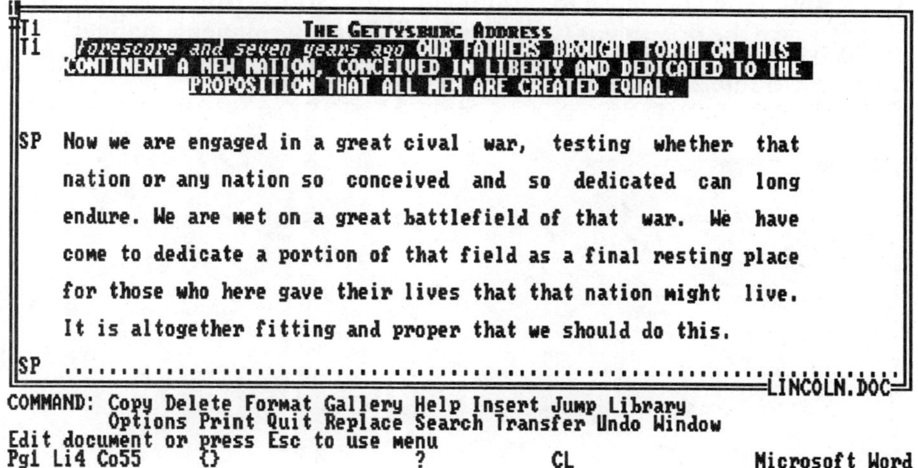

```
T1                        THE GETTYSBURG ADDRESS
T1     Forescore and seven years ago OUR FATHERS BROUGHT FORTH ON THIS
     CONTINENT A NEW NATION, CONCEIVED IN LIBERTY AND DEDICATED TO THE
                PROPOSITION THAT ALL MEN ARE CREATED EQUAL.

SP   Now we are engaged in a great cival  war,  testing  whether  that
     nation or any nation so  conceived  and  so  dedicated  can  long
     endure. We are met on a great battlefield of that  war.  We  have
     come to dedicate a portion of that field as a final resting place
     for those who here gave their lives that that nation might  live.
     It is altogether fitting and proper that we should do this.
SP   ..................................................................
                                                          LINCOLN.DOC
COMMAND: Copy Delete Format Gallery Help Insert Jump Library
         Options Print Quit Replace Search Transfer Undo Window
Edit document or press Esc to use menu
Pg1 Li4 Co55     {}                ?          CL              Microsoft Word
```

4. Press **Esc**. Type **U**. Word changes the format of the first paragraph back to its original style.

5. Place the text cursor at the end of the first paragraph by pressing arrow keys. Type **THIS IS SAMPLE TEXT**. Press **Esc**. Type **U**. Word removes the new text, but not the old. Notice the cursor appears at the end of the paragraph.

6. Press **Esc**. Type **U**. Word places the new text where you originally typed it.

```
T1                        THE GETTYSBURG ADDRESS

SP   Forescore and seven years ago our fathers brought forth  on  this
     continent a new nation, conceived in liberty and dedicated to the
     proposition that all men are created equal. THIS IS SAMPLE TEXT.

SP   Now we are engaged in a great cival  war,  testing  whether  that
     nation or any nation so  conceived  and  so  dedicated  can  long
     endure. We are met on a great battlefield of that  war.  We  have
     come to dedicate a portion of that field as a final resting place
     for those who here gave their lives that that nation might  live.
                                                          LINCOLN.DOC
COMMAND: Copy Delete Format Gallery Help Insert Jump Library
         Options Print Quit Replace Search Transfer Undo Window
Edit document or press Esc to use menu
Pg1 Li4 Co64     {}                ?                          Microsoft Word
```

7. Press **Esc**. Type **U**. Word removes the text.
8. Press **Esc**. Type **Q**. The DOS prompt appears. Notice Word does not ask if you want to save the document (you didn't make any permanent changes).
9. Turn to Module 28 to continue the learning sequence.

Module 47
WINDOW

DESCRIPTION

The Window command allows you to modify or add windows to the edit display. A window appears as the document edit area. Word usually surrounds it with a double line border. Word allows you to create up to eight windows at the same time. Word numbers each window. The number appears in the upper left corner. When you scroll text in one window, the text in the other windows stays the same, even if the other windows contain parts of the same document. You access this command by pressing Esc and typing W. To change the active window, press F1 while in the window area. Word cycles through the windows in numeric sequence.

```
COMMAND: Copy Delete Format Gallery Help Insert Jump Library
         Options Print Quit Replace Search Transfer Undo Window
Opens, closes, resizes, and moves windows
P1 D1 C1          {}              ?                     Microsoft Word
```

Word provides many shortcuts for mouse users. The mouse commands associated specifically with this form appear in Table 47-1. Generic mouse movements and commands appear in Appendix E.

TABLE 47-1. MOUSE COMMANDS

Action	*Pointing To*	*Result*
Push Left Button	Menu Selection	Word presents the requested form, submenu, or executes the requested command.
Push Left Button	Field	Word selects the field for change.
Push Left Button	Form Name	Word makes the requested changes and returns to the document.
Push Left Button	Window Number Indicator	Word selects the window.
Push Right Button	Multiple Choice Field	Word makes the requested changes and returns to the document.

Action	*Pointing To*	*Result*
Push Right Button	Fill in the Blank Field	Word places a positioning cursor on the left side for horizontal splits, top for vertical splits, and lower right corner for window moves.
Push Right Button	Window Number Indicator	Word goes into zoom mode. The selected window fills the entire screen even if others are present. The other windows exist, but do not occupy and display area.
Push Left or Right Button and Drag	Split Between Two Windows	Word moves the lower right corner of the uppermost and leftmost window in the direction of mouse drag.
Push Left or Right Button	Top Border	Window create a vertical split of the window bounded by the border.
Push Left or Right Button	Right Border	Window creates a horizontal split of the window bounded by the border.
Push Right and Left Buttons	Anywhere Except the Form or Window	Word cancels the current operation and returns to Main menu.
Push Right and Left Buttons	Top or Right Border	Window closes the window bounded by the border.

SPLIT The Window Split command allows you to create a new window. The form contains three commands. The Window Split Horizontal command creates a window by splitting the current one horizontally. The Window Split Vertical command creates a window by splitting the current one vertically. The Window Split Footnote creates a special, horizontally split window which displays the footnotes of the affected document.

The Window Split Horizontal form contains two fields. The At Line field contains the line number at which you wish to split the window. Most CGA and MDA displays contain only 25 total lines. Word provides a 40-line display for some EGA displays. Word provides a cursor you can use to position the window starting line when you press F1 in the At Line field. The Clear New Window field allows you to clear the window you create without using the Transfer Clear Window command. Select Yes to clear the window.

The Window Split Vertical form contains two fields. The At Column field contains the column number you wish to split the window at. Most displays use 80 columns.

Word provides a positioning cursor along the top of the window when you press F1 in the At Column field. The Clear New Window field allows you to clear the window you create without using the Transfer Clear Window command. Select Yes to clear the window.

The Window Split Footnote form contains a single field. The At Line field contains the line number at which you wish to split the window. Word provides the same features for this command as the Window Split Horizontal command.

MOVE The Window Move form contains three fields. The Window # field contains the number of the window you wish to move. The To Row field contains the row number of the lower right row of the window. The Column field contains the number of the lower right column of the window. You can obtain a positioning cursor by pressing F1 in either field.

CLOSE The Window Close command contains one field. The Window Number field contains the number of the window you wish to close. If you change a document, stylesheet, or glossary associated exclusively with the window, Word ask if you want to save them before actually closing the window.

APPLICATIONS

Use the Window command to manipulate up to eight windows. Using windows allows you to see several parts of the same document or several documents at the same time. Windows also allow you to move text from one document to another very easily since you can see the effect on both documents.

TYPICAL OPERATION

In this sample you use the Window command to open, move, and close windows showing different parts of the example document. Begin this example at the Main menu with LINCOLN.DOC loaded in the current window.

1. Press **Esc**. Type **W**. The Window menu appears.

```
WINDOW: Split Close Move

Divides current window; opens footnote window
P1 D1 C1            {}                ?                        Microsoft Word
```

2. Type **S**. The Window Split menu appears.

```
WINDOW SPLIT: Horizontal Vertical Footnote

Divides current window horizontally at specified line
P1 D1 C1            {}                ?                        Microsoft Word
```

3. Type **H**. The Window Split Horizontal form appears.

```
WINDOW SPLIT HORIZONTAL at line: 3█   clear new window: Yes(No)
Enter number
P1 D1 C1          {}             ?                    Microsoft Word
```

4. Press **F1**. The positioning cursor appears next to the style bar on the left side of the display.

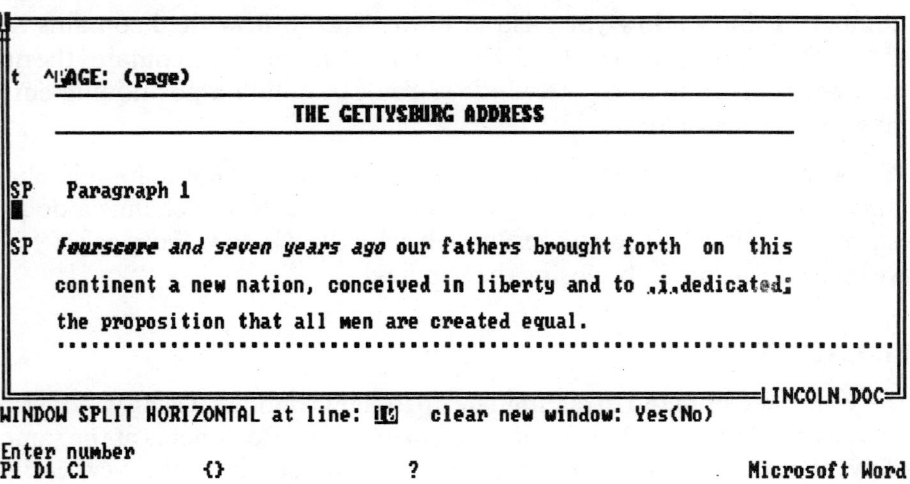

5. Press arrow keys to move the cursor to line 10. Press **Enter**. Word splits the current window.

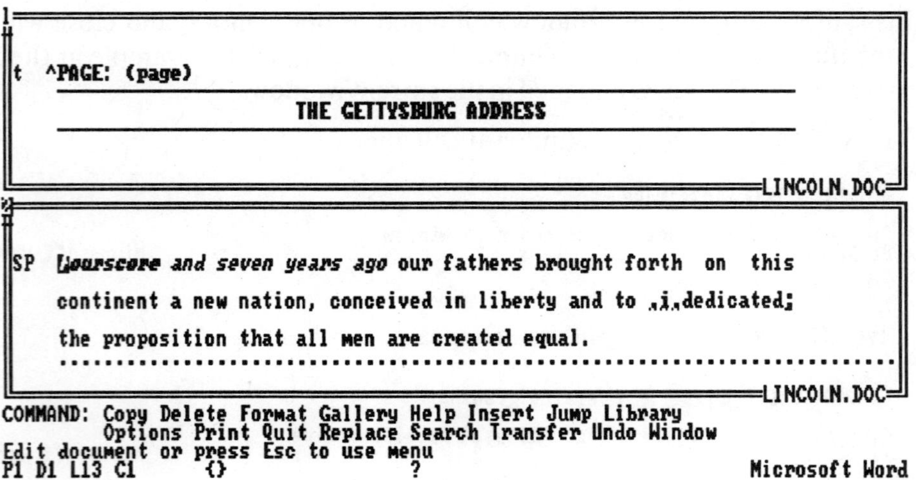

6. Press **Esc**. Type **T**, then **L**, then **New**. Press **Enter**. Word loads NEW.DOC in window 2. Notice window 1 still contains LINCOLN.DOC.

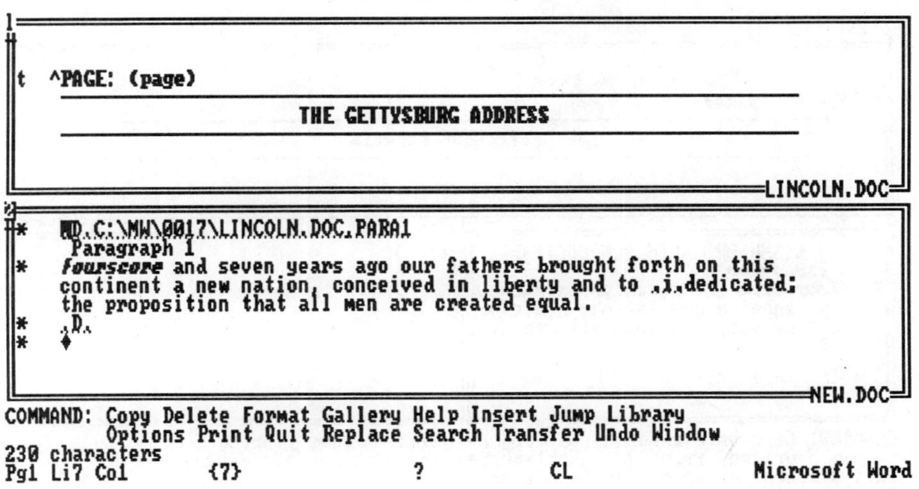

7. Press **Esc**. Type **W**, then **S**, then **V**. The Window Split Vertical form appears.

```
WINDOW SPLIT VERTICAL at column: 2█   clear new window: Yes(No)

Enter number
Pg1 Li7 Co1        {7}                ?           CL                Microsoft Word
```

8. Press **F1**. The positioning cursor appears.

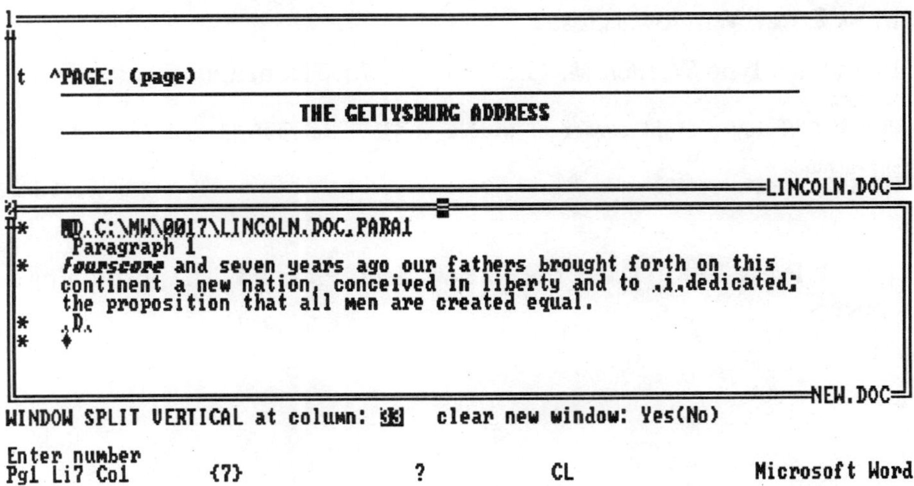

9. Move the cursor to column 34 by pressing arrow keys. Press **Tab** to select the Clear New Window field. Press **Spacebar** to select yes. Press **Enter**. Word creates a new window by vertically splitting window 2, then clears it.

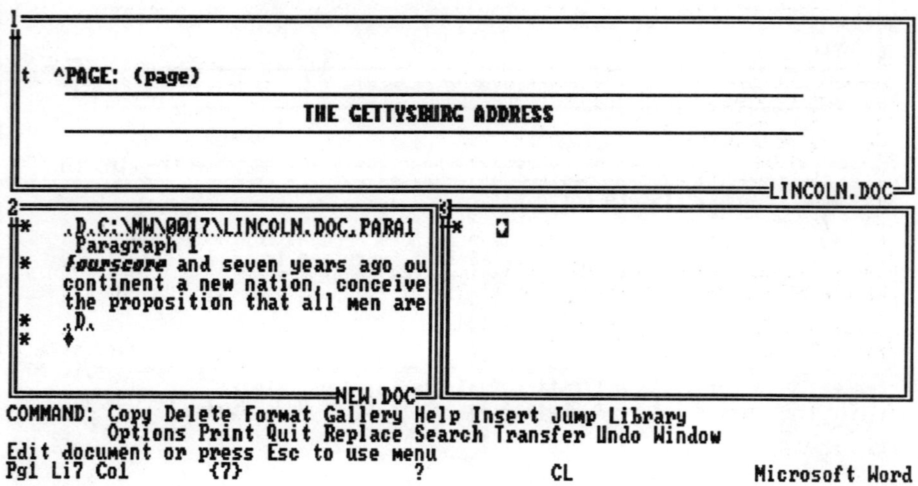

10. Press **Esc**. Type **W**, then **C**. The Window Close form appears. Notice Word suggests you close the last window opened.

```
WINDOW CLOSE window number: 3

Enter number
Pg1 Li7   Co1     {12}              ?                          Microsoft Word
```

11. Press **Enter**. Window 3 closes.

12. Press **Esc**. Type **W**, then **M**. The Window Move form appears.

```
WINDOW MOVE lower right corner of window #: 2     to row: 20   column: 79

Enter number
Pg1 Li7   Co1     {12}              ?                          Microsoft Word
```

13. Type **1**. Press **Tab** to select the To Row field. Press **F1**. The positioning cursor appears.

```
1
t   ^PAGE: (page)
                       THE GETTYSBURG ADDRESS

                                                              LINCOLN.DOC
2
*    .D.C:\MW\0017\LINCOLN.DOC.PARA1
      Paragraph 1
*    fourscore and seven years ago our fathers brought forth on this
     continent a new nation, conceived in liberty and to .i.dedicated;
     the proposition that all men are created equal.
*    .D.
*    ♦
                                                                NEW.DOC
WINDOW MOVE lower right corner of window #: 1    to row: 14   column: 79

Enter number
Pg1 Li7   Co1      {12}          ?                       Microsoft Word
```

14. Move the cursor to row 14 by pressing arrow keys. Press **Enter**. Word moves window 1.

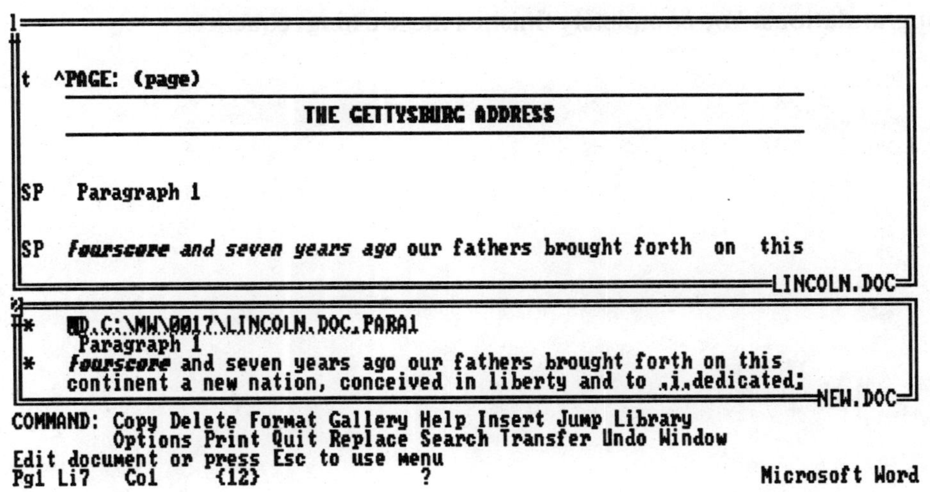

```
1
t   ^PAGE: (page)
                       THE GETTYSBURG ADDRESS

SP    Paragraph 1

SP   fourscore and seven years ago our fathers brought forth  on  this
                                                              LINCOLN.DOC
2
*    .D.C:\MW\0017\LINCOLN.DOC.PARA1
      Paragraph 1
*    fourscore and seven years ago our fathers brought forth on this
     continent a new nation, conceived in liberty and to .i.dedicated;
                                                                NEW.DOC
COMMAND: Copy Delete Format Gallery Help Insert Jump Library
         Options Print Quit Replace Search Transfer Undo Window
Edit document or press Esc to use menu
Pg1 Li7   Co1      {12}          ?                       Microsoft Word
```

15. Press **F1** to change the active window number to 1. Press **Esc**. Type **W**, then **S**, then **F**. The Window Split Footnote form appears.

```
WINDOW SPLIT FOOTNOTE at line: 3

Enter number
P1 D1 L7.5 C34    {12}          ?                        Microsoft Word
```

16. Type **7** and press **Enter**. Word splits window 1 horizontally at line 7. Notice how this split differs from the two previous splits.

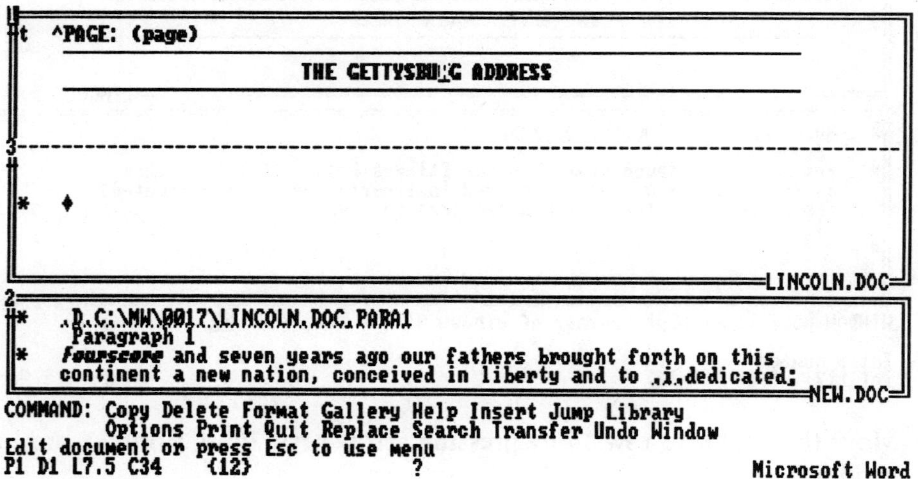

Congratulations! You completely finished the learning sequence.

Appendix A
MICROSOFT WORD TERMS AND DEFINITIONS

ASCII: (American Standard Code for Information Interchange) Word uses this code to store the text part of the document. The formatting information is stored as control codes interspersed with the text. When using the plain print driver, Word stores the entire document in standard ASCII format without control codes.

Column: A vertical division of a page into one or more sections for easier reading. You can divide pages into columns using the Layout option of the Format Division menu.

Division: A standard document partition. Word uses these partitions to limit the area defined by a stylesheet division entry. Divisions occur on several different boundaries: page, column, continuous (whole document), even (pages), and odd (pages).

Elite Font: A font providing 12 characters to the linear inch. You can select an elite font using the Character or Paragraph options of the Format menu, or using a character or paragraph stylesheet entry.

Footnote: A note referencing who wrote a text quote, commenting on the contents of a sentence or paragraph, or explaining a sentence or paragraph in greater detail. Word places footnotes on the same page as the footnote reference or at the end of the document.

Font: A set of characters (letters and numbers) with a consistent look and size. Word uses the paragraph font definition for standard characters and the character font definition for special characters within a paragraph. When using a laser printer, Word automatically downloads the fonts required to print a document. Word defines font size in points and font style by name (for example Courier).

Gallery: The stylesheet editor provided by Word. Using stylesheets allows documents to retain a more uniform appearance. The gallery allows the user to look at, add to, or change these stylesheet definitions.

Glossary: A special Word file used to store commonly used sections of text and macro definitions. Word allows the user to change, load, save, and combine glossary files as needed. The glossary always exists separately from a document. Word assumes NORMAL.GLY as the standard.

Gutter: The space between two columns of text. You can define the gutter width using the Layout option of the Format Division menu.

Hanging Indent: A paragraph where the second and following lines of text appear to the right of the first line. This paragraph is an example of a hanging indent. Some programs refer to a hanging indent as an outdent. You can adjust the size of a hanging indent using a paragraph entry in a stylesheet or the Paragraph option on the Format menu.

Indent: A paragraph where the second and following lines of text appear to the left of the first line. You can adjust the size of an indent using a paragraph entry in a stylesheet or the Paragraph option on the Format menu.

Macro: A series of recorded keystrokes used to perform a repetitive task. An example of a repetitive task using a macro is the heading used for correspondence. A macro could reduce the time required to produce a letter by setting up all the formatting characteristics and the heading automatically.

Margin: The white space surrounding text. You can define the margins of a page using the Margin option on the Format Division menu.

Outdent: See hanging indent.

Pica: A publishing unit of measurement for size and distances of text and graphics on a page. One pica equals twelve points (see Point) or 1/6 th of an inch.

Pica Font: A standard pica font provides 10 characters to the linear inch. You can select a pica font using the Character or Paragraph options on the Format menu, or using a character or paragraph stylesheet entry.

Point: A publishing unit of measurement often used to show the size of type. Twelve points equal one pica (see Pica).

Repaginate: Word normally keeps the document in one continuous piece until print time. You can change the page separations to match print time conditions using the Repaginate option on the Print menu.

Revision Marks: The method Word uses to record any changes made to a document. Using revision marks allows the user to change the document to its original condition at a later date. You can change the format on the revision marks using the Revision-Marks option of the Format menu.

Running Heads: A masthead that appears on every page of a document. The running heads for this book indicate the module names and numbers and appear in the upper corners of each page.

Stylesheet: A method of storing the formatting parameters of a document in an easy-to-change format. By changing the format definition for a paragraph, character, or division in a stylesheet, the user can instantly change the appearance of the entire document. You can access stylesheets using the Gallery option on the Main menu.

Thesaurus: Word provides a listing of words with similar meaning to the word currently pointed to by the cursor. This allows a user to vary the words used throughout a document and still convey the same meaning.

Window: Word uses windows to display more than one document or document section simultaneously.

Appendix B
DESKTOP PUBLISHING GUIDELINES

Microsoft Word is usually not considered a desktop publishing program; however, with the advent of easily downloaded "soft fonts" and the availability of inexpensive laser printers, Word can perform many functions previously reserved for desktop publishing programs. A word processing program like Microsoft Word provides many complex and robust features. You can change the style, font, and size of text. Version 5.0 allows pasting graphics or digitized photographs directly into a document. However, like all programs, you should follow certain guidelines when using Word.

Guideline #1: Use White Space

Determine the width and height of the page margins, headers, and footers. Most pages leave at least an inch-wide margin around the edges of the page. Use plenty of white space around headings to make them stand out from the rest of the page. Pages crammed with text almost dare the reader to understand it, let alone look at it.

Guideline #2: Remember that Microsoft Word is Not a Desktop Publishing Program

Remembering that Microsoft Word is in fact a word processing program, not a desktop publishing program, can help you determine where to draw the line on formatting capabilities. Word can perform many desktop publishing program tasks, but remembering that it has limited capabilities can save frustration for you and your reader from a poorly formatted document.

Guideline #3: Use a Minimum Number of Fonts on a Page

Most pages, such as those found in newspapers and magazines, mix two or three fonts on a single page. Too many fonts on a single page can be distracting. Also, choose fonts that look good together. Two wildly different fonts can be difficult to read.

Guideline #4: Use the Right Size Type for Your Text

Letters that look too small will be hard to read. Letters that look too large can waste page space. For headlines, use large type. For most text, use a smaller type size. The most common text type size is about 12 points.

Guideline #5: Use Line Spacing

The distance between each line should be large enough to prevent the lines from crowding one another. By leaving plenty of room between each line, you make all the lines easier to read. The most common spacing between single spaced lines is 1/2 the point size of the text font. (Example: if the text font is 12 points, the line spacing is 6 points.)

Guideline #6: Use Short Line Lengths

It's no accident that newspapers and magazines print articles in two or three columns per page. Short lines look more inviting to read than long lines, even if both fit in the same page space.

Guideline #7: Use Lines to Divide Your Pages

Even with the proper column and line spacing, a page might still look crowded. In these cases, use straight thin lines to divide columns from one another. Enclose graphics in boxes to separate them from the surrounding text. Your page will then look neater and more organized. The average line size is 1 point (1/72 inch). Make the lines as long as the text. Use lines to enclose graphics.

Guideline #8: Be Consistent!

Look at your favorite newspaper and magazine to see how each page uses the same layout. It has two or three columns per page and graphics in certain parts of the page. Inconsistency destroys the sense of order and structure of a page. A reader sensing this disorganization will likely turn the page or throw it away altogether.

Guideline #9: Identify the Purpose of Each Page

The purpose of a desktop publishing program (or a word processing program performing the same function) is to enhance the appearance of a document. You can do that by adding graphics, using different fonts, styles, and sizes, and organizing your page into columns and grids. Each element of a page must make the page inviting to read. Define a theme for each page, then make every item on the page reflect that theme. Eliminate any page element that does not do this.

Guideline #10: Use Role Models

Look at your favorite newspapers and magazines to see how they designed their pages. Copy their styles and use them yourself, enhancing or altering them slightly for your particular needs. The more you practice designing pages, the more skilled you will become. A word processing program with desktop publishing program capabilities, such as Microsoft Word, cuts out the tedium of designing pages, freeing you to focus on the creative aspect of page designing. By following the above guidelines, you can start producing documents that you can be proud of using your computer and Word.

Appendix C
USING GRAPHICS WITHIN A DOCUMENT

Even though version 4.0 of Microsoft Word does not provide a graphics capability (version 5.0 does), you can still leave space for graphics by using the line draw capability provided to outline the area where the graphic will be added. Then, when you print your document, you merely add your graphics to the outlined boxes. Graphics and text go hand-in-hand. There are many different types of graphics used in documents. Some graphics are computer generated (spreadsheet graphs, paint program art, etc.). You scan other graphics into the computer from photographs or other sources using a scanner. Whatever graphic source you use, the following rules will help you determine the best mix of graphics and text.

DEFINITIONS

Bit -mapped Graphics: A drawing composed of bits. This type of drawing requires more space and is less flexible than vector graphics. It requires less time to load, manipulate, and print than vector graphics.

Bitonal: See line drawing.

Blow-Up: A drawing or photograph that is enlarged to show greater detail.

Continuous-tone Images: Images that use a large variety of shades. An example of a continuous-tone image is a photograph.

Cropping: Removing uninteresting or unimportant parts of photographs or drawings. This usually allows more text or a blown-up version of the photograph or drawing on the page.

Dithering: Most laser printers produce only one color. Dithering forms dots of various sizes to approximate different halftones.

Dots Per Inch: The dots produced by a printer, scanner, or graphics display per linear inch. Many laser printers produce 300 dots per inch. Dot matrix printers usually produce from 120 to 180 dots per inch. Scanners produce from 80 to 300 dot-per-inch images.

Gray Scale: The range of gray values produced by a printer scanner or graphics display.

Halftones: The process of converting continuous-tone images into a pattern of dots. A screen with a fixed number of dots per inch approximates the gray scale for that drawing section. Screen dot-per-inch values range from 65 to 120 lines per inch. The printer approximates the halftones using dithering.

Isometric Drawing: One type of three-dimensional drawing. It is a line drawing representing the way the actual object would appear to the human eye. The parts closer to the viewer appear larger, while the parts farther away are smaller. It shows three connected sides of the object.

Line Drawing: A drawing without halftones or any type of other shading. An example of a line drawing is the blueprints drawn by drafters.

Orthographic Drawing: A two-dimensional drawing. It shows only one side of an object.

Pixel: One dot on a display or scanner. The number of bits per pixel determines the number of colors read or displayed by the device. If, for example, a monitor has 4 bits per pixel, then it is capable of displaying 16 colors.

Raster Graphics: Images stored using raster graphics use mathematical representations for various parts of a drawing. There are equations that represent circles, arcs, squares, rectangles, and lines. The memory required by raster graphics is significantly less than bit-mapped graphics. Because they are smaller, computers transmit and load raster graphics faster than bit-mapped graphics. You can easily scale raster graphics with no loss in resolution (mathematic equations have no resolution). Bit-mapped graphics display and print faster than raster graphics because the computer does not compute each line position.

Resolution: The number of dots or pixels displayed or read per linear inch by displays, printers, and scanners. Resolution is an important factor in the final appearance of text or graphics. The higher the resolution, the less jagged a graphic appears.

Vector Graphics: See raster graphics.

GENERAL GUIDELINES

1. Use graphics that emphasize the accompanying text. Graphics that do not emphasize the text lead the reader's attention away from your message to the graphic image. A graphic that does emphasize the text, explains what words can't. Effective graphics sometimes reduce or eradicate the need for text.

2. Use significant graphics. Graphics which contain irrelevant elements detract from the overall graphic effect.

3. Be sure your graphics are clear. Forcing the reader to decipher poorly written text is one way to lose reader interest. Forcing the reader to look at poor graphic images is the other. Never use blurred or indistinguishable graphics.

4. Use graphics of the correct size. Graphic images that are too large for the reader to look at in one glance are usually too large. If a graphic is too small, the reader may not even look at it. A good rule of thumb is to look at the graphic at arms length. If you can see the whole graphic and still see all the details, it is probably the right size.

5. Use lines to separate the graphic from the text. Using a light line to separate small graphics from the surrounding text gives the reader an area to look at. Do not use lines when the graphic extends the entire width or length of the page. Of course, there are exceptions to every rule.

Appendix D
USING FONTS WITHIN A DOCUMENT

Some versions of Microsoft Word come equipped with a Bitstream soft font generator to produce fonts for your laser printer. Bitstream also sells many typeface add-ons for their product. In addition, Word allows you to use any cartridge or soft font add-ons you already possess using the print driver description files talked about in Appendix F. To use fonts effectively requires many years of schooling and experience to study their effect on the reader. By following a few simple rules and learning some typesetting terms you can produce effective results on simple documents.

DEFINITIONS

Alignment: This is the way text lines up with the margin. Another name for alignment is justification. There are four recognized alignment types: right justified (left side ragged, right side aligned), left justified (left side aligned, right side ragged), center justified (text aligns with the middle of the page) and justified (both right and left sides aligned).

Ascender: The portion of a lowercase letter that goes above the X-height.

Baseline: The lower limit of a line of text. It does not include the descender portion of lowercase letters (g and j for instance). Most measurements of letter height (except point size) use the baseline as a point of reference.

Centered Text: See alignment.

CPI: This is an abbreviation for characters per inch. It provides a measure of how many monospaced characters will fit in one linear inch.

Descender: The portion of a lowercase letter that extends below the baseline.

Elite: A unit of measure for monospaced fonts equal to 12 CPI.

Em: A unit of measure for printer's type. It specifies a character about as wide as it is high. Printers used em because the letter M is about as wide as it is high.

En: A unit of measure for printer's type. It specifies a character about half as wide as it is high. Printers used en because the letter N is about half as wide as it is high.

Flush: Refers to text that aligns with either the left or right margin.

Folio: The current page number. It often appears with the chapter title or some other text.

Font: A complete set of letters, numbers, and symbols of a specific point size and typeface. A complete font description tells the point size, typeface, and any special font characteristics (for example: Times Italic 14 point).

Footer: One or more lines of text appearing at the bottom of every page of a document. The page number often appears as a footer.

Greeking: The method a desktop publishing program uses to display text position when text is too small to read due to zooming. Microsoft Word uses this technique for the page preview option. Greeking usually consists of small boxes and squares used to approximate the text appearance.

Header: One or more lines of text appearing at the top of every or alternate pages of a document. The chapter or book title often appear as the header. Some books use the chapter title on alternate pages with the book title.

Hyphenation: The determination of where a word breaks between lines of text. The hyphen (-) character separates the beginning of the word from the ending. Word uses hyphenation to make individual lines of text more appealing by reducing the space between letters and words.

Hyphenation Zone: The area between the end of text and the right margin where a word breaks naturally. If a word is too long to fit on the line, Word checks to see if the word contains a hyphen point within the hyphenation zone.

Inside Margin: The edge next to the binding in a book. It is the right margin on left-hand (even-numbered) pages and the left margin on right-hand pages. The inside margin is usually wider than the outside margin to accommodate binding.

Justified Text: See alignment.

Kerning: The space between two letters. Proportionately spaced letters have equal spaces between each letter. Monospaced letters center each character within a specific space. The space is equal for all letters; therefore, the space between each letter is different.

Leading: The space between the baseline of one line of text and the next line. Normally, this space is equal to the point size of the letter plus 1/6th more. For example, when using 12-point type, you would use 14-point leading. This allows 2 points of space between lines.

Line Spacing: See leading.

Monospacing: A typeface in which each character uses exactly the same amount of space. Typewriters use monospaced fonts to alleviate mechanical problems introduced by proportionally spaced fonts.

Oblique: A skewed or slanted typeface like italic.

Orphans: The top line of a paragraph is an orphan when a page break separates it from the rest of the paragraph. This detracts from page appearance (especially on multi-column text).

Outside Margin: The left margin of a left-hand page or the right margin of a right-hand page. The outside margin is usually less than the inside margin by the amount taken by binding.

Pica: A unit of measure equal to 1/6 inch or 12 points. It also refers to monospaced fonts with 10 CPI spacing.

Pitch: The space each character of a monospaced font requires. The three most common sizes are 10, 12, and 15 characters per inch.

Point: The smallest unit of typographic measurement. There are 12 points to a pica and 72 points to an inch.

Proportional Spacing: A typeface which allows each character to occupy only the space it needs. The space between each character is equal. Proportional spacing closely approximates the way most people write. It is also easier to read than monospaced fonts.

Roman: An unslanted typeface.

Rules or Ruled Lines: Lines drawn on a page to separate columns of text or graphics from text. These lines can be any size, style, or thickness.

Sans Serif: A typeface that does not contain any lines crossing the letter ends. Examples of sans serif letters include Helvetica and Swiss.

Screen: A screen used to produce different shades of gray on art. You produce a screen by placing black dots on a white background. The screen darkness varies as a percentage of white to black. A 100 percent screen is solid black and a 10 percent screen is light gray.

Script: A typeface which looks like handwriting or calligraphy. Some examples of script include Zapf Chancery and Park Avenue.

Serifs: Short lines crossing the ends of the main cross-members of a character. Examples of letters that use serifs include Times Roman, Bookman, and New Century Schoolbook. Publishers use these fonts in book text because they are easier to read than sans serif fonts in small sizes.

Twips: A unit of measure related to dot matrix printers. One twip equals 1/1440th of an inch or 1/20th of a point. Word uses the twip as a standard measure for its print driver description files (talked about in Appendix F).

Typeface: The formation of a group of letters. It includes the size, shape, orientation, thickness, and general appearance of the letter.

X-Height: The height of the lowercase letter x in a specified typeface.

GENERAL GUIDELINES

1. Don't Use More Than Two Typefaces On a Page. When you use too many different typefaces, the fonts draw the reader to the lettering rather than the material itself. This detracts from the general appearance of the writing. It does help to use a sans serif typeface for the chapter title and headings, and a serif typeface for the text.

2. Do Use Type Size, Thickness, and Obliqueness to Enhance Page Appearance. When you want to emphasize a particular point within the text, use italic type. When you want to emphasize the chapter title, heading, and sub-headings, use bold type. Use a larger type size for the title and heading.

3. Do Use a Serif Typeface for Text. The serifs on Times Roman guide the reader's eyes from one letter to the next. A serif typeface is usually easier to read in small type sizes because the bowls (the circular portions of letter) do not close as easily. Most text is very readable between 8 and 12 points in size.

4. Do Regulate Letter Kerning. If character spacing is too close together, they become hard to read. In addition, they bleed together when copied. If character spacing is too far apart, words loose their cohesiveness and become hard to read.

5. Do Use Bold, Sans Serif Letters for Titles and Headings. When you present a page of text to the reader, you want the reader drawn into the page. Use bold titles between 16 and 24 points to draw the reader's attention to the headings within the text. Using sans serif type makes the heading look less fussy. Then use bold headings one or two point sizes larger than the text to draw the reader into the text.

6. Do Regulate Letter Leading. Use spacing between lines of text to add or detract from its importance. If line spacing is too close together, it becomes unreadable and messy looking. If line spacing is too far apart, the paragraph looses cohesiveness. You also waste page space. Within limits, line spacing can add feeling to the page presentation.

Appendix E
USING MICROSOFT WORD WITH A MOUSE

Even though you can use Microsoft Word with the keyboard, it is easier and faster to use with a mouse. This appendix shows you the steps required to use a mouse with Word. The end of this appendix explains problems you might encounter using a mouse.

There are three simple rules to remember when using the mouse with Microsoft Word. First, the left mouse button always selects the object pointed to by the mouse cursor. Second, the right mouse button always selects the default selection within a menu. Using this button when the mouse cursor points to a menu selects all the default settings. For example, if you point to the Format option on the Main menu and press the right mouse button, the character format dialogue box appears. Third, pressing the middle button on a three-button mouse or the right and left buttons on a two-button mouse cancels the current selection. As with anything else, there are probably a few exceptions to these rules, but Word uses them very consistently throughout the program.

USING YOUR MOUSE

The example below shows some of the tasks you can perform in Word using a mouse.

1. Make sure you have the right kind of mouse. Any Microsoft™, Logitech™, Mouse Systems™, or compatible mouse will work with Microsoft Word.
2. Install your mouse using the manufacturer's directions. Make sure you install any special drivers that you need to make Microsoft Word work.
3. Turn on your computer and load Microsoft Word. You should see a mouse icon that looks like an arrow. This icon points to the text you modify when using Word. This is the text/menu selection cursor.

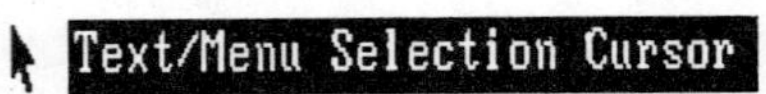

4. Point to one of the menu options with the mouse icon. If the menu is not visible, place the cursor in the lower right corner and press the Left Mouse Button. Press the Left Mouse Button, another menu or a dialogue area will replace the menu.
5. Move the mouse icon out of the menu/dialogue area and press the Middle (3-button mouse) or both Right and Left (2-button mouse) Mouse Buttons, the menu will disappear.
6. Move the mouse almost to the left side of the display. The cursor does not change shape, but the arrow points right instead of left. This is the line selection cursor used to select an entire line of text at a time.

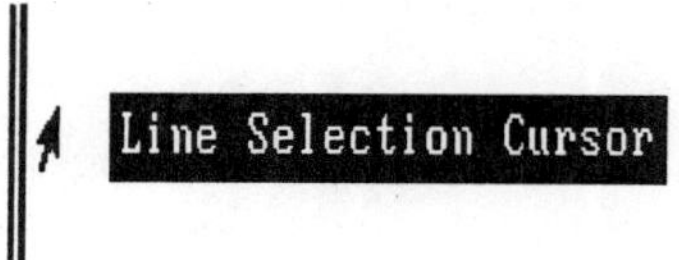

7. Move the mouse completely to the left side of the display. The cursor changes into a double arrow shape. This is the document position cursor. Use it to move up or down within the document. Press the left arrow to move up; the right arrow to move down.

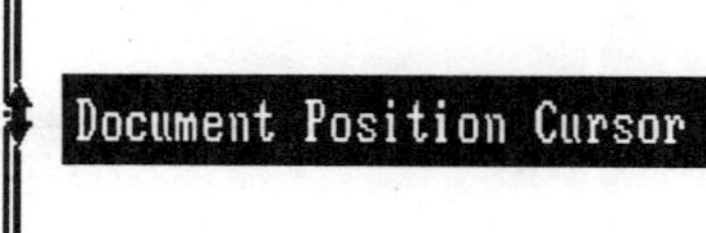

8. Press the Left Mouse Button. Notice the cursor icon changes into an up arrow shape. Word emits a beep when you are at the top of the document.
9. Press the Right Mouse Button. Notice the cursor icon changes into a down arrow shape. Word emits a beep when you are at the bottom of the document.
10. Move the mouse to the right side of the display. The cursor changes into a box shape. This is the horizontal split cursor. Use it to split the current display into two displays, change the size of two displays, or to remove the display at the cursor position.

11. Press the Left Mouse Button. Word adds another window to the display.

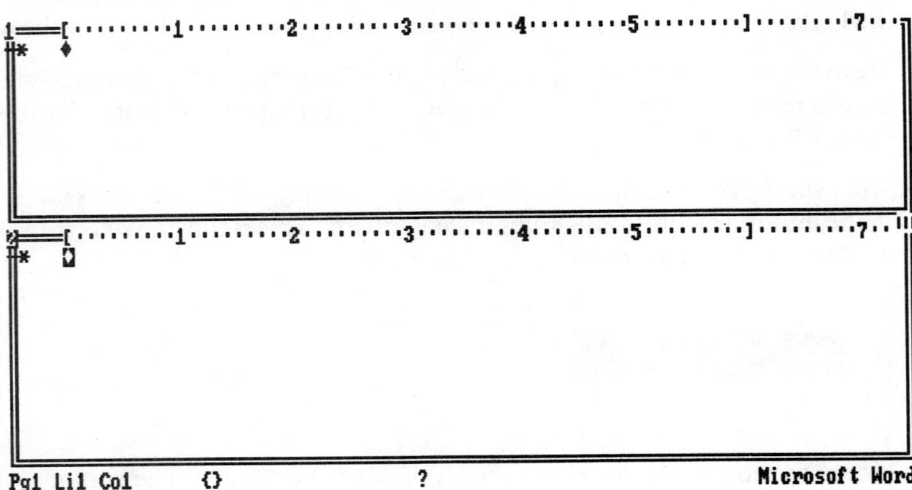

12. Move the mouse until a crossed double arrow icon appears (one pointing up and down, and one pointing left and right).

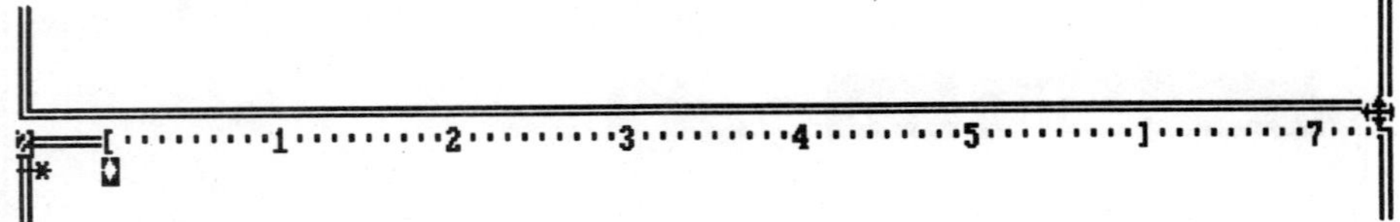

13. Press the Middle (for 3-button mice) or Left and Right (for 2-button mice) Mouse Buttons, then move the mouse pointer up or down. Notice the window changes size when you release the mouse button.
14. Move the mouse to the lower window and press the Middle (for 3-button mice) or Left and Right (for 2-button mice) Mouse Buttons. Notice the lower window disappears and the upper window fills the display.
15. Move the mouse to the top of the display. Notice the mouse icon changes into a box shape. This is the vertical split cursor. Use it exactly like the horizontal split cursor.

16. Point to the Format option and press the Left Mouse Button. If the menu is not visible, place the cursor in the lower right corner and press the Left Mouse Button. The Format menu appears.

```
FORMAT: Character Paragraph Tab Border Footnote Division Running-head Stylesheet
        sEarch repLace revision-Marks
Sets character format (bold, italic, hidden, etc.) and fonts
Pg1 Li1 Co1      {}            ?                         Microsoft Word
```

17. Point to the Division option and press the Left Mouse Button. The Division menu appears.

```
FORMAT DIVISION: Margins Page-numbers Layout line-Numbers

Sets margins, page length, and running head position for current division
Pg1 Li1 Co1      {}            ?                         Microsoft Word
```

18. Point to the Margins option and press the Left Mouse Button. The Margins dialogue box appears.

```
FORMAT DIVISION MARGINS top: 1"     bottom: 1"     left: 1.25"  right: 1.25"
              page length: 11"      width: 8.5"    gutter margin: 0"
         running-head position from top: 0.5"     from bottom: 0.5"
Enter measurement
Pg1 Li1 Co1      {}            ?                         Microsoft Word
```

19. Point to the Width option and press the Left Mouse Button. Then type 10 and press Return. The menu disappears and a double line of dots appear on the display.

20. Press Up Arrow. Then move the mouse to the bottom of the display. This is the horizontal position cursor. Use it to move horizontally when the entire document will not fit in the display.

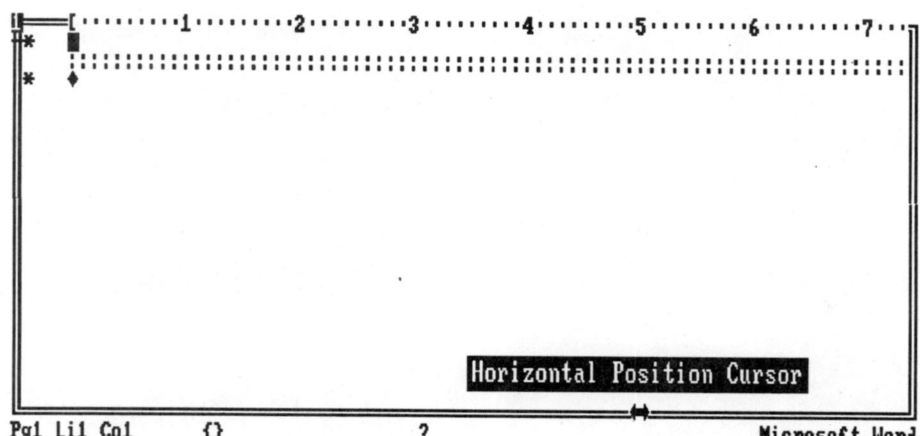

MOUSE FAULT ISOLATION

There are several problems that can occur during installation of your mouse and after you begin to use it. When your mouse fails to work, the manufacturer's manual is always the final authority on how to fix it. The steps below will help you find problems not always covered in the manual.

1. Check your mouse for physical damage. A damaged mouse will probably not work. Not only look for damage on the mouse itself, but for frayed cabling as well.
2. Check your mouse driver. Make sure you install it correctly. Most mouse manufacturers provide instructions on how to do this.
3. Some mouse programs require you to indicate the mouse serial port connection. Make sure you install the mouse in the correct port. Make sure you run the installation program or use a command line parameter to tell the mouse software which port to use.
4. Make sure the ball on the bottom of your mouse is clean. Some mouse manufacturers provide instructions on how to clean the ball. Use these instructions if the ball feels too slick or dirty.

CAUTION

Perform this step with the power switch set to off and the power cord disconnected. Failure to observe this precaution may result in electrical shock.

5. Check the connection between your mouse and the serial port for a serial mouse or mouse card for a bus mouse. Open the computer and make sure the mouse (for a bus mouse) or serial card seats correctly in the PC expansion bus.

Appendix F
CREATING AND MERGING PRINT DRIVERS

INTRODUCTION

Microsoft Word provides two different programs for maintaining and creating print drivers. By using these two programs, you can create a print driver for every printer conceivable. All you need is the manufacturer's manual explaining the printer control codes and characteristics. The first program, MakePRD, assembles and disassembles existing drivers. The second program, MergePRD, combines two assembled drivers together. This appendix will show you how to create and maintain your own print drivers for Word.

DISASSEMBLING AND ASSEMBLING WORD DRIVERS

Word uses a unique format for its print drivers. The MakePRD utility reads a text file containing print driver information and creates a binary file for Word to use. The same driver creates text files from binary files provided on your Word disks. Table F-1 a listing of the text file entries contained in a print driver description file.

The header portion of the print driver description file contains printer specific information. This includes the minimum left/right movement of the print head (dxaMin), the minimum up/down movement of the print roller (dyaMin), the kind of printer, and various flags. The flags tell Word how to format a page for printing. For example, microspace justification allows Word to place equal spacing between text elements. If the printer does not support microspace justification, then Word uses whole character widths between words to create justified text. Every print driver description file must contain a header.

The font description portion of the print driver description file contains information about the fonts supported by the printer. Since every printer supports at least one font, every print driver description file must contain at least one font description. Each font description contains the font number, a character translation table pointer if required, the number of point sizes supported by the font, a description of the characteristics of each point size the font supports, and the name of the font. You must include a font size description for each point size supported by a font. The font size description contains the actual font size in points, the width of the font, control codes for beginning and ending use of the font, and control codes for using various font attributes (like italics and bold).

The character width table pertains only to special and proportional character sets. Since each character requires a different amount of space, you must tell Word what those requirements are. Using this method, Word can support any font and any font size, even fonts you create yourself. The character width table begins with W followed by the number of the table.

Number the tables sequentially beginning at zero. Next comes a statement telling the font size, and the beginning and ending character ASCII code supported by the font. Finally, you list each supported character ASCII code followed by a colon and the amount of space required referenced to dxaMin. For example, if you wanted to list the letter D, which is 15 dots wide, then you would write 68:15.

The character translation table allows you to print characters not normally supported by you printer using characters your printer does support. For example, if your printer doesn't support foreign characters, you could superimpose two characters to produce the required character. To produce an emphasized letter a tell Word to print an a, then backspace, then print an ' (apostrophe). The character translation table begins with T followed by the number of the table. Number the tables sequentially beginning at zero. Next comes a statement telling the beginning and ending character ASCII code referenced by the table. Finally, you list each supported character ASCII code followed by a colon and a control string Word sends to the printer.

Since Word allows you to describe character conversion control strings, you could effectively create soft fonts for your printer. You would do this by using a character conversion table to change the printer mode to graphics, then provide a bit-mapped pattern for the printer to follow. Because of printer limitations, this technique provides a very limited number of fonts.

The final element in a print driver description file is the printer control sequence description (PCSD). The PCSD controls various aspects of printer operation as shown in table F-1. There are two types of PCSDs. The first type, short, uses no magic or value numbers. The second type, long, uses both magic and value numbers. Some printers use odd sequences of characters not conforming to a standard printer. If your printer, for example, uses ASCII code 65 for zero and 66 for one, then use a magic value of 65. Word automatically adds this value to each character printed for the specified attribute. The value number tells Word the maximum number the printer accepts with certain control character sequences. Use this entry only with the magic number.

MERGING WORD DRIVERS

Before you can merge two print drivers together, they must describe exactly the same printer. In some cases, you can change the header information (tells Word the printer characteristics) and use the driver as is. A good example of this is adding a generic plain font to your driver. This way you can convert your document to ASCII without changing drivers (only fonts). In other cases, the two printers are completely different so you cannot merge the drivers together. Since Word checks the print drivers before allowing you to use them, you will never inadvertently use two dissimilar drivers to create a new one.

TABLE F-1. PRINT DRIVER TEXT FILE STRUCTURE

Name	*Required?*	*Value*	*Description*
Header:			
dxaMin	Yes		Use this value to indicate the smallest space the print head can move. When using dot matrix printers, this value is in twips (1/1440 inch). When using laser printers, this value is in parts per inch. For instance a value of 300 equals 1/300 inch.
dyaMin	Yes		Use this value to indicate the smallest space the print roller can move. Always express this value in twips (1/1440 inch).
Printer Type	Yes	0	MSPRINT-type PRD File
		1	Dot Matrix Printer
		2	Daisywheel Printer
		3	Other Types of Printers
		4	PLAIN.PRD
		5	Laser Printer
Microspace	Yes	0	Always On (Justification)
		1	Always Off
		2	Off in Draft Mode
		4	Half-width Correction for Proportionally Spaced Fonts
		6	Off in Draft Mode, Half-width Correction for Proportionally Spaced Fonts
		8	Use Units Per Inch Instead of Twips for both dxaMin and dyaMin.
		16	Use Character Width Tables (described below).
Special Flags	Yes	0	No PostScript Mode
		2	PostScript Mode (for Printer Type 0). Use / (backslash) Instead of ' (apostrophe) as the Text Escape Character for Adobe PostScript.
Serial Interface	Yes	49152	ETX/ACK-type Communications Protocol
		40960	XON/XOFF-type Protocol
WidthTSwap	Yes	0	No Swapping of Character Width Tables

Name	Required?	Value	Description
		1	Leave Only One Character Width Table in Memory
Download Flag	Yes	0	No Downloading
		1	Download Fonts Before Printing
		2	Send Setup File Before Printing
		3	Download Fonts and Send Setup File Before Printing
Linedraw	Yes	0 - 63	Use Font# for Linedraw Characters
		64 -127	Perform Linedraw Using Vertical Bar and Hyphen. Adjust Vertical Spacing.
	128+		Perform Linedraw Using Vertical Bar and Hyphen. Do Not Adjust Vertical Spacing.
Font Description: (One Required for Each Printer Font)			
{F#	Yes	0 - 15	Modern a - Modern p
		16 - 31	Roman a - Roman p
		32 - 39	Script a - Script h
		40 - 47	Foreign a - Foreign h
		48 - 55	Decor a - Decor h
		56 - 63	Symbol a - Symbol h
CTP	Yes	Nil	No Character Translation Table Required (Table Format Described Below).
T#			Table Number to Use for this Font (Each Table Uses Successive Numbers Starting at 0).
cPSDs	Yes		Number of Sizes for the Font
PSDs	Yes		One required for each font size. Each PSD contains the elements listed below.
FontSize	Yes		Font Size in Half Points (120/Font Pitch) * 2
Wtps	Yes	##/W#	Width of each character in units described by dxaMin when using mono-spaced fonts. When using proportional fonts, enter W plus the number of a character width table instead.
beginmod	Yes		This entry consists of modification value and a control code sequence. Enter the modification value first. Then enter the control code sequence used by the printer to produce this font. The modification values appear below.
		0	Default, No Special Modification
		1	Indicates No Bold Attribute Available for this Font.
		2	Use the set character spacing command contained the printer control sequence description (PCSD) section. This is not normally required

Name	*Required?*	*Value*	*Description*
			when using dot matrix printers or proportionally spaced fonts.
		4	The set character spacing command contained in the PCSD section is doubled.
		5	Ignore the control character string in draft mode.
endmod	Yes		This entry contains the modification value and a control string required to return the printer to its default state after using this font. Use the modification values described above.
beginItalicmod	Yes		This entry contains the modification value and a control string required to set the printer for italics mode printing. Use the modification values described above.
endItalicmod	Yes		This entry contains the modification value and a control string required to end printer italics mode printing. Use the modification values described above.
beginBoldmod	Yes		This entry contains the modification value and a control string required to set the printer for bold mode printing. Use the modification values described above.
endBoldmod	Yes		This entry contains the modification value and a control string required to end printer bold mode printing. Use the modification values described above.
begin ItalBoldmod	Yes		This entry contains the modification value and a control string required to set the printer for a combination of italics and bold mode printing. Use the modification values described above.
endItalBoldmod	Yes		This entry contains the modification value and a control string required to end printer italics and bold mode printing. Use the modification values described above.
DLF (Download Fonts Flag)	Yes		This entry ends with the download flags value as listed below.
FontName	Yes		This entry ends with a string identifying the previously described font.
}F	Yes		Identifies the end of the font description section for the previously described font.
Character Width Table: (Only Required When Referenced in Font Description)			
{W#	No		Identifies the beginning of the character width table. Number the tables sequentially beginning with zero.
FontSize#	No		Identifies the average font size in half points.
chFirst#	No		Identifies the ASCII code of the first character included in the width table.

Name	Required?	Value	Description
chLast#	No		Identifies the ASCII code of the last character included in the width table.
chNum:chWidth	No		Contains the character ASCII code followed by the character width. Use the minimum horizontal movement of the printer as a reference for width.
}W	No		Identifies the end of this particular character width table.
Character Translation Table: (Only Required When Referenced in Font Description)			
{T#	No		Identifies the beginning of the character translation table. Number the tables sequentially beginning with zero.
chFirst#	No		Identifies the ASCII code of the first character included in the translation table.
chLast#	No		Identifies the ASCII code of the last character included in the translation table.
chNum:TransStr	No		Contains the character ASCII code followed by the character translation string. Use a caret (^) followed by the left bracket ([) to designate an escape sequence. Use a ^ followed by a letter to designate control characters 1 through 26.
}T	No		Identifies the end of this particular character translation table.
Printer Control Sequence Description (PCSD):			
{P	Yes		Identifies the beginning of the PCSD.
byte:#	Yes		Identifies the PCSD byte being described. The byte values appear below.
mod:#	Yes		Contains a control code string required to perform a certain function. For example, resetting the printer.
	0 - 3		Printer reset code at the beginning of document.
	4 - 7		Printer reset code at the end of document. Mod 1 - Suppress form feed when canceling print.
	8 - 13		Sets page length (part 1) in lines (normally 66 lines on an 8 1/2 by 11 inch page). Mod 0 - Word uses line feeds to get to the bottom of the page. Mod 1 - The printer uses a form length switch rather that a control sequence. Word outputs a form feed at the end of the page. Mod 2 - Uses Qume hex format of two characters. The first character contains the tens value; the second character contains the ones value.

Name	*Required?*	*Value*	*Description*
			Mod 3 - Uses NEC7710 format; count of new lines.
			Mod 4 - Uses ASCII format. Word outputs a variable length ASCII string.
	14 - 17		Set page length (second part). Word outputs any control string provided after the first parameter.
	18 - 23		Set line spacing (first part). The line spacing equals dyaMin + the magic number.
			Mod 1 - EpsonMXG temporary line space. Affects the spacing of only a single line. Line spacing equals dyaMin * 3.
			Mod 2 - Suppresses line feed after carriage return.
			Mod 3 - Suppresses carriage return before line feed.
			Mod 4 - ASCII format
			Mod 5 - Xerox 2700 format. Word converts parameter into units of dyaMin * 5.
			Mod 7 - Incremental line feed. Word moves the carriage one unit of dyaMin for each control sequence.
	24 - 27		Set line spacing (second part).
			Mod 7 - Tandy format. Uses a two character control sequence to move the carriage instead of a carriage return.
	28 - 33		Set character spacing (first part). Word uses a character spacing equal to dxaMin + magic number. Word uses extra spaces if desired spacing is greater than the value number.
			Mod 1 - Relative movement command.
			Mod 3 - Epson format. Word places the printer in graphics mode, then tells the printer the number of graphics characters to follow. Word outputs 0s (nulls) for the graphics values.
			Mod 4 - ASCII format.
			Mod 6 - Okidata format. Word uses graphics mode to space characters as in mod 3. Word does not output the graphics bits and restores the current font after exiting graphics mode.
			Mod 8 - Hewlett-Packard Laserjet format. Relative movement command.
			Mod 9 - Xerox 2700 and DEC LN03 format. Relative movement command. Word outputs the parameter in ASCII.
			Mod 10 - Epson LQ series format. Absolute positioning command.

Name	Required?	Value	Description
			Mod 11 - Brother format. Uses set character spacing command to explicitly set each space.
	34 - 37		Set character spacing (second part).
			Mod 1 - Brother format. Restores current font after changing character spacing.
	38 - 41		Begin bin 1. Word uses this entry for sheet feeders only. It outputs the begin command at the beginning of each page and end command at the end of each page.
	42 - 45		End bin 1.
	46 - 49		Begin bin 2.
	50 - 53		End bin 2.
	54 - 57		Line begin. Word outputs this value at the beginning of each line.
	58 - 61		Line end. Word outputs this value at the end of each line.
	62 - 65		Text begin. Used for MSPRINT only. Contains character sequences Word outputs other than normal control codes.
	66 - 69		Text end.
	70 - 73		Begin bin 3.
	74 - 77		End bin 3.
	78 -127		Reserved
	128-131		Begin Bold
			Mod 1 - BS Pass (double strike)
			Mod 2 - CR Pass
			Mod 3 - Print Wheel Change
			Mod 6 - C. Itoh F10 format. CR pass 1 then pass 2 one unit of dxaMin back.
			Mod 7 - IBM Quietwriter format. CR pass then code sequence after CR.
	132-135		End Bold
	136-139		Begin Italic
			Mod 3 - Print Wheel Change
			Mod 4 - Use Underline Instead
	140-143		End Italic
	144-149		Begin Underline
			Mod 1 - BS Pass. Word uses underscore characters.
			Mod 2 - CR Pass
			Mod 3 - Epson format. Uses single density graphics mode.

Name	*Required?*	*Value*	*Description*
			Mod 4 - Control sequence doesn't underline spaces. Use ASCII underline character instead of spaces where required.
			Mod 6 - CR Pass with BS Correction
	150-153		End Underline
	154-159		Begin Strikethrough
			Mod 1 - BS Pass. Word uses hyphen characters.
			Mod 2 - CR Pass
			Mod 3 - Epson format. Uses single density graphics mode.
			Mod 6 - CR Pass with BS Correction
	160-163		End Strikethrough
	164-169		Begin Double Underline
			Mod 1 - BS Pass. Word uses underscore characters unless control sequence specified.
			Mod 2 - CR Pass
			Mod 3 - Epson format. Uses single density graphics mode.
			Mod 4 - Word uses underlines.
			Mod 6 - CR Pass with BS Correction
	170-173		End Double Underline
	174-179		Begin Superscript
			Mod 2 - CR Pass. Uses set line spacing to perform vertical spacing.
	180-183		End Superscript
	184-189		Begin Subscript
			Mod 2 - CR Pass. Uses set line spacing to perform vertical spacing.
	190-193		End Subscript
	194-255		Reserved
magic:#	No		Specifies a value Word adds to every character for the function described by the byte value.
value:#	No		Specifies the maximum value accepted by the printer for a control code sequence.
}P	Yes		Identifies the end of the printer description table.
E	Yes		Identifies the end of the printer description file.

MAKEPRD TYPICAL OPERATION

In this example you change the plain print driver (used to convert documents to ASCII text) so that the header matches EPSONRX.PRD. Begin this example at the DOS prompt.

1. Type **MAKEPRD** and press **Enter**. The MakePRD utility asks for a PRD file name.

2. Type **PLAIN.PRD** and press **Enter**. The MakePRD utility asks for a text file name.

```
C:\WORD>MAKEPRD

PRD Editor 1.50 of July 14, 1987
Name of PRD file : PLAIN.PRD
Name of Text file: PLAIN.TXT
```

3. Type **PLAIN.TXT** and press **Enter**. The MakePRD utility asks if you want to convert from text to PRD format, or PRD format to text.

```
C:\WORD>MAKEPRD

PRD Editor 1.50 of July 14, 1987
Name of PRD file : PLAIN.PRD
Name of Text file: PLAIN.TXT
Select PRD to Text conversion (Press T)
    or Text to PRD conversion (Press P):
```

4. Type **T** and press **Enter**. The MakePRD utility displays a conversion complete message.

```
C:\WORD>MAKEPRD

PRD Editor 1.50 of July 14, 1987
Name of PRD file : PLAIN.PRD
Name of Text file: PLAIN.TXT
Select PRD to Text conversion (Press T)
    or Text to PRD conversion (Press P): T
Conversion Complete

C:\WORD>
```

5. Type **WORD PLAIN.TXT** and press **Enter**. The Word Main menu appears with PLAIN.TXT already loaded. Table F-1 provides a complete listing of the elements of a PRD text file.

```
[.........1.........2.........3.........4.........5.........].........7...
*   ;MAKEPRD 1.50
*   dxaMin:144 dyaMin:240 PrinterType:4
*   Microspace:0 SpecialFlags:0 SerialInterface:40960
*   WidthTSwap:0 DownloadFlag:0 LineDraw:128
*
*   {F0
*   CTP:NIL
*   cPSDs:1
*
*   FontSize:24
*   Wtps:1 1 1 1
*   beginmod:0
*   endmod:0
*   beginItalicmod:0
*   endItalicmod:0
*   beginBoldmod:0
*   endBoldmod:0
*   beginItalBoldmod:0
*   endItalBoldmod:0
*   DLF:0
*   FontName:Pica
*   }F
                                                              PLAIN.TXT
Pg1 Li1 Co1       {}                 ?            CL          Microsoft Word
```

6. Select the dxaMin entry. Delete the old entry using **Del**. Type **12**.
7. Select the dyaMin entry. Delete the old entry using **Del**. Type **20**.
8. Select the PrinterType entry. Delete the old entry using **Del**. Type **1**.
9. Select the Microspace entry. Delete the old entry using **Del**. Type **1**.
10. Select the Font Description entry, {F0. Delete the 0 using **Del**. Type **4**.
11. Select the FontName entry. Delete the old entry using **Del**. Type **Plain**.
12. Press **Esc**. The Word Main menu appears with the cursor on the first selection.
13. Press **Q**. Word asks if you want to save the file.
14. Type **Y**. The DOS prompt appears.
15. Type **MAKEPRD** and press **Enter**. The MakePRD utility asks for a PRD file name.
16. Type **PLAIN.PRD** and press **Enter**. The MakePRD utility asks for a text file name.
17. Type **PLAIN.TXT** and press **Enter**. The MakePRD utility asks if you want to convert from text to PRD format, or PRD format to text.
18. Type **P** and press **Enter**. The MakePRD utility displays a message asking if you want to overwrite the existing PRD file.
19. Type **Y** and press **Enter**. The MakePRD utility displays a conversion complete message.

Congratulations! You have just modified the PLAIN.PRD print driver.

MERGEPRD TYPICAL OPERATION

In this example, you take the print driver created using the MakePRD utility and merge it with the EPSONRX.PRD print driver. To perform this procedure using the example files, modify the PLAIN.PRD print driver file using the procedure above. Begin this procedure at the DOS prompt.

1. Type **MERGEPRD** and press **Enter**. The MergePRD Main menu appears.

```
C:\WORD>MERGEPRD

MERGEPRD 1.10 - Microsoft Word Printer Description (.PRD)
Merging Utility
Copyright (c) Intuition Systems Corporation, 1987.  All
Rights Reserved.


                 MERGEPRD - Microsoft Word .PRD Merging Utility

                 P) Enter .PRD list
                 C) List current .PRD list with available fonts
                 E) Enter/edit desired font/size entries
                 F) Display current font/size entries
                 O) Create output .PRD file
                 Q) Quit program

                 Enter selection:
```

2. Type **P** then **PLAIN.PRD**. Press **Enter**. The MergePRD utility displays an adding PRD to list message.

```
Enter Input .PRD Filename: PLAIN.PRD

Testing PRD file PLAIN
PRD file added to list.
```

3. Type **EPSONRX.PRD** and press **Enter**. The MergePRD utility displays an adding PRD to list message.
4. Press **Enter**. The MergePRD utility main menu appears.
5. Type **C**. A listing of PRD files and associated fonts appear.

```
Font  PRD File   Generic     Font Name      Sizes
 #
 0    PLAIN      Modern e    Plain          12
 1    EPSONRX    Modern a    Pica            8 12 14 16
 2    EPSONRX    Modern b    PicaD           8 12 14 16
 3    EPSONRX    Modern c    Elite          10 15
 4    EPSONRX    Modern d    EliteD         10 15
Press a key to continue...
```

6. Press **Enter**. The MergePRD Main menu appears.
7. Type **E**. The Enter/Edit Font Entries menu appears.

```
Enter/Edit Desired Font/Size Entries

A) Add new Font/Size Entry
D) Delete existing font/size entry
F) Display current font/size entries
L) Change linedraw font
R) Return to main menu

Enter selection:
```

8. Type **A**. The MergePRD utility asks which font to add.

```
Add - Enter Font # (0-4): 0

  0   PLAIN      Modern e    Plain           12

Enter Sizes desired, separated by spaces, then press Enter
(ALL = All Sizes): ALL
```

9. Type **0** then press **Enter**. The MergePRD utility displays the font name, generic name, and point sizes available.
10. Type **ALL** then press **Enter**. The MergePRD utility asks for the next font number.
11. Repeat steps 9 and 10 above for fonts 1 through 4. Press **Enter**. The Enter/Edit Font Entries menu appears.
12. Press **F**. The MergePRD utility displays the fonts added to the new printer driver file.

```
Font  PRD File   Generic     Font Name     Selected Sizes
 #
  0   PLAIN      Modern e    Plain         12
  1   EPSONRX    Modern a    Pica           8 12 14 16
  2   EPSONRX    Modern b    PicaD          8 12 14 16
  3   EPSONRX    Modern c    Elite         10 15
  4   EPSONRX    Modern d    EliteD        10 15
Press a key to continue...
```

13. Press **Enter**. The Enter/Edit Font Entries menu appears.
14. Type **D**. The MergePRD utility asks which font to delete.
15. Type **4** and press **Enter**. The MergePRD utility displays a font deleted message. The Enter/Edit Font Entries menu appears.

```
Delete - Enter Font # (0-4): 4

  4   EPSONRX    Modern d    EliteD            10 15
Font/Size entry deleted.

               Enter/Edit Desired Font/Size Entries

               A) Add new Font/Size Entry
               D) Delete existing font/size entry
               F) Display current font/size entries
               L) Change linedraw font
               R) Return to main menu

               Enter selection:
```

16. Type **F**. The MergePRD utility shows font number 4 deleted.

```
Font  PRD File   Generic     Font Name       Selected Sizes
 #
 0    PLAIN      Modern e    Plain           12
 1    EPSONRX    Modern a    Pica             8 12 14 16
 2    EPSONRX    Modern b    PicaD            8 12 14 16
 3    EPSONRX    Modern c    Elite           10 15
Press a key to continue...
```

17. Press **Enter**. The Enter/Edit Font Entries menu appears.
18. Type **A**. The MergePRD utility asks which font to add.
19. Type **4** then press **Enter**. The MergePRD utility displays the font name, generic name, and point sizes available.
20. Type **ALL** then press **Enter**. The MergePRD utility asks for the next font number.
21. Press **Enter**. The Enter/Edit Font Entries menu appears.
22. Type **R**. The MergePRD Main menu appears.
23. Type **F**. The MergePRD utility displays all the selected fonts, generic names, and point sizes.

```
Font  PRD File   Generic     Font Name       Selected Sizes
 #
 0    PLAIN      Modern e    Plain           12
 1    EPSONRX    Modern a    Pica             8 12 14 16
 2    EPSONRX    Modern b    PicaD            8 12 14 16
 3    EPSONRX    Modern c    Elite           10 15
 4    EPSONRX    Modern d    EliteD          10 15
Press a key to continue...
```

24. Press **Enter**. The MergePRD Main menu appears.
25. Type **O**. The MergePRD utility asks for an output filename.

26. Type **NEW.PRD** and press **Enter**. The MergePRD utility displays reading file messages as it reads the original print drivers, then displays a creating output PRD file message. The DOS prompt appears.

```
Enter Output .PRD Filename (with .PRD extension): NEW.PRD

Reading data from PRD file PLAIN
Reading data from PRD file EPSONRX
Creating output PRD file NEW.PRD

End of program execution...

C:\WORD>
```

Congratulations! You have just created a new print driver.

Appendix G
CREATING A FORM LETTER

INTRODUCTION

Form letters let you create multiple documents that are nearly identical except for specific information such as a name or address. To create a form letter with Microsoft Word, you must create two documents: a main document and a data document.

The main document contains the actual letter. The data document contains the information that Microsoft Word will insert in separate copies of the main document, such as names and addresses.

THE MAIN DOCUMENT

When creating form letters, the main document differs from a normal Word document. First, a main document must contain a DATA instruction line, which specifies the filename of the data document. The DATA instruction line must appear as the first line of the document and must be surrounded by chevrons (<< >>) such as:

<<DATA A:NAMES.DOC>>

Press Ctrl+[to create the left chevron (<<).

Press Ctrl+] to create the right chevron (>>).

Second, the main document contains field names, which appear within chevrons as well. Some example field names might be <<name>>, <<state>>, <<company>>, or <<item number>>. These field names correspond to field names specified in the data document.

THE DATA DOCUMENT

The data document contains a header record and multiple data records. The header record lists the types of field names used in the main document, such as name, state, or address. The data records contain the actual information identified by the field names.

For example, a typical header record might look like the following:

name,street,city,state,zip

A typical data record might look like the following:

John Smith, 123 Main Street, San Diego, CA 92123

You can create the data document directly in Microsoft Word, or you can import a comma-delimited ASCII file created from a database file. If you create a data document from an ASCII file, you must include the header record.

MERGING THE MAIN DOCUMENT WITH THE DATA DOCUMENT

After creating both the main document and the data document, you use the Print Merge command to combine the two documents together. Word gives you a choice of printing directly to the printer or to a separate document. Print to a separate file if you wish to review and make minor editing to each document. Print directly to the printer if you do not need to review or edit the main document. Follow these steps to print directly to the printer:

1. Load the main document.
2. Press **Esc**, **P**rint, **M**erge, **P**rinter and press **Return**.

Microsoft Word begins printing.

Follow these steps to save form letters in a separate document.

1. Load the main document.
2. Press **Esc**, **P**rint, **M**erge, **D**ocument.

Microsoft Word prompts you for a filename. Type the name you wish to give the new merged document.

3. Press **Return** to start merging.

SPECIAL MERGE INSTRUCTIONS

When merging the data document with the main document, Microsoft Word prints exact copies of the main document text with information from the data document. However, you may want to create form letters that contain slightly different information, depending on certain conditions.

One way to do this is by merge printing to a separate document, and then editing each page of this new document. While suitable for short documents, this approach is time-consuming and tedious for longer documents.

To overcome these problems, Microsoft Word provides special merging instructions for printing form letters. The six types of special merging instructions are: IF/ELSE/ENDIF, SET, ASK, SKIP, NEXT, and INCLUDE.

IF/ELSE/ENDIF

Sometimes you may wish some form letters to contain certain text while you may want other form letters to contain different text. Rather than edit each form letter individually, use the IF/ELSE/ENDIF instructions.

The IF instruction checks a condition. If the condition is true, then Word includes the text within the letter. If the condition is not true, Word includes the text following the ELSE instruction. Two examples are as follows:

<<IF condition = true>> print this text <<ENDIF>>

<<IF condition = true>> print this text <<ELSE>> print this text instead <<ENDIF>>

SET AND ASK

Sometimes you may want to use an existing main document but may not want to create a data document. To do this, you can use the SET instruction in three ways, placed in the main document:

<<SET field name = "value">>

This SET instruction sets a field name to a constant value, enclosed within quotes.

<<SET field name = ?>>

This SET instruction prompts you for a value to assign a specific field name.

<<SET field name = ?Enter data for field name>>

This SET instruction prompts you for a value to assign a specific field name, and also provides a prompt. The above example would display the prompt, "Enter data for field name."

The ASK instruction works similar to the SET instruction. Unlike the SET instruction, which assigns a value to a field name throughout a document, the ASK instruction prompts you for a value before printing each copy of a merged document.

The ASK instructions can appear in two ways:

< <ASK field name = ?> >

This ASK instruction prompts for a value. Word will assign to the field name the value that you type in.

< <ASK field name = ?Enter data> >

This ASK instruction prompts for a value and displays the prompt "Enter data."

INCLUDE

Microsoft Word can also merge two documents together into a single document. If you have two existing Word documents and want to create a third document out of the two documents, use the INCLUDE instruction.

In the main document, add the INCLUDE instruction as follows:

< <INCLUDE filename> >

where filename is the name of the second document. Word will now include the second document into the first.

Appendix H
USING MACROS

INTRODUCTION

Macros store multiple keystrokes in a glossary file. Rather than type these keystrokes by hand, you can choose the macro glossary file. After choosing a macro glossary file, Word types the keystrokes automatically. As an alternative, you can assign a macro glossary file to a specific keystroke combination, such as Ctrl-N. Whenever you press this keystroke combination, Word will automatically run your macro.

The most common uses for macros include typing repetitive text, such as names and addresses, or for performing specific tasks, such as formatting a document or creating indexes. For any repetitive task, use a macro to save you time and perform the task accurately as well.

CREATING MACROS

Word provides two ways to create a macro. You can have Word record your keystrokes as you type, or you can create a separate Word document and specify the exact keystrokes for the macro to run. Of the two, having Word automatically record your keystrokes as you type them is the easiest. Note that macros cannot record mouse actions, but can only record keystrokes.

RECORDING MACROS

Follow these steps to record a macro:

1. Press **Shift-F3** to start recording a macro. When recording a macro, Word displays the RM (Record Macro) message at the bottom of the screen.
2. Type the keystrokes you want to record. Be careful not to type the wrong keystrokes.
3. Press **Shift-F3** to stop recording the macro. Word displays the "COPY to: { }" message at the bottom of the screen.
4. Type the filename that will hold your macro. If you want to assign a keystroke combination to your macro, type the caret symbol (^) and the keystroke combination, such as Ctrl-P. Press **Return**.

WRITING MACROS

Although it's easier to record a macro, writing a macro can contain comments and special IF and WHILE instructions that let the macro choose alternate actions, depending on each document. To write a macro, follow these steps:

1. Load a document.
2. Type your macro. Enclose each keystroke within brackets, such as <F6> or Home.
3. Highlight the macro commands, using the mouse or F6.
4. Press **Esc** and then **C**opy or **D**elete to store the macro in the glossary. If you choose Copy, Word leaves the macro text in the document. If you choose Delete, Word removes the macro text from the document.
5. Type the macro name followed by the optional keystroke combination, such as ^ <Ctrl P>.
6. Press **Return** to store the macro in the current glossary.

WRITING MACRO INSTRUCTIONS

Macro instructions can be as simple as typing names and addresses, or as complex as searching a document for specific words and creating customized form letters automatically. For creating complex macros, Word provides nine different macro instructions.

ASK

The ASK instruction pauses and waits for the user to type in an answer.

<<ASK name = ?>>
<<ASK name = ?Enter name>>

COMMENT . . . ENDCOMMENT

The COMMENT . . . ENDCOMMENT instructions let you insert notes to yourself on how the macro works. For short notes, use the COMMENT instruction by itself. For long notes, use the COMMENT instruction, type the explaination, then use the ENDCOMMENT instruction.

<<COMMENT Short note>>

<<COMMENT>>

Longer note that lets you add more detail. You start a comment with the <<COMMENT>>instruction and end it with the <<ENDCOMMENT>>instruction.

<<ENDCOMMENT>>

IF . . . ELSE . . . ENDIF

The IF . . . ELSE . . . ENDIF instructions let Word perform different tasks, depending on certain conditions.

```
<<IF condition = TRUE>>
     Do this
<<ENDIF>>
<<IF condition = TRUE>>
     Do this
<<ELSE>>
     Do this instead
<<ENDIF>>
```

MESSAGE

The MESSAGE instruction displays a message to the screen, while the macro runs. The typical use for the MESSAGE instruction is to let a user know that a macro is running, so the user doesn't type on the keyboard.

```
<<MESSAGE Macro working . . . Please wait>>
```

PAUSE

The PAUSE instruction temporarily stops a macro from running so the user can perform an action. To continue running the macro, the user must press Return. To stop the macro from continuing, press Esc.

```
<<PAUSE>>
<<PAUSE Highlight text to delete>>
```

QUIT

The QUIT instruction halts the macro. Use this instruction with the IF instruction to stop a macro if certain conditions are true or not.

```
<<QUIT>>
```

REPEAT . . . ENDREPEAT

The REPEAT . . . ENDREPEAT instructions repetitively runs instructions a specific number of times. Using these instructions prevents you from having to write repetitive instructions.

```
<<REPEAT 3>>
     Types this line three times before quitting.
<<ENDREPEAT>>
```

SET

The SET instruction assigns values to field names. The ASK and the SET instructions work the same except that the ASK instruction requires input from the user while the SET instruction does not.

Once defined by the SET or ASK instruction, a value remains until reassigned by another SET or ASK instruction.

```
<<SET variable = expression>>
<<SET name = "John Smith">>
```

WHILE . . . ENDWHILE

The WHILE . . . ENDWHILE instructions repeat instruction while some condition remains true. Unlike the REPEAT . . . ENDREPEAT instruction, the number of times the WHILE . . . ENDWHILE instructions execute is not known in advance.

```
<<WHILE condition = TRUE>>
     Do this
<<ENDWHILE>>
```

CREATING AUTOEXEC MACROS

Microsoft Word lets you create macros that run automatically whenever you load Microsoft Word. To create such a macro, you must name them AUTOEXEC. If you store an AUTOEXEC macro in the NORMAL.GLY glossary, Word will run this macro automatically whenever you start the program.

Appendix I
EXAMPLE MACROS FOR MICROSOFT WORD 5.0

Microsoft Word contains macro features to customize the program so it works the way you want it to. To help you get started creating your own macros, work through the following sample macro examples.

You will create six different macros: three for working in the outline view and three for working in the document view.

OUTLINE MACROS

These three outline macros only work when you are in the outline view. To shift to the outline view from the document view, press Shift-F2.

The Collapse Outline Heading Macro

To create this macro, you must write each step of the macro in the document. Make sure you are in the outline view.

1. Type the following outline:

INFORMATION
    Books
    Magazines
    Training classes
SOFTWARE
    Word processors
    Spreadsheets
    Databases
    Desktop publishing
HARDWARE
    Monitors
    Printers
    Hard disks

2. Press **Ctrl-PgDn** to move the cursor at the end of the document.
3. Press **Shift-F2** to show the document view.
4. Type the following to write a macro:

   NOTE

   To display the left chevron (< <), press Ctrl-[. To display the right chevron (> >), press Ctrl-].

```
<Shift F5>
<Ctrl PgUp>
<<WHILE selection     “”>>
        <Keypad  ->
        <down>
<<ENDWHILE>>
```

5. Press **F6** and highlight the entire text you just typed in step 4. Press **F6** again.
6. Press **Esc** and type **D**. Word prompts you for a glossary name.
7. Type **Collapse** ^ and press **Ctrl-C**. Word displays the entire macro name as collapse ^ < ctrl c >.
8. Press **Enter**.
9. Press **Ctrl-C** to run the macro. The macro collapses the outline so that only the main headings appear.

The Expand All Outline Heading Macro

To create this macro, you will use Microsoft Word's macro recording feature. Make sure you are in the outline view.

1. Press **Shift-F3** to start recording the macro.
2. Press **Shift-F10** to select the entire outline.
3. Press the **gray asterisk** (*) near the keypad.

4. Press **Shift-+**. Make sure you use the gray + key and not the + key shared with the = sign. This command expands any text belonging to an outline heading. In this example, there is no text to an outline heading.
5. Press **Shift-F5**. The outline expands.
6. Press **Shift-F3** to stop recording of the macro. Word prompts for a macro name.
7. Type **Expand ^** and press **Ctrl-E**. Word saves the macro under the name of expand ^ <ctrl e>.

The Outline Heading Alphabetical Sorting Macro

This macro sorts the main headings of an outline in alphabetical order. To create this macro, you must have previously created the collapsing macro.

1. Press **Ctrl-PgDn** to move the cursor at the end of the document.
2. Press **Shift-F2** to show the document view.
3. Type the following: **<Ctrl C> <Shift F10> L A <Enter>**
4. Press **F6** and highlight the entire text you just typed in step 3.
5. Press **Esc** and type **D**. Word prompts you for a macro name.
6. Type **sort ^** and press **Ctrl-S**. Word saves the macro under the name of sort ^ <Ctrl s>.
7. Press **Ctrl-S** to watch the macro run. The macro first collapses all outline subheadings, then sorts the main headings alphabetically.

DOCUMENT MACROS

These three macros work only if you are in the document view.

Creating Bookmarks

This macro quickly creates a bookmark using the first word appearing to the right of the current cursor location.

1. Type the following:

   The bookmark feature of Microsoft Word lets you quickly jump to different places in a document. By doing this, you can quickly mark information that you may want to find again without having to scroll through the entire document page by page.

2. Press **Ctrl-PgDn** to move the cursor to the end of the document.
3. Type the following macro for creating bookmarks:

   <F8>
   <Esc>
   F
   K
   <<PAUSE Enter bookmark name>>
   <Enter>

4. Press **F6** and highlight the entire text you typed in step 3.
5. Press **Esc** and type **D**.
6. Type **Makebook** ^ and press **Ctrl-B.**
7. Press **Enter.**
8. Place the cursor before the word "Microsoft" on the first line of the document.
9. Press **Ctrl-B**. Microsoft Word marks the word "Microsoft" as a bookmark and asks for a bookmark name.
10. Type **Microsoft** and press **Enter.**

Jumping to Bookmarks

Microsoft Word lets you create bookmarks and jump to them from anywhere in a file. Unfortunately, once you jump to an existing bookmark, there is no way to return to your previous location.

This macro lets you jump to an existing bookmark. When you want to return to your previous location, press Enter. Word will return you back to your original location.

1. Press **Ctrl-PgDn** to move the cursor at the end of the document.
2. Type the following macro:

```
<<SET echo = "off">>
<F8>
<Esc>
F
K
xyz
<Enter>
<Esc>
J
K
<<PAUSE Jump to which bookmark?>>
<Enter>
<<PAUSE Hit the Enter key to return to previous
location>>
<Esc>
J
K
xyz
<Enter>
<Esc>
F
K
<Enter>
Y
```

3. Press **F6** and highlight the entire macro text you typed in step 2.
4. Press **Esc** and type **D**.

5. Type **View ^** and press **Ctrl-V.**
6. Press **Enter.**
7. Move the cursor to the word "document" at the beginning of the last line in the text you typed for step 1.
8. Press **Ctrl-V.** Word asks at which bookmark you want to jump.
9. Type **Microsoft** and press **Enter.** Word moves the cursor to highlight the word "Microsoft."
10. Press **Enter.** Notice that Word now returns the cursor back to the word "document" in the last line.

Viewing Disk Directories

Microsoft Word provides a DOS shell, allowing you to temoporarily exit to DOS without exiting Word first. You can customize macros to perform frequently needed DOS commands, such as viewing a directory.

The following macro prompts you for a drive and directory to display, then performs the DIR ¦ MORE command. You can modify this macro to perform a different DIR command or to run a different DOS command altogether.

1. Press **Ctrl-PgDn** to move the cursor to the end of the document.
2. Type the following macro:

```
<<ASK variable = ?Enter drive and directory to display>>
<Esc>
L
R
DIR <<variable>> ¦ MORE
```

3. Press **F6** and highlight the entire text you just typed in step 2. Press **F6** again.
4. Press **Esc** and **D.** Word prompts you for a glossary name.
5. Type **Dir ^** and press **Ctrl-D.** Word displays the entire macro name as Dir ^ <ctrl d>.
6. Press **Enter.**

7. Press **Ctrl-D** to run the macro. The macro prompts for a drive and directory to display.
8. Type **C:** if you have a hard disk, or **A:** or **B:** if you only have floppy drives.
9. Press **Enter**. Word displays the DIR ¦ MORE command on the screen. Press **Enter** to run this command. Word displays the directory on the screen.
10. Press **Enter** to return to Microsoft Word.

Appendix J
IMPORTING AND EXPORTING MICROSOFT WORD DOCUMENTS

INTRODUCTION

Microsoft Word can save and use documents created by other word processors such as WordPerfect, WordStar Professional, or the Macintosh version of Microsoft Word. No matter which type of word processor you have been using, you can use Microsoft Word to edit all your existing files. Microsoft Word can import and export three types of file formats besides its own format: ASCII, Rich Text Format (RTF), and DCA format.

ASCII FILES

Any word processor, whether it runs on an IBM PC, Atari ST, Amiga, or Macintosh, can create ASCII files. ASCII files contain only text. Any special formatting such as underlining, boldfacing, italics, or stylesheets will be lost when storing a document as an ASCII file.

Microsoft Word can create ASCII files as Text-only, and ASCII files as Text-only-with-line-breaks. Text-only only saves the carriage return at the end of each paragraph. Text-only-with-line-breaks saves a carriage return at the end of each line.

Word processors for other computers (Atari ST, Amiga, Macintosh) usually create ASCII files as Text-only. Other IBM PC word processors, such as WordStar or WordPerfect, usually create ASCII files as Text-only-with-line-breaks.

To export an ASCII file, choose Transfer Save or press Ctrl-F10. Then choose the option Text-only or Text-only-with-line-breaks.

RICH-TEXT FORMAT (RTF)

The rich-text format is Microsoft's own word processing format. If you need to transfer documents between different Microsoft products, such as the Macintosh versions of Microsoft Word or Microsoft Works, use the rich-text format instead of ASCII. Unlike ASCII, the rich-text format retains all special formatting such as underlining or italics.

To export a rich-text format document, choose Transfer Save or press Ctrl-F10. Then choose the RTF option. Word will automatically save the newly converted file with a .RTF extension unless you specify another extension.

To import a rich-text format document, run the RTFDOS.EXE program that comes on the Word Utilities disk 3. You can run this program in four ways:

1. Type **RTF_DOS**. Type in the Microsoft Word document you want to convert and the filename to hold the converted document.
2. Type **RTF_DOS filename1 filename2** where filename1 is the name of the Microsoft Word document you want to convert, and filename2 is the name of the new RTF document.
3. Type **RTF_DOS /S**. The /S command prevents Word from prompting you for a stylesheet if it does not find one.
4. Type **RTF_DOS /G**. The /G command prevents Word from displaying any prompts or error messages during document conversion.

You may convert multiple documents from Word format to RTF format by specifying wildcards. For example, to convert all Word documents on drive A to RTF documents on drive B, you would type the following:

RTF_DOS A:*.DOC B:*.RTF

DCA FORMAT

The WORD_DCA.EXE program on the Word Utilities disk 3 converts DCA documents to Word documents and Word documents to DCA documents. You can load the WORD_DCA.EXE program in three ways:

1. Choose **T**ransfer **G**lossary **L**oad and load the MACRO.GLY file. Run the dca_load.mac macro to convert a DCA file to Word, or dca_save.mac to save a Word file to DCA format.
2. Type **DCA_WORD** from the DOS prompt, press **Enter,** and follow the displayed instructions.

3. Type **DCA_Word** from the DOS prompt followed by the input and output filenames. To convert from DCA to Word format, type:

   WORD_DCA -i=inputfile1 -c=dca,msw -o=outputfile1

   where -i specifies the Word file to convert, -c specifies the conversion from DCA to Word, and -o specifies the converted filename.

   To convert from Word to DCA format, type:

   WORD_DCA -i=inputfile1 -c=msw,dca -o=outputfile1

   where -i specifies the DCA file to convert, -c specifies the conversion from Word to DCA, and -o specifies the converted filename.

Appendix K
CAPTURING SCREEN IMAGES

INTRODUCTION

Microsoft Word can capture images from the screen and store them directly in Word documents. To capture screen images for Microsoft Word, you must run the CAPTURE.COM program. This program can capture both text and graphic images. If you capture a graphic image, you may save any part of the screen. If you capture a text image, you must save the entire screen.

USING THE CAPTURE.COM PROGRAM

Before running the CAPTURE.COM program, you may want to change the program's default settings. To change the settings, type:

    CAPTURE /S

To load the program, type:

    CAPTURE

To remove the program from memory, type:

    CAPTURE /E

CAPTURING A SCREEN IMAGE

After loading the CAPTURE.COM program, you may run any program you wish. To capture a screen image, press Shift-PrtScr. The program displays a filename at the top of the screen. Press Enter to accept this default filename, or type any valid filename. If you are capturing a graphic image, the filename will have a default extension of .SCR. If you are capturing a text image, the filename will have a default extension of .LST.

With graphic images only, you have the option to clip part of the screen. You will see clipping lines appear around the boundaries of the screen. Use the right/left and up/down arrow keys to move the clipping lines around the image you want to capture. Press the Tab key to activate the different clipping lines.

To increase the movement of the clipping lines, press the gray plus (+) key on the numeric keypad. To decrease the movement of the clipping lines, press the gray minus (−) key on the numeric keypad.

To move two clipping lines towards or away from each other simultaneously, press the Insert key. To move only one clipping line at a time after pressing the Insert key, press the Delete key.

You will hear a beep when the program has completely captured a screen image. If you want to cancel the screen capture, press Esc before you hear a beep.

PASTING SCREEN IMAGES INTO A DOCUMENT

To paste a screen image in a Word document, load Word and move the cursor to the desired location for the screen image. Next, choose **L**ibrary **L**ink **G**raphics. Word will prompt you for the filename.

> **NOTE**
>
> The CAPTURE.COM program saves screen image files in the directory of the currently running program. For example, if you capture a screen image from your graphics program, the CAPTURE.COM program stores the file in the directory of your graphics program. Then if you capture a screen image from a spreadsheet program, the CAPTURE.COM program stores the file in the directory of the spreadsheet program.

When prompted for a filename, type the filename or highlight it from the listed directory on the screen. Press Enter to paste the screen image into your Word document. Word will not show the screen image. Instead, Word will display hidden text that shows the screen image filename, its dimensions, and its file format.

VIEWING A PASTED SCREEN IMAGE

Word provides two ways to view a screen image you have pasted into a Word document. Choose **P**rint **P**review to see the page preview, or print the document on a printer.

ADDING BORDERS TO SCREEN IMAGES

Word can display borders or shading around pasted screen images. To do this, move the cursor on the line containing the screen image (.G.) and choose **F**ormat **B**order. Choose the type or border or shading intensity, then press Enter.

ADDING CAPTIONS TO SCREEN IMAGES

Add captions by typing them directly following the line containing the screen image (.G.). If the screen image has borders, press Shift-Enter to include the caption within the border.

Appendix L
EXERCISES

1. About This Book
   a. How much memory do you need to run Microsoft Word?
   b. Name three advanced writing features of Microsoft Word.
   c. What type of video display do you need to run Microsoft Word?
   d. What type of mouse will work with Microsoft Word?

2. Microsoft Word Overview
   a. How can Microsoft Word's outliner help you overcome writer's block?
   b. Name four editing features that Microsoft Word provides.
   c. How can Microsoft Word work with spreadsheet files created by Lotus 1-2-3, Excel, or Multiplan?
   d. Give two uses for linking documents together.
   e. How can Microsoft Word help you write long manuscripts?
   f. How many windows can Microsoft Word display on the screen at one time?
   g. How can the print preview feature save you time?
   h. How can you see special formatting such as underlining or italics in Microsoft Word?
   i. Explain the difference between ASCII files and Microsoft rich-text format (RTF).
   j. Name the four basic mouse commands.
   k. How can Micrsoft Word work with Microsoft Windows?

3. A Sample Session With Microsoft Word
   a. What three features does this sample session show about Microsoft Word?
   b. How can you switch between an outline and a document?
   c. How can you switch between text and graphics mode?
   d. How can you collapse and expand an outline?
   e. How can you choose the Spell-checking command?

4. Copy
   a. Name two places where the Copy command stores text.
   b. How can you tell when the scrap is empty?
   c. What is the keyboard shortcut for choosing the Copy command?
   d. When would you store text in a glossary? In the scrap?

5. Delete
   a. Name two places where the Delete command stores text.
   b. How can you see a list of glossary files while in the Delete form?
   c. Explain why the Delete command works faster than using the Backspace key.
   d. What happens to the contents of the scrap when you delete new text?

6. Format Border
   a. What does this command draw around a paragraph?
   b. How can you change the style of the line that Microsoft Word draws?
   c. How can you use color to enhance a document's appearance?

7. Format Character
   a. How do you select text for using this command?
   b. How does Microsoft Word show where hidden text appears in a document?
   c. How can your printer affect the character styles that Microsoft Word can print?
   d. Give two uses for the strikethrough modifier.

8. Format Division
   a. Name the four groups of characteristics that this command affects.
   b. What is the gutter margin?
   c. Name the five different numbering schemes that Microsoft Word provides.
   d. How can you change the width between columns?
   e. Name the three line numbering options of Microsoft Word.
   f. Explain how the line numbering option can be useful for creating legal documents.

9. Format Footnote
   a. Where does Microsoft Word place footnotes in a document?
   b. Give two reasons for using footnotes.
   c. Which command lets you change the position where Microsoft Word prints a footnote?

10. Format Paragraph
    a. Name the four justification options.
    b. What does Microsoft Word do to spacing between words when using the Justified selection?
    c. Name the three indenting options.
    d. Name the three options that affect the number of spaces between paragraphs.
    e. How can you prevent page breaks and column breaks from splitting paragraphs in half?
    f. Which option changes the way Microsoft Word prints paragraphs?

11. Format Replace
    a. How can the Format Replace command quickly change character formats within a document?
    b. Will this command work with text formatted using a stylesheet?
    c. How can you have Microsoft Word ask you for confirmation before replacing a character style?
12. Format Revision-Marks, Format Annotation, Format Bookmark
    a. Explain the purpose of revision-marks.
    b. How can the format annotation command display the time, date, and author's initials?
    c. How can the format annotation command help multiple writers work on the same document?
    d. Give one use for bookmarks.
13. Format Running-Head
    a. Where can this command place headings on pages?
    b. Which keys do you press for the default running-head at the bottom of the page? At the top of the page?
    c. How can you print running heads only on odd or even numbered pages?
    d. How many lines can a running head contain?
14. Format Search
    a. How can you quickly find a paragraph that uses a particular style?
    b. Give two reasons you might need to use this command.
    c. Does this command work with formats created by stylesheets?
15. Format Stylesheet
    a. What is the default key for choosing formats from a stylesheet?
    b. How can you see a listing of stylesheets in the current directory?
    c. How can you quickly format a paragraph?
    d. Why would you need to use stylesheets?
    e. How can stylesheets work together with macros to create documents quickly?
16. Format Tab
    a. Name the three commands provided by Format Tab.
    b. How can you use the decimal tab selection for creating tables?
    c. What are the four leader characters that Microsoft Word provides?
    d. How can you quickly clear all active tabs?
    e. Give two uses for the vertical line tab.

17. Gallery Copy
    a. Where does this command store formatting parameters?
    b. When would this command be useful?
    c. How does the gallery scrap relate to the main program scrap?
18. Gallery Delete
    a. How many styles can the Gallery scrap contain?
    b. Why would you want to remove unneeded styles from an existing stylesheet?
    c. What happens to a style in the scrap if you copy or delete another style to the scrap?
19. Gallery Exit
    a. What does Microsoft Word use the gallery for?
    b. What is the default stylesheet if a document does not use a specialized stylesheet?
    c. When you choose this command, does Microsoft Word ask if you want to save any modified stylesheets?
20. Gallery Format
    a. How does this command choose a user interface based on the type of highlighted text chosen?
    b. How can you create special effects by choosing various options together?
    c. How can lines enhance the appearance of a document?
    d. How can the dot leader character help create a table of contents quickly?
21. Gallery Help
    a. What type of help does this command provide?
    b. Which key can you press to get context-sensitive help? Non context-sensitive help?
    c. How is the Gallery Help command similar to the Help command from the Main menu?
22. Gallery Insert
    a. How does this command affect an existing stylesheet?
    b. What does the Key Code field change?
    c. Name the three Usage field style types.
    d. Explain the use of the Variant field.
    e. How can you add comments to specific styles within a stylesheet?

23. Gallery Name
    a. Name the three parameters that the Gallery Name command can change.
    b. How can you quickly create new styles using the Gallery Name command with the Gallery Copy command?
    c. Give two reasons why you would want to rename styles in an existing stylesheet.
24. Gallery Print
    a. How can this command help you keep track of the different styles in an existing stylesheet?
    b. Which printer driver does this command use?
    c. Give one reason why you would use this command.
25. Gallery Transfer
    a. What type of information does this command retrieve and send to disk?
    b. How can you see a listing of existing stylesheets in the current directory?
    c. What happens if you edit a stylesheet but don't save it before exiting Microsoft Word?
    d. Do you need to save a stylesheet if you switch between the Gallery and the Main menu?
    e. Explain the difference between the Clear and the Delete commands.
    f. How can you combine stylesheets together in a single document?
    g. How can you see a listing of stylesheets in another directory or drive?
26. Gallery Undo
    a. How can this command help if you accidentally remove a style from a stylesheet?
    b. Under what conditions would this command NOT recover an accidentally removed style?
    c. What types of formatting changes does this command affect?
27. Help
    a. Name the three ways to access Help.
    b. Explain when you would need to use the Tutorial command and when to use the Index command.
    c. Can you get help on using Microsoft Word at any time?
28. Insert
    a. Where does the Insert command retrieve text from?
    b. Name the six standard entries of this command.
    c. What is the difference between changing and non-changing dates and times placed in a document?
    d. Which key lets you quickly make multiple copies of the scrap contents?

29. Jump
    a. Name the four items that the Jump command can move to quickly.
    b. What happens if you jump to a page that does not exist?
    c. What happens when you select a footnote reference with the text cursor and then choose the Jump command?
    d. How does the Jump command work similarly between the footnote and annotation commands?
    e. How can you find a listing of current bookmarks?

30. Library Autosort
    a. What does this command do to selected text?
    b. When would you normally use this command?
    c. Name the four fields that change the way the Library Autosort command works.

31. Library Document-Retrieval
    a. How can this command sort documents based on the summary sheet information?
    b. Explain how the Query command choses documents to display.
    c. Which command lets you look at documents in the current query directory without performing any actions on them?
    d. How many documents can you load at a time?
    e. How can you open a document so that you can only read it but not make changes to it?
    f. How can you print multiple documents?
    g. How many levels of information can the View command display?
    h. Name the three options for copying documents between different drives or directories.

32. Library Hyphenate
    a. How does this command affect the appearance of your document?
    b. How can you create optional hyphens?
    c. When do optional hyphens appear on the screen?
    d. How can you have Microsoft Word automatically hyphenate words or ask if you want to it to hyphenate a word first?
    e. Explain how justified text may need improvements in letter spacing.

33. Library Index
    a. How can you specify which words to include in an index?
    b. How can you avoid having Microsoft Word print out the special index codes?

c. Name the four options the Library Index command provides for formatting an index.
d. Name two methods for marking index entries.

34. Library Link
    a. What type of information can this command place in your documents?
    b. How do bookmarks affect the amount of text this command imports from another Microsoft Word document?
    c. Name four different types of files that Microsoft Word can import into a document.
    d. How can you see graphics imported into a Microsoft Word document? Describe two ways.
    e. Name the three options for placing graphics within a frame.
    f. From which programs can Microsoft Word import a spreadsheet?
    g. What will Microsoft Word do to spreadsheet references throughout a document if the spreadsheet numbers change?

35. Library Number
    a. What type of numbering style does Microsoft Word use unless you specify otherwise?
    b. Which types of paragraphs will Microsoft Word NOT number?
    c. Give two uses for the Library Number command.

36. Library Run
    a. When would you want to use this command?
    b. Why shouldn't you run programs, from this command, that use lots of memory?
    c. How do you return from the DOS prompt back to Microsoft Word?

37. Library Spell
    a. Where does Microsoft Word begin checking the spelling of a document?
    b. What happens if you begin the spelling check in the middle of a document?
    c. Which key can you press to access spell checking without using the menus?
    d. How can you add your own words to Microsoft Word's spelling dictionary?
    e. Where does Microsoft Word display the text cursor if you choose the Exit command in the middle of spell checking?
    f. Can Microsoft Word check for abnormal capitalization or punctuation errors as well as for incorrect spelling?
    g. How can you reverse the effect of the last spelling correction?

38. Library Table
    a. Describe the two ways this command can create tables.
    b. What are the two most common tables you might create?
    c. Can Microsoft Word include page numbers in an automatically created table? Explain how.

39. Library Thesaurus
    a. How can this command help you write more effectively?
    b. Name the keys to press which runs this command without using the menus.
    c. Describe the three types of information the thesaurus window displays.
    d. How can synonyms help reduce letter spacing within justified paragraphs?

40. Options
    a. Name the two groups of options and what they do.
    b. How does the ruler change tab stops and margins without using the Format command?
    c. What happens if you set the Show Layout option to Yes?
    d. How does the Show Line Breaks option affect columnar text?
    e. Explain how you can display the style used by a paragraph or division, on the left side of a window.
    f. When should you display a document in graphics mode? In text mode?
    g. When using an Enhanced Graphics Adapter (EGA) or Virtual Graphics Array (VGA), how can you increase the number of lines that appear on the screen at once?
    h. What is the Autosave feature used for?
    i. How can you hide the main menu from view?
    j. Give three reasons for modifying Microsoft Word using the Option command. Give three more reasons for NOT modifying Microsoft Word from its installed default settings.

41. Print
    a. Name the three places where Microsoft Word can send output to.
    b. Which option lets you send typewritten characters directly to the printer, essentially turning your computer into a typewriter temporarily?
    c. How can you create form letters?
    d. Explain what the queue does.
    e. When would you need the Repaginate command?
    f. How can the Print Preview Jump command let you move quickly within a document?
    g. How does the Print Preview Facing-Pages command differ from the 2-Page command?

42. Quit
    a. What happens if you change a document, glossary, or stylesheet and then choose Quit?
    b. If you quit without saving changes to a document, glossary, or stylesheet, what happens to these changes?
43. Replace
    a. Where does Microsoft Word begin searching for text within a document?
    b. Explain the difference between the Case option and the Whole Word option. When would you use either one?
    c. How can you use this command to remove text?
44. Search
    a. How does this command differ from the Replace command?
    b. What happens when Microsoft Word finds the first occurrence of a text string?
    c. Which key can you press to continue searching for a text string?
    d. How can you change the direction that Microsoft Word searches for text?
45. Transfer
    a. Why would you want to open a file as read-only if you were using Microsoft Word on a network?
    b. Which key can you press to see a listing of Microsoft Word documents in the current directory?
    c. What is the difference between saving a file as text only and as text only with line breaks?
    d. What is the advantage of rich-text format (RTF) over text only format?
    e. How does the Clear command affect stylesheets and glossaries?
    f. Why does Microsoft Word ask you to confirm whether you want to delete a file with the Delete command?
    g. How can the Merge command link two or more documents together?
    h. Which command lets you place previously saved macros and text scraps into memory?
    i. How can you perform the function of the Transfer Save, Transfer Glossary Save, and Gallery Save using only one command?
46. Undo
    a. What does the Undo command do?
    b. Under what conditions will the Undo command NOT work?
    c. Besides restoring text, what else will the Undo command restore?

47. Window
    a. How many windows can Microsoft Word display at once?
    b. Which key lets you switch between different windows?
    c. Name the two ways you can split a window in half.
    d. What does the Window Split Footnote command create and display?
    e. How can you move a window on the screen?
    f. What happens if you change a document in a window and then attempt to close the window without saving your changes?
    g. Give five reasons for using two or more windows.

Index

Books From Wordware

Computer Books

Desktop Publisher's Dictionary
LARRY S. BONURA
Discover the language of desktop publishing with this comprehensive, one-stop reference to the terms used in this exploding industry. More than 4,000 terms, words, and abbreviations, from typography to binding and finishing, are clearly defined and frequently clarified by illustrations. Related terms and concepts are identified for easy cross-reference. Perfect for office, home, or school, this is an indispensable tool for today's contemporary professional. This is the perfect companion volume to *Wordware's Desktop Publisher's Thesaurus*.
1-55622-106-1 • **$21.95**
hardbound • 456 pages • 6 x 9

Desktop Publisher's Thesaurus
LARRY S. BONURA
Discover an authoritative source of desktop publishing synonyms, antonyms, and related words that reflects the contemporary vocabulary of this expanding industry. The desktop publishing terms associated with a single concept are now together in one reference. More than 3500 words are presented in a dictionary format with A to Z entries. This is the perfect companion volume to *Wordware's Desktop Publisher's Dictionary.*
1-55622-118-5 • **$21.95**
hardbound • 320 pages • 6 x 9

Handbook of Desktop Publishing
A Guide for Business and Professional People
JOHN C. SANS, JR.
This excellent information source examines the hardware and software capabilities, limitations, and purposes of desktop publishing. Sound advice, financial implications, and investment tips on acquiring, operating, and maintaining an inhouse publishing system are detailed. This handbook introduces Macintosh and IBM terms, principles, tools and techniques. Checklists and cost justification formulas help estimate your current and future needs while determining whether desktop publishing is for you.
0-915381-95-8 • **$19.95**
softbound • 192 pages • 7 1/2 x 9 1/4

Lotus 1-2-3 Release 3
JOHN MUELLER
A complete, in-depth reference with dozens of practical examples. This book provides coverage for the many new features of the long-awaited Release 3 from Lotus Development Corporation.
1-55622-160-6 • **$21.95**
softbound • 320 pages

Microsoft Excel 1.5
For the Macintosh
PAUL SCHLIEVE and JON YOUNG
Learn to use the powerful spreadsheet, charting, and graphing capabilities of Excel for the Macintosh. Illustrated training demonstrates how to link worksheets, build applications, and create macros using this full-featured worksheet environment. Hands-on exercises provide helpful experience in creating and customizing presentation-quality graphs and charts.
1-55622-110-X • **$21.95**
softbound • 288 pages

Microsoft Works 1.05
ROBERT H. MARTIN
All the vital information you need to command this popular integrated software package can be found in this example-rich guide. Clear descriptions, applications, and illustrations provide thorough information on using the word processing, spreadsheet, database, and communication features. Applications are discussed in depth with adaptable examples. Build your knowledge level from scratch or expand your skills with this easy-to-use, fully annotated quick reference guide.
1-55622-061-8 • **$21.95**
Fall 89 • softbound • 416 pgs

Microsoft Windows 2.0
ROBERT E. WHITSITT II and
LANA K. BRYAN
This comprehensive reference/tutorial now includes the latest updates of version 2.0. Learn to work with several applications simultaneously and shift among them easily and quickly. Complete and clear descriptions of the Program Information File (PIF) Editor, Print Spooler, and Clipboard features are included. Depend on this valuable guide to master the fundamentals as well as the subtle details of this popular, new operating system.
1-55622-069-3 • **$19.95**
softbound • 304 pages

MS/PC-DOS 4.0
Sixth Edition
RUSSELL A. STULTZ
This complete, timesaving reference contains all the significant updates to the world's most popular operating system. The novice-to-expert DOS user is led keystroke-by-keystroke through a sequence of exercises designed to provide hands-on experience. Use the new text-based DOSSHELL to initiate powerful DOS utilities. Each command is detailed in brief, easy-to-understand modules which make this book an indispensable reference.
1-55622-111-8 • **$21.95**
softbound • 272 pages

Novell NetWare 2.15
TIMOTHY K. McDONALD
Step-by-step techniques clearly demonstrate the fundamentals of this networking operating system from installation to operation. Master NetWare's user commands to effectively store, protect, and share company data and resources among personal computers. Learn to adapt essential software programs to NetWare's LAN for custom applications. Tips on a variety of security and printer options are included. A complete guide for effective communications between centralized personal computers. Reviewed for accuracy by Novell Corporation.
1-55622-065-0 • **$21.95**
softbound • 256 pgs

PageMaker 3.0
BENNIE R. LOWERY, Ed.D. and
PHYLLIS MOORE
From basic setup to final printout, examples and illustrations clarify every stage of page composition. The authors step through all the procedures required to create professional publications by utilizing style sheets and templates. Learn to flow text around graphics and modify graphics through enhanced image control. This excellent tutorial is also an alphabetical reference to the features found in PageMaker 3.0. (For the IBM PC.)
1-55622-073-1 • **$21.95**
softbound • 368 pages

Ventura 2.0
GEORGE SHELDON
All the skills, techniques, and tips needed to master this top-selling desktop publishing program can be found in this comprehensive tutorial reference. Fully illustrated throughout, working examples demonstrate the enhanced user interface and technical publishing features designed to make desktop publishing more functional and easier to use. Step-by-step learning begins with a blank file that you develop into an impressive professional-quality document. New and experienced users will find the reference value of this book indispensable.
1-55622-104-5 • **$21.95**
softbound • 336 pages

WordPerfect 5.0
JORDAN GOLD
Taste the latest, most significant capabilities of this top-selling word processing package. Create and save standard formats for document elements. Learn to size, rotate, crop, and position imported graphics. Preview pages that use a variety of fonts, sizes, column layouts, and graphics. New menu structure and mnemonic command selection is completely outlined. Hands-on exercises demonstrate the full macro language needed to create complex macros.
1-55622-063-4 • **$19.95**
softbound • 416 pages

WordStar Professional
Release 5
RUSSELL A. and DIANNE STULTZ
Master a host of new WordStar features including advanced page preview, footnotes/endnotes, windowing, TelMerge, ListMerge, and many more. Practical hands-on activities demonstrate the new user interface and the pull-down menus used to initiate the latest functions. This step-by-step learning guide is also a complete reference to the all-new advanced document features now available in WordStar 5.0.
1-55622-074-X • **$21.95**
softbound • 304 pages

AutoSketch 1.03

PAUL SCHLIEVE and TOM BERGHAUSER

The authors of the popular *Illustrated AutoCAD* bring you detailed information on this entry-level, full-functioned, precision drawing tool. This complete AutoSketch introduction gets you up and running in about one hour. Hands-on activities step through the easy-to-use pull-down menus and dialog boxes that control sophisticated graphics manipulation functions. Details on how to import AutoSketch drawings to AutoCAD for additional refinements are included.

1-55622-113-4 • **$21.95**
May • softbound • 304 pages

C Programming (ANSI)

2nd Edition

J. EMMETT BEAM

For programmers who design text processors, database managers, spreadsheets, business applications, and operating systems. This book includes the emerging ANSI standard of the C programming language. Uncover the intricacies of programming techniques, C compilers, common errors, data types, and numbering systems. Examples provide hands-on experience entering code, compiling, and running powerful programs. Logical explanations and clear format make this guide popular with novice and expert C programmers.

1-55622-068-5 • **$21.95**
softbound • 450 pages

dBASE IV

RUSSELL A. STULTZ

Grasp the power and flexibility of dBASE IV commands, functions, system memory variables, and SQL commands as you work through the hands-on examples contained in this clearly written book. Fully operational, annotated programs help you create and use menu bars, pop-ups, windows, macros, user-defined functions, and more. Practical development activities probe the Control Center, and WYSIWYG report, label, query, view and application generators. Explore the latest programming techniques of this top-selling database management program. Ideal for learning and teaching, this book is an in-depth reference for the dBASE IV developer.

1-55622-116-9 • **$21.95**
softbound • 450 pages

pfs:First Publisher 2.0

JOHN MUELLER and WALLY WANG

Now you can master the skills necessary to create typeset-quality books, brochures, newsletters, and more. Capabilities like resizing, cropping, graphics, and font functions are demonstrated with concise, easy-to-follow applications. Appendices feature instructions on converting MacPaint graphics into First Publisher and vice versa. A special section details how to use Laserjet soft fonts on a dot-matrix printer.

1-55622-119-3 • **$21.95**
softbound • 320 pgs

Q&A 3.0

2nd Edition

THOMAS B. CALVERT

An excellent simple-to-complex tutorial for programming in plain English. Utilize the latest techniques of this sophisticated business management system to gather information, create and revise data, and generate reports. Discover the ease of using a natural language interface, database, word processor, filer, and report generator. Each application is thoroughly explained with ready-to-implement examples providing working models.

1-55622-155-X • **$21.95**
softbound • 352 pgs

Turbo Pascal 5.0

PAUL SCHLIEVE

Newly updated with the expanded features of 5.0, including source-level debugging, this language reference-tutorial provides hands-on instruction and sound advice for both the novice and expert Turbo Pascal user. Program examples make excellent models for your programming needs. Original and expanded features are demonstrated with short, easy-to-perform activities, which are easily found for quick reference.

1-55622-107-X • **$21.95**
softbound • 384 pgs

Business Professional Books

The Business Side of Writing
RUSSELL A. STULTZ
If you regard writing as a business rather than an art, this book can provide the reference information you need for a successful career in writing or publications management. These guidelines help organize and refine your approach to project planning, cost estimating, project research, financial control, development, and production. Mr. Stultz addresses the tools, techniques, methodologies, and processes to plan, manage, and automate publications development and production with emphasis on the bottom line.
1-55622-157-6 • **$15.95**
hardbound • 224 pages • 6 x 9

How to Develop Company Policies
MICHAEL A. REAVES
To protect company assets and ensure the achievement of company goals, every business, large or small, needs operational guidelines. This practical handbook helps you construct and revise company policies while promoting order, direction, and acceptance. You will learn to establish and achieve consistent objectives while keeping the regulatory, legal, economic, operational, ethical, and morale issues in mind. This book is full of written sample policies that make ideal models for developing or revising your own.
1-55622-156-8 • **$24.95**
hardbound • 352 pages • 6 x 9

MegaTraits
12 Traits of Successful People
DR. DORIS LEE MCCOY
Dr. McCoy traveled extensively to interview over 1,000 "successful" people. Interviews with such people as Charlton Heston, Malcolm Forbes, and Ronald Reagan led Dr. McCoy to discover 12 traits of success. She sought consistencies and success patterns from which you can benefit. Are there specific points to help all of us become more successful? The answer is a resounding YES! There are traits consistently found in the lives of successful people. Discover how you too can develop and utilize these unique attributes. *MegaTraits* illustrates how you can make these successful qualities a part of your life.
1-55622-056-1 • **$17.95**
hardbound • 304 pages • 6 x 9

Innovation, Inc.
Unlocking Creativity in the Workplace
GROSSMAN, RODGERS, and MOORE
Unlock your hidden potential to reach a new plane of creative thinking. Seek new avenues of problem solving by elevating your ability to conceive ideas. Techniques and exercises in this book expand your creativity. The authors take you on a journey designed to spark confidence by reorganizing your thinking processes and patterns. Learn to use innovative thinking to inspire fresh ideas and formulate imaginative concepts.
1-55622-054-5 • **$14.95**
softbound • 256 pages • 6 x 9

Business Emotions
A New Business Concept
RICHARD M. CONTINO
Revolutionize your thinking, conditioning, and approach. Learn why emotions are a controlling factor in every success and failure situation. This practical book will guide you through the maze of hidden psychological issues in a simple and straightforward manner. Achieve predictable, positive, and immediate results. The author introduces unique concepts in and practical techniques for emotional awareness, self-analysis, and effective business functioning.
1-55622-058-8 • **$14.95**
softbound • 184 pages • 6 x 9

Steps to Strategic Management
A Guide for Entrepreneurs
DR. RICK MOLZ
This book will help the entrepreneur uncover opportunities for a more successful business. A fictitious person, business, and product illustrate how this system works. Nine key steps to strategic management are developed and followed by real-world business applications. This system is used worldwide by sophisticated organizations of all types and sizes. The case example approach and readable style make this strategic method easy to understand and apply.
1-55622-050-2 • **$13.95**
softbound • 184 pages • 6 x 9

Other Books from Wordware Publishing, Inc.